Neuroeconomics

Neuroeconomics: A Guide to the New Science of Making Choices

PETER POLITSER, MD, PhD

Brown University
Department of Family Medicine

OXFORD
UNIVERSITY PRESS

2008

OXFORD
UNIVERSITY PRESS

Oxford University Press, Inc., publishes works that further
Oxford University's objective of excellence
in research, scholarship, and education.

Oxford New York
Auckland Cape Town Dar es Salaam Hong Kong Karachi
Kuala Lumpur Madrid Melbourne Mexico City Nairobi
New Delhi Shanghai Taipei Toronto

With offices in
Argentina Austria Brazil Chile Czech Republic France Greece
Guatemala Hungary Italy Japan Poland Portugal Singapore
South Korea Switzerland Thailand Turkey Ukraine Vietnam

Published by Oxford University Press, Inc.
198 Madison Avenue, New York, New York 10016

www.oup.com

Oxford is a registered trademark of Oxford University Press

Library of Congress Cataloging-in-Publication Data

Politser, Peter E.
Neuroeconomics : a guide to the new science of making choices / by Peter Politser.
p. cm.
ISBN 978-0-19-530582-1
1. Cognitive neuroscience. 2. Decision making—Physiological aspects.
3. Decision making—Mathematical models. 4. Neuroeconomics. I. Title.
QP360.5.P65 2006
153.8'3—dc22
2005034753

9 8 7 6 5 4 3 2

Printed in the United States of America
on acid-free paper

Dedicated to my wife, Lillian, and my father, Dr. R. Elliot

Preface

What happens in the brain when people make decisions about money? Recent interest in this question has spread with the velocity of information through highly circulated publications (see Figure P–1). According to some TV and news reports, the new field called neuroeconomics will tell us how people buy and invest.

Yet, the media attention has also provoked controversy. Some people argue that knowledge of the brain will add nothing to existing methods that predict peoples' choices. Others say that the predictions will be so important that marketers will use them to control peoples' minds.

Unfortunately, the speculation about the field's possible future has often overshadowed its present status and the challenges it faces. As a young field, it has not yet blown the lid off traditional theories of decision making. Nor has it yet led to the demise of human autonomy. But it has contributed knowledge about many important economic concerns: from risk to ambiguity, from fairness to morality, from individual pleasure to social norms. Its contributions come from respected scientists, including two Nobel Laureates. Already, it has produced two of its own journals (see Figure P–1a). At least 14 related articles appeared in *Nature* over a two-and-a-half-year span. Over 4 years, at least 26 appeared in *Science*. These and other widely read papers have ignited the interest of many disciplines from marketing and finance to management and education, to psychology and political science, as well as mental health, and the law.

In fact, many issues that the field now faces arise not from publicly debated controversies about its potential but from the fact that so many people from diverse areas have migrated toward the new field. As they venture into the new territory of neuroeconomics, the strange new languages of different disciplines are often foreign to them. Also, people worry about the dangers of travel across its difficult terrain. They see the mixed layers of evidence and uncertainty that neuroeconomic methods have unearthed. Along the muddy, unfamiliar routes, they often come across conflicting findings. Some fear that they will take the wrong turn when they decide what findings to believe. Others look at the colorful new brain "maps" and are unsure how to read them or how to follow the complicated written explanations. And for most of them, it is hard to get

(a)
- Television/radio: ABC (3), NBC, Fox, PBS
- Newspapers: *Pravda, London Financial Times, Le Monde Diplomatique, NY Times (4), The Wall Street Journal, USA Today, Boston Globe, LA Times, US News, Associated Press, Chicago Tribune, LA Times, Dallas News, Cape Cod Times, Pittsburgh Live*
- Periodicals: *Times, Newsweek, The New Yorker, Scientific American, Forbes, Money, Magazine, The Economist, The American Economic Review*
- Scientific Articles:
  - *Nature* (14 in 2½ years, 2005–2007)
  - *Science* (26 in 4 years, 2003–2007)
- Dedicated Journals: *The Journal of Neuroscience, Psychology and Economics* and *The Journal of Neuroeconomics*

(b)
- Are you wired for wealth?
- Looking inside the brains of the stingy
- There is a Sucker Born in Every Medial Prefrontal Cortex
- Hijacking the Brain Circuits With a Nickel Slot Machine
- The Why of Buy
- In Search of the Buy Button

Figure P–1 (a) Selected Neuroeconomic Reports. (b) Selected Neuroeconomics Headlines.

good directions. No interdisciplinary or understandable guidebook exists to help orient them.

The present text outlines such a guidebook. It surveys the landscape of neuroeconomic research in understandable terms for those new to the field. First, it enables the reader to glimpse the forest. It categorizes decision capacities and the branches of study that address them. Then it critically examines the health of some trees in the forest—the economic and behavioral economic methods for studying the capacities. Finally, it answers the unavoidable cries that arrive when one exits the strange new laboratory environment and re-enters the real world—the demands for behavioral evidence of the field's relevance. The book examines the importance of neuroeconomic variables to the behavioral disorders associated with poor decisions.

The results also specifically illustrate how neuroeconomic methods may help us to

- *discover the neural correlates of specific elements of choice* through models of desire, regret, expectation, context, learning, and aversion to risk or ambiguity;
- *measure biological responses to monetary risk and reward* using various methods to estimate the "exchange rates" that convert gains or losses in monetary currencies into the electrical "currencies" in the brain;
- *recognize some underpinnings of inconsistency in values* involving what we recall, experience, expect, or want;

- *clarify mysterious questions about responses to reward and penalty,* such as why some people delay a kiss or hasten an electric shock;
- *integrate diverse theories of anticipatory emotion* through the unexpected coincidence of behavioral, economic, and biophysical models of "quality adjusted life minutes" (QALMs). Such models reach beyond correlates of neural activity, toward interactivity.

Finally, the book seeks new methods to inform debates about the value of neuroeconomic methods. Somewhat as the field of epidemiology has categorized medical experiments, it describes the different methods of study and the levels of evidence they provide.

Ultimately, such a framework for interpreting neuroeconomic studies may increase understanding and reduce speculation about the significance of new results. So before rushing to get a glimpse of the future of neuroeconomics before it arrives, let us briefly interrupt your regularly scheduled news about the field. Turn off the television. Put down the paper. Disconnect from your internet news channel. Let's take a closer look at the neuroeconomics and see what all the excitement is about.

Acknowledgments

This book would not have been possible without the support of my family—including my father, Elliot, and my wife, Lillian, to whom the book is dedicated. For their comments at varying stages of the book, I thank Trevor Robbins, Martin Paulus, Monica Ernst, Robert Zeilinski, Kent Berridge, and several anonymous referees. In addition, I wish to credit Harvey Fineberg, with whom I taught a course in health decision science at Harvard. The present book combines recent neuroscience findings with some didactic materials originally from that course and others. I also express my appreciation to the many staff at Gateway and the Community Counseling Center who supported me during the book's preparation. I am grateful to Lisa Meloy, who provided invaluable editorial expertise; my editor at Oxford, Catharine Carlin; and developmental editor Steve Holtje. Although I also wish to thank many of the previously mentioned researchers, who helped me see the path to this book, none should be held responsible for any of the ideas expressed in it, which are my own.

Contents

Neuroeconomics

1

Introduction: Toward a Biological Science of Making Choices

Today, the field of neuroeconomics may appear quite new. Yet the most basic motivations for the new theory may have developed on a fertile plain between the Tigris and Euphrates rivers thousands of years ago. Long before Euclid had developed a general science of geometry, the Babylonians who lived on this plain had few general theories and instead used empirical observations to solve most problems. As a result, they estimated the area of a circle to be $3r^2$, not πr^2.[1] In fact, to understand the meaning of "π" and realize his error, a Babylonian statistician would need to travel forward in time by a millennium to read a geometry book by Euclid. From the insights of Euclid, he then could have learned the limitations of empirical statistics without theory.

From later historical events, however, scientists also learned the problems of pure theory. For example, several thousand years after Euclid, Descartes developed a more complex theory to explain the geometry of rational choice. His theory suggested that one needed only to think to be rational. And he would not learn how bodily feelings also guide decisions unless, like the Babylonian statistician, he could read a book centuries in the future titled *Descartes' Error*.[2]

The errors of Descartes' theory and the Babylonians' empiricism led to a lesson that would later motivate the development of neuroeconomics, teaching us that a reliance on either pure theory or empirical statistics can lead to misconceptions. Similar misconceptions had previously beset the theory of economics and the empiricism of neurobiology.

For instance, many economists had overlooked the neural and psychological processes underlying choices somewhat as Descartes had disregarded the role of bodily feelings in decisions. With the notable exception of empirical economists, many others had refused to let the inconsistency of empirical research mar the perfection of their models. Yet, it was unclear how much longer they could withstand the relentless weathering of psychological research. It had unraveled most empirical support for the fraying axioms of the economic theory. Thus, to preserve the theory's clarity, power, and generality, it needed modifications that had more empirical support.

Also, somewhat like the Babylonians who collected empirical data to define the area of a circle, neuroscientists sought to understand behavior through vast amounts of descriptive data—from changes in neural activities and biochemical interactions to cellular and even subcellular processes. However, in the studies of executive functions and other decision-related neural processes, it was easy to get lost in the details of the findings, and without much theory, it was hard to see how the conclusions could predict actual choices.

THE FIRST GENERATION OF NEUROECONOMICS

Thus, economics provided a clear and testable theory with faltering empirical support, while neurobiology provided detailed empirical research without clear theories that make testable behavioral predictions. In the past, when two fields, such as these, have had complementary limitations and strengths, syntheses of the two fields have often emerged. Such integration occurred with neurobiology and computer science in the field of neurodynamics; with electronics and chemistry in a new area of photolithography; with molecular and computational biology in the field of bioinformatics; and with genetics and neuroscience in pharmacogenomics, the human genome project, and related investigations into the causes of mental disorders. Such new fields integrate the strongest features of their parent disciplines to address many difficult problems.

For similar reasons, as neurobiology and economics alone did not solve many puzzles of decision making, a more integrated view emerged. An initial glimpse of the field in the mid-1990s suggested how economic and neurologic studies together might help us understand human abilities. As described in Antonio Damasio's book, *Descartes' Error*, patients with damage to the prefrontal cortex (PFC) made extremely poor choices in gambling tasks, as well as in their own affairs.[3] According to physiologic measures, they also failed to anticipate the outcomes of their choices. Hence, the PFC appeared to be needed to generate the bodily feelings that guide our decisions. The research that followed suggested that other brain circuits also played a role in decision making, and that body of research was recognized in a book by Paul Glimcher as the field of neuroeconomics.[4]

Neuroeconomics stimulated hopes almost unthinkable by its predecessors. Rather than merely guessing peoples' values from their choices and the assumptions of a problematic theory, economic analyses now could directly monitor biological responses to reward and punishment, and even unarticulated motivations. Rather than evaluating models merely by their correlations with hypothetical choices, economists could now also evaluate models based on their consistency with neurobiologic research. Thus, they could use knowledge of the brain to refine the economic theories in their heads.

At the same time, researchers could use the economic ideas in their heads to understand the brain.[5] With clearer, more testable economic ideas, they could search for meaningful determinants of neural activities during decision making. They could uncover logical components of decisions, somewhat as Euclid had revealed the geometric determinants of areas.

THE SECOND GENERATION OF NEUROECONOMICS

The surging optimism led to a tidal wave of press coverage. Yet, in the wake of the tidal wave, the new field was left with a big clean-up job with many previously unforeseen obstacles. For instance, the seminal research on patients with PFC lesions had fascinated scientists and journalists alike because these patients did not merely make poor economic choices in a lab. They also appeared to make painfully incompetent choices in real life. Yet, in many later studies of specific neural deficits, the evidence about the patients' lives outside of the lab appeared sketchy and anecdotal. Case histories about individual patients were prone to biases. Also, the studies could examine only a limited range of neurologic lesions and uncover a small number of distinct decisional impairments.

So many investigators sought other methods to study a wider variety of specific functions in a more controlled manner. In research by Shultz, Dayan, and Montague, single neuron recordings clarified how animals learned to expect different values from their choices.[6] In research by Glimcher, Platt, Knutson, Gehring, and Willoughby, important economic variables—such as value and probability—had representations in neural and functional magnetic resonance imaging (fMRI) recordings.[7] While it was important to look at the correlates of such variables from the neoclassical economic model, however, that model poorly predicted many choices. And unlike the lesion studies, these correlational ones could only speculate about the findings' importance outside of the lab.

Fortunately, several streams of research helped these and other researchers move toward a second generation of neuroeconomic research. They enlarged the range of decision-making variables and populations by traveling beyond the immediate territory between neurobiology and economics and through other vast regions linking economics with psychology and psychology with neuroscience (see Figure 1–1).

First, a broad channel of *behavioral economic* research had connected psychology and economics. A Nobel Laureate, Daniel Kahneman, with his coauthor, the late Amos Tversky, had previously challenged many traditional economic assumptions about decisions, and their work motivated many alternative behavioral models of choice. These models identified a broader set of psychological variables that better described how people actually make decisions. They provided a more varied and valid set of variables that could broaden neuroeconomic studies in ways summarized by Weber, Johnson, Dickhaut, McCabe, Camerer, Loewenstein, and Prelec.[8] Likewise,

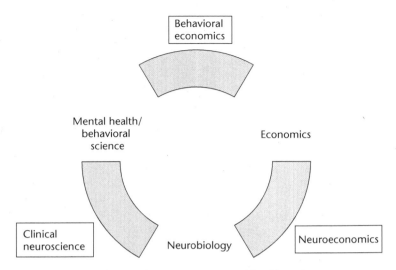

Figure 1–1 Streams of research connecting mental health and economics.

in many studies, the neurobiological correlates of cooperation in economic games broadened our understanding of human behavior in social settings, as illustrated by Camerer, Cohen, Sanfey, Delgado, Rilling, Cohen, Phelps, McCabe, and Smith, another Nobel Laureate.[9]

Yet, other behavioral research by Kahneman considered a broader variety of goals in decision making beyond individual acquisitiveness or wealth, including various types of well-being.[10] They included the feelings of happiness that we recall, experience, or anticipate. Berridge and Shizgal identified some neurobiologic correlates of these different forms of well-being.[11]

Second, a torrent of research connecting the neurosciences and psychology enabled us to enlarge the range of patients studied by neuroeconomists. In particular, the clinical, cognitive, and affective neurosciences clarified the neural dysfunctions seen in many mental disorders. Although the brain dysfunctions in these disorders were often less clear than in patients with neural lesions, such populations had already clarified mechanisms of attention, motivation, and adaptation in the cognitive and affective neurosciences. Now, they also promised to broaden the spectrum of decision processes accessible to neuroeconomists as well as to clarify the effects of neurochemical changes.

Hence, many neuroeconomic studies of decision making in mental disorders followed. In specific studies of such linkages, Bechara and Damasio tested whether addicts' poor economic choices were due to altered neural responses to the experience of reward and punishment.[12] Robbins, Rogers, Ernst, Grant, London, Bernheim, and Rangel suggested how people with substance abuse or misbehaving adolescents make choices that ignore negative consequences, much as reported for the patients with neurologic lesions.[13] Paulus and Nestler studied other reward system disturbances in mental illnesses as well as possible sources of pathological values—such as the long-term molecular and cellular changes in the brains of addicts as they develop increasing preferences for drugs.[14]

With such expansions of the field using new populations and a wider variety of measures, the field became an even more interdisciplinary one, embracing neurobiology, economics, computational neuroscience, and many different branches of psychology. At the same time, however, it was also expanding in many other ways, using a multitude of methods: from studies of single neuron recordings in animals to fMRI activities in groups of interacting people, from magnetoencephalography to evoked signals in the electroencephalogram (EEG), from biochemical circuitries envisioned in positron emission tomography (PET) scans to measures of biochemical metabolites in the urine.

TOWARD A THIRD GENERATION OF NEUROECONOMICS

Unfortunately, whereas expanding the breadth of methods, models, and populations did certainly enrich the capacities of neuroeconomics, such growth did not solve many other problems. As the range of neuroeconomic studies expanded, they became more dissimilar. Since the studies used many different types of subjects, measures, models, and tasks, one often could not tell the reasons for different results. Also, two studies might seem similar when they actually assessed very different abilities; and some measures confounded multiple capacities. Beyond this, some of the same words, such as risk attitude, were used with different meanings. Thus, the results of the latest, breaking findings were sometimes as enigmatic as they were exciting.

Clearly, the readers of neuroeconomic studies needed to better understand the differences between possible decision-making models and study methods. They needed help in understanding results, avoiding misinterpretations, resolving conflicting findings and building a coherent body of knowledge. Yet, no guidebook existed to describe the field's methods as well as their values and limitations.

Neuroeconomics begins to fill these gaps. It provides a new framework to help us understand different components of human decision-making capacities, including those based on economic theory (called efficacy) and those more closely tied to behavioral economic data (called effectiveness). Also, it shows how specific neuroeconomic methods illuminate different decision-making variables as well as their neural and behavioral correlates.

In the process, the book shows what neurobiologic studies may add to economic models. It suggests how these studies explain some violations of economic axioms. It shows how these studies may ultimately clarify the neural plausibility of different behavioral economic models. And it demonstrates similarities between psychological, economic, and neurophysiological models, thereby enriching the connections outlined in Figure 1–1.

Beyond this, the book shows how a very different field—epidemiology—may now help address many obstacles to further progress. Somewhat as the field of epidemiology has categorized medical studies, the book identifies the different types of neuroeconomic methods. In the proposed classification framework, different studies involve different layers of evidence about human decisional capacities. Higher-level studies better answer questions about the global performance of subjects. Lower-level studies better identify specific sources of poor performance. Finally, the book outlines the contents of a more complete science of the neuroepidemiology of decision making—a science that may ultimately enable a more unified and coherent third generation of neuroeconomic research.

DISCLAIMERS

This initial guidebook presents only a thin slice through the psychology, economics, and neurobiology of decision making. It describes in detail only a few biologically tractable models. Mainly, it considers those having parameters that have been the topic of study in neurobiology and psychology. As such, the book does not describe many important cognitive models related to heuristics and biases in judgment or process tracing models. It also omits many neurobiologic models of action and consciousness from the field of computational neuroscience. Moreover, it only briefly covers topics related to cost-effectiveness, consumer choice, and social interaction.

Similarly, the present book is primarily about neuroeconomic methods and does not discuss many important substantive topics in economics. Also, this book does not detail many vital issues surrounding the topic of rational choice, for example, whether one should use economic methods to describe how people *do* or *should* make choices or only to predict aggregate behavior. I consider these controversial, interdisciplinary debates in a forthcoming volume titled *Neurorationality*.

In addition, although the book will present evidence about the behavioral correlates of neural dysfunctions, such evidence often is correlational, which does not prove that the dysfunction caused a particular behavioral disorder. To adequately discuss the many issues surrounding studies of the neurobiologic correlates of mental disorders, a separate book would be required.

Furthermore, the book does not address many complexities of study design or data analysis that are peculiar to specific neurobiologic methods, for example, fMRI. Regrettably, it will also leave many important questions about the neurobiology of decision making unanswered. It lacks a detailed discussion of the literature on executive functions related to decision making and can only briefly mention the details and issues raised by many of the neuroeconomic studies it reviews. Clearly, current neuroeconomic studies are often difficult to generalize beyond a particular experimental context. Also, neurobiologic research is advancing so quickly that many of the substantive findings in the book may be obsolete by the time it is read.

Often, however, the biggest problem of a fledgling science is not the lack of current answers to the questions that we ask but rather the fact that we ask the wrong questions. For example, if we ask what brain circuits compute expected utility, but the brain is not really computing that, then our answer may mislead us. Likewise, if two studies both ask about the neural determinants of risk preferences but they measure entirely different decision-making components, then we will often end up with unclear results that are difficult to integrate and interpret. Thus, we require a framework that can clarify the meaning and limitations of current neuroeconomic research. We also require a science that teaches us how to ask the pertinent questions. To assist such learning is a major purpose of this book.

2

What Are the Components of Choice?

The view of "neuroeconomics" presented here is defined in terms of its approach rather than its content. The aim is not to describe all of the elements of neuroeconomics nor to cover all of the minute-to-minute changes in neurobiological knowledge. The framework to be presented merely outlines a style of inquiry, and as such will inevitably oversimplify the determinants of choice. A more detailed analysis of one particular aspect of choice will be presented in chapters 3 and 4 to illustrate how we can begin to develop the rudimentary elements described here.

EFFICACY AND EFFECTIVENESS: TWO CENTRAL CONCEPTS OF THE NEUROECONOMIC APPROACH

The neuroeconomic model proposed here uses two basic concepts: the *efficacy* and *effectiveness* of a decision-maker's performance. Previously, these epidemiologic concepts have been applied in a single, and very different, context: to study the performance of medical technologies, such as treatments and diagnostic tests. Efficacy describes a technology's impact upon an individual's health and well-being under ideal conditions.[15] By contrast, effectiveness studies describe the technology's value in patients who actually walk into a doctor's office. Typically, such studies do not control for many external factors that could affect outcomes, but they portray the technology's impact in clinical practice more realistically.[16]

The neuroeconomic approach introduced in this chapter applies efficacy and effectiveness concepts very differently. It uses them to assess the performance of an individual rather than the performance of a test or treatment.[17] Neuroeconomic efficacy provides a method in the madness. Efficacy evaluations use economic concepts to describe some necessary mental capacities, which, when impaired, lead to irrational behavior.

By contrast, neuroeconomic effectiveness describes the madness in the method: the factors that economic efficacy overlooks. While some of these factors go beyond the range of neuroeconomic analysis, the "effectiveness" concepts to be discussed derive from behavioral economic theories. These theories, in part, reveal capacities required for action when one considers inherent limitations in human decisional capacities. The next section outlines approaches based on these two concepts.

The Method in the Madness: Efficacy

Freud Meets the Godfather

Economic decision theory suggests three global levels of performance: diagnostic, management, and outcome efficacy. The following example illustrates these efficacy concepts heuristically and later demonstrates some additional factors that a more realistic effectiveness evaluation needs to consider.

In the movie *Analyze This*, Robert De Niro plays an unhappy mobster who goes into the emergency room following a heart attack—or so he thinks. He complains of intense chest pain, heart palpitations, sweating, and shortness of breath. An intern examines him, runs some tests, then returns and says he has good news.

"You're just fine! You only had a panic attack!" says the intern.

De Niro, who prides himself on being a cold-hearted killer, replies, "What do you mean? Look at me! Do I look like a guy who panics?"

Recalling the Cliff Notes on doctor-patient communication, the intern replies, "It's nothing to be ashamed about."

But De Niro responds: "Listen you stupid *#!*!$. I got a *!#*-ing heart attack!"

The young doctor, intent on making an accurate diagnosis, tells him, "Not according to your EKG."

De Niro then gently pulls the shades on the office window, approaches the young healer, and brutally beats him to a pulp.

Later, after months of therapy with a psychologist played by Billy Crystal, De Niro's character might have admitted that the mere diagnosis of a panic attack should not have inflamed his anger to this degree. A simple diagnosis—even for a coke-snorting, combustibly aggressive criminal such as De Niro—falls short of sufficient grounds for assault. On the other hand, he had every right to question the diagnosis. Hardened criminals usually are not the type of sensitive souls prone to "panic attacks."

Economic efficacy concepts help illuminate the possible origins of De Niro's symptoms and behaviors.[18] As a mobster, De Niro must respond skillfully to dangers and choose decisively between alternative courses of action. For example, when he senses a threat, should he flee or stay? In part, his success in making a choice depends on his ability to interpret bodily signals of possible dangers, including his rapid heartbeat, profuse sweating, and shallow breathing. He must experience and respond to such signals when danger really is present. Yet he must avoid overresponding with panic when danger is not present.

As shown in Figure 2–1a, De Niro's ability to deal with his problems depends on his diagnostic efficacy, management efficacy, and outcome efficacy. Figure 2–1b further details these components. Diagnostic efficacy involves his abilities to perceive stimuli (S) and to "diagnose" (Dx) problems from these perceptions—for example, to determine the likelihood of danger. Management efficacy involves his ability to react to his perceptions—to make decisions and implement the proper actions to deal with the danger (A). Outcome efficacy involves his ability to derive benefit from the stimuli he perceives and the actions he takes—for example, to enjoy the relief that results from reducing his risk. These components derive from those previously identified in the economic model.

Diagnostic Efficacy: The Ability to Perceive and Diagnostically Evaluate Stimuli

Guns and Sausages. The first necessary condition for higher levels of rationality is diagnostic efficacy—the ability to revise one's "diagnostic" estimates of uncertainties after being exposed to a stimulus, such as a signal indicating possible danger. These estimates may be reflected either in peoples' conscious beliefs or in their unconscious mind-sets. Somewhat as Moliere's Monsieur Jourdain could speak prose without knowing he was doing so, De Niro might act as if he believed the likelihood of danger were high without realizing that either.

In any case, diagnostic efficacy requires the ability to perceive stimuli accurately and then to diagnose their significance (represented by the line from S to Perception to Dx in Figure 2–1b). More specifically, it requires the ability to appropriately revise one's estimates of the probability of danger

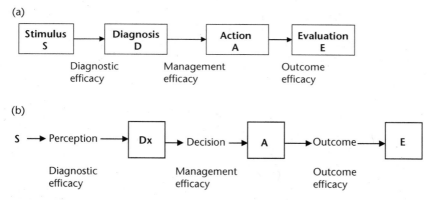

Figure 2–1 (a) Overview of the efficacy hierarchy. The arrows denote the fact that each level is necessary for the next—diagnostic efficacy is necessary for management efficacy and management efficacy for outcome efficacy. (b) Refinement of the components of efficacy. S = stimuli, Dx = diagnoses, A = actions, E = evaluations.

after an ambiguous object has been spotted.[19] Consider one of the perceptual problems that De Niro might face. Suppose that he sees what appears to be a mobster in the distance carrying something in his arms. It might be a gun. Or it might just be a kielbasa, a type of sausage that is usually harmless even when pointed directly at someone. From his perceptions of these stimuli, De Niro should form a mental image of the object the mobster is carrying. His perceptual accuracy is partly dependent upon his discriminatory sensitivity. He must efficaciously distinguish signal from noise; in other words, he must extract, and then focus upon, the relevant features of the ominous object, ignoring irrelevant details. The quality of his perceptual abilities roughly resembles the quality of reception on a radio. A poor radio has background noise that makes it difficult to distinguish the true signal coming from a radio broadcast. A better radio, however, eliminates the noise and produces clearer signals.

Some neuroeconomic studies have focused on this level of the hierarchy and clarified the neural sources of diagnostic efficacy. For example, Cohen, Usher, Ashton-Jones, McClure, and other investigators at Princeton have studied the neural sources of discriminatory sensitivity—the ability to distinguish signal from noise.[20] They have found that a brain structure called the locus coeruleus (LC) modulates some discriminations. The ability to "tune in" to a clearer signal is greatest at modest resting levels of LC activity, which occur at moderate levels of arousal. The ability to discriminate a specific signal declines at high levels of activity and arousal. Also, learning alters discriminatory sensitivity, in part via changes in different dopamine system signals. Different signal changes modulate the degree of resting and reactive behavior of LC neurons. High reactive or low resting levels at rest both increase discriminatory sensitivity.[21]

Accordingly, when De Niro learns danger signals and experiences a moderate level of arousal, his ability to detect signals and distinguish between a gun and a sausage may actually improve. But distant guns and sausages may all start looking alike at very high levels of chronic arousal. Such levels, which may reflect learned responses to possible danger—as when De Niro saw his father murdered at age 12—are characteristic of posttraumatic stress disorder (PTSD).

De Niro's diagnostic efficacy also depends on the higher-level inferences he draws from his perceptions about the likelihood of danger. Once he recognizes a signal, he also must interpret what he sees. After seeing a mobster holding an object that might be a gun, for instance, the neural structures representing De Niro's perceptions may "report" to associative areas of his brain that help him "diagnose" the problem and estimate the likelihood of danger (or his perceptions may induce unconscious mind-sets through faster neural signaling pathways).[22] How much his estimates of the likelihood of danger should rise depends on how often his perceptions err (how often he thinks he sees a gun when it is really a sausage or a sausage when it is really a gun). However, he may be overconfident or underconfident and revise his beliefs too much or too little.[23] When exposed to fear-provoking stimuli, patients with panic disorder overestimate the chances of negative consequences.[24] Chapter 3 will discuss measures of calibration and the revision of predictions, which are components of diagnostic efficacy.

Management Efficacy: The Ability of Perceptions and Diagnostic
Beliefs to Change Actions

> I don't believe in the after life, although I am bringing a change of underwear.
>
> Woody Allen

While necessary, diagnostic efficacy is not a sufficient criterion for efficacious action. After seeing a gun, for example, De Niro may demonstrate diagnostic efficacy and revise his estimates of the chances of danger appropriately (see Figure 2–2a). His thinking, however, may actually have little impact on his decisions and actions. Therefore, management efficacy, the ability to translate thoughts into actions, is also essential (Figures 2–2a).[25]

While diagnostic efficacy enables De Niro to use information to recognize a problem, management efficacy ensures that he has the capacity to do something about it. According to an economic model of management efficacy, the capacity to act depends on one's ability to select an appropriate threshold for action. This threshold should vary according to the prior likelihood of danger (i.e., De Niro's beliefs about the possibility of danger before he sees anything resembling a gun). It should also depend on De Niro's prospective evaluation of the severity of possible errors. Note that while De Niro might revise his estimates of the probability of danger accurately, his threshold for acting might still be too high (Figure 2–2b). In these circumstances, he would then often fail to act, since he believes the gangster carries a sausage when he really has a gun.

Conversely, if De Niro could revise his estimates of the probability of danger accurately, his threshold for acting might still be too low (Figure 2–2c). He would then act as if the gangster had a gun when he really carried a

(a)

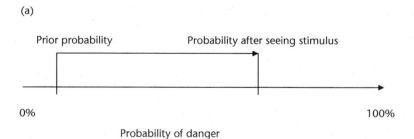

Figure 2–2 (a) Diagnostic efficacy. Shown is the increase in the perceived probability of danger after seeing an ambiguous object. The degree of change is determined by the likelihood ratio, as defined in note 19.

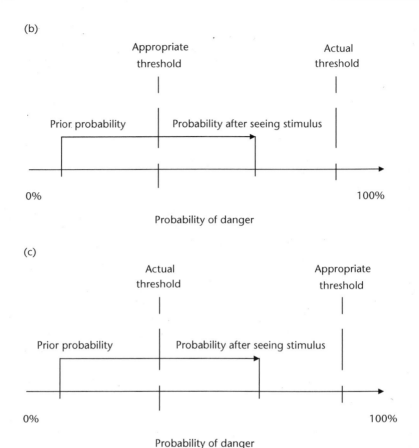

Figure 2–2 (*Continued*) (b) Management efficacy problem: Inappropriate inaction. Note that the person may revise his estimates of the probability of danger appropriately, as in Figure 2–2a, yet still fail to act appropriately. In the efficacy model, whether or not the person acts should depend on whether the danger probability exceeds the appropriateness threshold. If it does, the person should act; otherwise he should not. But the above diagram shows that the person's actual threshold for action may be greater than the appropriate one. So the probability of danger can exceed the appropriateness threshold, meaning that he should take action, yet he may not take action because the probability does not exceed the person's actual threshold. (c) Management efficacy problem: Inappropriate action. In this case, the appropriateness threshold exceeds the actual one. So he may take action because the probability of danger exceeds the actual threshold, yet he should not take action, because the probability does not exceed the appropriateness threshold. Note also that the person's actual threshold may vary across time, and so it may sometimes exceed the appropriateness threshold, as in Figure 2–2b, yet at other times fall short of it, as in Figure 2–2c. The person then may appear to act inconsistently and make both kinds of errors: inappropriate action or inaction.

sausage. Although this outcome would be significantly less disheartening than a bullet in the chest, it would still leave something to be desired. If De Niro ran away from a sausage, he would risk being considered a coward (or a vegetarian). And if the mobster were bringing the kielbasa to him as a token of respect and admiration, he might also miss out on a good lunch.

Hence, De Niro should consider both the probabilities and anticipated costs of the two types of decision errors in order to find an appropriate threshold that balances their risks. This task, however, requires mental simulation, the ability to forecast and evaluate the possible types of decision errors. Usually, when proceeding from diagnostic evaluations (Dx) to decisions and actions (A), people mentally simulate possible actions and the outcomes, which are represented by the additional loop in Figure 2–3. In this process, people first consider hypothetical decisions, actions, and outcomes that could result from the actions (denoted by the arrow from $Decision_H$, to A_H to $Outcome_H$). Then they evaluate how they might feel if the hypothetical outcomes actually occurred (E_H).[26] The simulation of hypothetical outcomes can strengthen their abilities to make choices (through the connection of E_H to Decision in Figure 2–3).

Many experiments have examined the neural correlates of such anticipatory evaluations. For instance, patients with lesions to the front, middle (ventromedial) part of the frontal lobe of the brain have decreased skin conductance responses (SCRs) when awaiting the outcome of a gamble.[27] Thus, even when they have diagnostic efficacy and can identify the risks they face, they are unable to use this information to change their actions appropriately. Other measures related to management efficacy have included reports of the accuracy of choice in gambling tasks according to external criteria (e.g., percent choice of advantageous gambles).

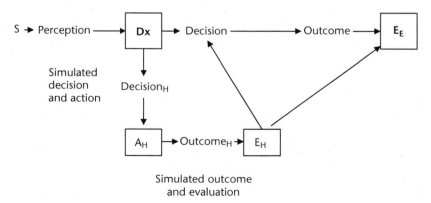

Figure 2–3 Refinement of the components of efficacy: simulated evaluation. S = stimuli, Dx = diagnoses, A = actions, E_E = experienced evaluations, A_H = hypothetical actions, E_H = hypothetical evaluations.

Additional disturbances in management efficacy can occur. For example, some patients with dementia or schizophrenia may be unable to formulate a decision. Patients with attention deficit/hyperactivity disorder may be able to formulate a decision but unable to keep track of their goals long enough to translate their intentions into actions. As a result, they often proceed to other unplanned activities and appear distracted. Likewise, some patients with antisocial personality can keep track of their goals but cannot inhibit an action after receiving diagnostic information.[28] Depressed patients may realize that action is required but lack the motivation to act. And some patients with bipolar disorder and mood instability often act erratically due to changing motivations. Such appeared to be the case in *Analyze That* (the sequel to *Analyze This*) when De Niro's character began having mood swings. As if auditioning for a musical based on *The Sopranos*, he began alternately weeping like a child and then singing tunes from *West Side Story* to his fellow inmates at Sing Sing.

Outcome Efficacy: The Ability of Actions to Improve
Subjectively Evaluated Outcomes

If an individual has both diagnostic and management efficacy, then he also possesses the judgment to appraise risks as well as the ability to act after exposure to a stimulus. Although information from the stimulus may change thoughts and actions, it still may prove to be of little use. What one also needs is outcome efficacy, the ability to achieve good outcomes and to experience them as beneficial—the capacity to profit from information hedonically rather than just managerially. While management efficacy determines whether an individual can choose actions that best serve his interests, outcome efficacy determines the extent to which they actually do.

To be sure, the degree to which De Niro can expect to satisfy his interests depends on his environment as well as his emotional capacities. Environmental factors, such as the type of job he has, may determine the usefulness of his skills. For example, in *Analyze That*, when De Niro decides to reform himself through gainful—and legitimate—employment, he tries out his abilities in several new nonmob-related jobs: as a car salesman, a jeweler, and a waiter. However, his keen abilities to perceive and manage danger are of little use in positions outside of the mob. For example, as a florist, if De Niro saw someone approaching with an oblong object, it is not likely to be a gun but rather a bouquet of flowers. Accordingly, his worst-case scenario would be that a dissatisfied customer is coming to complain about wilted petals. The customer would be more likely to shout than to shoot. So it would not matter much whether De Niro stayed or left or how skillful he was in detecting approaching weaponry and managing mortal dangers. If he makes a mistake as a florist, he will not be pushing up daisies; he will be putting them back in a vase.

However, internal capacities still are important in determining the ultimate impact of outcomes when they occur. A critical aspect of outcome efficacy concerns the extent to which imagined outcomes can actually change evaluations—for example, the extent to which the person can reap the rewards of the outcomes when they occur.

Losses of such outcome efficacy often occur in depression. For example, depressed patients often experience anhedonia—the loss of the ability to actually experience pleasure from outcomes. Thus, if a severely depressed patient musters the energy to complete a task, he will usually be unable to enjoy its completion. Depressed individuals often complain, "no matter what I do, it doesn't matter." This experiential aspect of outcome efficacy has been measured in some controlled experiments involving hypothetical gambling tasks. By measuring the SCR that occurs after an outcome, such as a win or loss, researchers attempt to measure one's capacity to experience outcomes. This capacity involves the relationship between an individual's internal goals and the actual, rather than simulated, environmental outcomes, as discussed in the section on management efficacy.

Note that, while some psychiatric diagnostic criteria do consider capacities to experience outcomes, the classical economic model does not. That economic model considers only the consistency of one's choices with one another, according to principles of rationality. Thus, it considers only capacities up to the level of management efficacy. A more extended economic model advocated by Bentham does consider outcome experiences and will be discussed further in chapter 4.

Value and Limitations of the Efficacy Hierarchy

In this basic, highly simplified model, each of the three global levels of efficacy is necessary for the next, higher level (see Figure 2–1a). Diagnostic efficacy is required for management efficacy. One must be able to revise appraisals of information in order to respond effectively to changing assessments. (De Niro had to be able to see the mobster and assess the likelihood of danger in order to act to preserve his safety.) Likewise, management efficacy is required for outcome efficacy. One must first be able to act in order to derive benefit from outcomes. (De Niro had to have sufficient motivation to flee a dangerous situation before experiencing the relief of finding safety.)

Due to the necessity of diagnostic efficacy for higher levels of efficacy, the most basic diagnostic errors will likely produce a "ripple effect" that leads to management errors and poor outcomes. Indeed, some economic decision analyses have shown that diagnostic errors are often more severe than such other errors as the failure to set a proper threshold for action. More precisely, simulations, based on the type of expected utility model discussed in chapter 3, show that the amount of utility loss due to an inaccurate threshold has limits, whereas the possible loss from a failure to revise information and make appropriate diagnostic estimates has no limit.[29] Therefore, the assessment of diagnostic efficacy takes priority in this model. And in some contexts, knowledge of severe perceptual and diagnostic impairment might even decrease the need to make more difficult determinations of management efficacy. Such impairment could suggest that the person's performance is likely to be very low in many areas.[30]

At the same time, while the neuroeconomic efficacy framework clarifies the hierarchical—and to an extent, sequential—nature of some human abilities, it does not include all such abilities. The efficacy assessments sacrifice some realism in order to obtain clarity. In addition, while efficacy assessments that utilize questionnaires or other structured evaluations may control factors affecting performance that are unrelated to the specific ability being tested, they do not determine how these abilities are used in realistic settings in which people (a) have limitations of attention and need to allocate it cost-effectively, (b) use actions to communicate commitments to significant others, and (c) consider outcome evaluations not merely as the end result of their decision processes but also as signals to take further action.

To capture these and other factors important to our adaptation, we also require effectiveness evaluations, which test a broader set of skills. The following section introduces a few of these skills.

The Madness in the Method: Effectiveness

> When I woke up this morning my girlfriend asked me, "Did you sleep well?" I said, "No, I made a few mistakes."
>
> Steven Wright

Beyond Diagnostic Efficacy: The Cost-effective Use of Limited Mental Resources

Even if one's perceptions and diagnoses are usually accurate and lead to appropriate actions and good outcomes, the struggle to attain these outcomes might prove too costly. The process may exhaust limited time and mental resources that could have been spent more profitably elsewhere. In such cases, the decision-making process has efficacy but lacks cost-effectiveness (CE in Figure 2–4). The CE is roughly the (incremental) cost of using information to improve actions divided by the expected gain.[31]

The consideration of cost-effectiveness adds yet another element to performance and builds upon the previously discussed efficacy concepts; as before, the prior levels of diagnostic, management, and outcome efficacy are necessary for the next level—cost-effectiveness. That is, diagnostic efficacy, which determines whether an individual can revise his beliefs appropriately, is necessary for management efficacy. Management efficacy, which requires that the individual knows whether an action serves his best interests, is necessary for outcome efficacy. And outcome efficacy, which enables him to know how much an action will serve those interests, is necessary for cost-effectiveness—his ability to prioritize attention and allocate his mental resources. Before utilizing a particular mental resource, he must implicitly consider the time, effort, or attention required, and determine whether that cost is justified by the expected benefits.

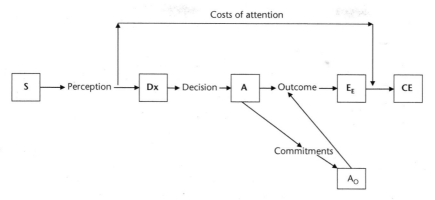

Figure 2–4 Some components of effectiveness: beyond diagnostic and management efficacy. S = stimuli, Dx = diagnoses, A = actions, E = evaluations, CE = cost-effectiveness, A_O = actions of others. This figure illustrates how the costs of attending to stimuli may affect the person's cost-effectiveness (CE) and how signals of one's commitment to a course of action can influence the actions of others (A_O), which in turn affects outcomes for oneself.

According to this extension of the simpler efficacy model, a person should behave as if allocating a limited budget of mental resources. If he does so efficiently, then he can expect to benefit most. For example, if De Niro is performing a "high-cost" activity, such as practicing a difficult arpeggio on the piano, and then sees a mobster approaching, he will probably need to stop playing the piano and shift his attention to the approaching threat. But if he is merely humming a few bars of the "Theme from the Godfather," a familiar tune requiring little attention, he might be able to continue with the "low-cost" activity of humming and still be able to watch the approaching mobster through the window.[32]

Cost-effectiveness plays an important role in some mental disorders. If information were free, for example, an economically rational De Niro would want all the information he could get about the dangers of his situation. He might even benefit from an awareness of his own bodily signals of danger— his rapid heartbeat, his sweaty palms, his shallow breathing. If properly calibrated, these signals can help him gauge the risks and decide what to do. Such information, however, comes at a cost. Because patients with panic disorder have abnormally sensitive fear networks in the brain, information can actually command more attention than it warrants, distracting them from real dangers.[33,34] People with panic disorder often pay a high price for the negligible benefits that accrue from their internal perceptions.

The price of information is just as high for obsessive-compulsive patients. They often cannot attend to urgent matters because they spend every waking hour attending to possible disturbances in the order, safety, and cleanliness of their homes. Disturbances in brain function appear related to their preoccupation. When some patients with obsessive-compulsive disorder (OCD) touch a dirty object, images of their brains reveal abnormal activity in regions (such as the *cingulate* gyrus and *caudate* nucleus) that play a role in attention.[35]

In addition, evidence suggests that attention mechanisms, such as working memory, are highly inefficient in schizophrenic patients. In simple tasks, these patients need to exert much more effort than people without the illness. Such effort is correlated with increased frontal brain activity.[36] While earlier reports suggested schizophrenics had decreased frontal brain activity (called hypofrontality), later reports suggest that this only occurs in more complex tasks, as if to reflect their inattention and lack of effort when overwhelmed.

In such cases, dopamine system activity may play an important role in determining the perceived costs required to obtain a reward. Depletion or inhibition of dopamine in the nucleus accumbens (NAc) does not affect the physical effort that animals will exert to obtain a high reward option alone. But it does lower the physical effort that animals will exert to obtain a high (vs. low) reward option.[37] Conceivably, then, dopamine activity in the NAc affects the perceived incremental cost-effectiveness of one choice versus another.

Beyond Management Efficacy: Commitment and the Value of Actions as Social Signals

Crooks and Cry Babies.   In the efficacy framework, actions determine outcomes. However, actions also send a signal indicating one's commitment to a course of action (A). Such actions strategically influence the actions of others (A_O) in order to produce better outcomes (see the connection from A to A_O to outcome in Figure 2–4). For example, if rational people follow only their own immediate self-interests, they will avoid conflicts, such as mob wars, in which both parties are likely to lose. However, De Niro's assistant warns him that he cannot appear weak and that he sometimes must fight. If De Niro's rivals, such as "Lou the Wrench," suspect his weakness—if they learn that he has lost his nerve, developed panic attacks, and now breaks down crying during sentimental TV commercials—then he's dead. Assuming he could not retaliate, they certainly would have struck. If he appears to be a "mad dog" killer, on the other hand, the other mobsters would fear reprisal, and De Niro might actually find safety. In this instance, then, an apparently irrational act of aggression could paradoxically achieve a rational goal.

To help motivate De Niro to be a "mad dog," the rewards for such reprisals appear to be built into the brain. In economic "trust" games, when one person "punishes" another—even at a cost to himself—after the other person repays too little, a reward region called the NAc is still activated.[38] So revenge may have once "tasted sweet" to De Niro, even when it appeared to be counter to his interests. However, people may sometimes also calculate whether the loss in personal income is worth the pleasure of reprisal. Evidence suggests that different brain regions may sometimes attenuate the desire for revenge and enable us to weigh its costs and benefits. When the punishment is costly to the other player, the caudate is activated in proportion to the size of the punishment.[39] By contrast, when the punishment is also costly to the punisher, the ventromedial prefrontal cortex (VMPFC), including the orbitofrontal cortex (OFC), is activated.

Perhaps troubled by the utilitarian conflict between self-interest and revenge, De Niro seeks therapy. Believing that revenge is the only truly honorable goal, his initial desire in therapy is to free himself of panic attacks and other heart-felt sentiments in order to liberate the latent psychopath within him. Along the way, however, he discovers the value of having a heart. His fear and guilt signal a commitment to cooperation that makes others believe he will not exploit them. He discovers that, in noncompetitive situations, others are more likely to behave cooperatively to arrive at a mutually advantageous outcome.

Some research suggests that his newfound benevolence may also be related to activity in the caudate.[40] In multiround trust games, activity in the caudate correlates initially with an "intention to trust" signaled by their decisions and occurring afterward. However, as the game continues, the activity eventually begins occurring prior to the decision. Thus the player may actually develop a mental model for the other's behavior, which can then help guide decisions.

Other regions may also contribute to the capacities to form mental models of others' intentions. For instance, the difficulty of the autistic in "reading minds" appears linked to deficits in what some have termed the brain's "mind-reading" center (an area of the PFC called Brodmann area 10). This area is preferentially activated when people cooperate in economic games.[41] Because they cannot imagine the thoughts and feelings of their competitors, autistics often propose unfair offers to them in economic games.[42] Likewise, since they are unaware of others' intentions, autistics have trouble responding to spiteful actions, deceit, and lies.

The lack of empathy of criminals such as De Niro's character may not be related to such a fundamental deficit in reading minds. Rather, their deficits in the frontal cortex may reduce autonomic responsiveness. Their low anxiety sensitivity, which produces almost the opposite of panic, may contribute to noncooperative, antisocial behaviors.[43] In the opinion of some researchers, these apparently "heartless" criminals kill, steal, and destroy property to get their hearts going a bit faster—to begin to feel again.

Beyond Outcome Efficacy: Predictions as Evaluations and Evaluations as Predictions

The sections on management and outcome efficacy discussed the role of anticipatory predictions in guiding the selection of acts and the estimation of the degree of benefit from them. However, such predictions can also produce evaluations—they can have an intrinsic affective value (shown by the contribution of hypothetical evaluations, E_H, to experienced evaluations, "E_E", in Figure 2–3).[44] For example, feelings of hope are important to well-being,

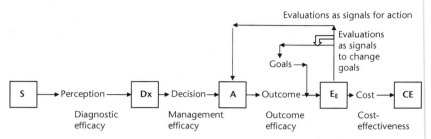

Figure 2–5 Other components of effectiveness: Beyond outcome efficacy. This figure illustrates the role of evaluations as signals for action (connection of E_E to A) or as signals to change goals (connection of E_E to Goals). Note that the anticipatory judgment of cost-effectiveness would simulate this entire process, resulting in a hypothetical evaluation of cost-effectiveness (E_H). S = stimuli, Dx = diagnoses, A = actions, E_E = experienced evaluations, CE = cost-effectiveness.

and their loss often contributes to depression. Feelings of dread are also important and may contribute to excessive pain sensitivity.

Likewise, just as predictions can become evaluations, evaluations can become predictors. For example, many negative emotions—such as depression, pain, disgust, or anger—are not just end states. They also signal the need to change goals or act differently. While these emotions may have a negative impact in the short term, they might produce a positive effect by helping us avoid even more negative outcomes in the long term (see the connection between E_E and A in Figure 2–5).

De Niro discovers that his usual outlets for anger have become ineffective. Formerly able to kill and mutilate his colleagues in a happy-go-lucky way, he now is troubled by these activities and becomes frustrated. However, while his frustration may have had negative value in the short term, it ultimately leads to a search in psychotherapy for more successful actions that would produce better long-term outcomes. His therapist helps him learn alternative anger management strategies, such as "hitting" a pillow when he is angry. And when the angry "hit man" De Niro pulls out his gun and shoots the pillow, he does feel soothed. Later, he even stops pulverizing his physicians. He thereby overcomes his short-term frustration and avoids more negative future outcomes such as imprisonment.

In addition to leading to new management strategies, negative evaluations also prompt people to change goals, which turns negative evaluations of outcomes into positive ones (see the connection from E_E to goals in Figure 2–5). In other words, if people do not get what they like, they learn to like what they get. For instance, when De Niro's panic attacks interfered with his success as a mobster, he questioned and then gave up his lifelong goal to be the best mobster he could possibly be. Although it once may have been hard for him to imagine, he learned that he could live a rich and fulfilling life even without the violence, viciousness, and vengeance he had once loved so dearly.

3

The Efficacy of Evaluation: What Are the Economic Elements of the Ability to Evaluate Risk and Reward?

While the previous section provided an overview of some general categories of decision-making capacities, chapters 3 and 4 illustrate more detailed neuroeconomic models of some of the capacities. They consider economic and behavioral economic models of our abilities to anticipate and experience outcomes.

Following the more general framework for identifying elements of efficacy in chapter 2, the present chapter will consider in more detail the economic components of the capacity to evaluate outcomes. Since the neoclassical economic model considers rational choices to depend only on the ability to anticipate outcomes, the present chapter will consider the diagnostic and management components of anticipation. For the sake of brevity and in order to describe possible evaluation inconsistencies, the topic of outcome efficacy will be covered in chapter 4. The following sections describe possible measures of diagnostic and management evaluations as well as their neural correlates and possible disturbances. As a starting point for readers, the chapter will greatly simplify the discussion of neurobiological findings and economic models. It will reserve discussion of more complex and realistic models, as well as a more detailed discussion of the neurobiology, for chapter 4.

DE GUSTIBUS NON EST DISPUTANDUM?

ARE TASTES REALLY INDISPUTABLE?

For much of the past century, economists have held that values are indisputable, that one cannot quarrel about tastes. They found no way to measure values directly and gave up arguing about what they could not directly assess. Many economists even doubted that one could ever improve these inexact inferences. As W. S. Jevons stated, "I hesitate to say that men will ever have the means of measuring directly the feelings of the human heart."[45]

Some philosophers added to the pessimism about the prospect of measuring tastes by demonstrating how difficult it is to identify their origins. If asked why you like anchovies, for example, you might say that you like the salty taste. But you are likely to have much more trouble saying why you like the salty taste. And since tastes and values often escape explanation, they have sometimes been seen as mystical entities that cannot be measured or studied scientifically. The philosopher Robert Pirsig has poked fun at the belief that values are mysterious and indeterminate. "Any person of any philosophic persuasion who sits on a hot stove," he writes, "will verify without any intellectual argument whatsoever that he is in an undeniably low-quality situation [and that] the value of his predicament is negative." He continues, "This low quality is not just a vague, wooly headed, metaphysical abstraction. It is an experience. It is not a judgment about an experience. It is not a description of experience. The value is itself an experience. As such, it is completely predictable. It is verifiable by anyone who cares to do so."[46]

Recent progress in neuroscience may make the experiment that Pirsig proposes unnecessary for some individuals. One can now measure the origins of some of our feelings about outcomes in a way that many economists and philosophers never thought possible. For instance, some neurobiologic research has shown that the feelings of dread we experience when we think about sitting on a hot stove may derive from the same circuits in the brain that mediate the pain we felt when we sat on it in the first place.[47]

At the same time, however, neurobiologic research also has confirmed what many philosophers believe—that there is more to our evaluations of stimuli than the mere sensations we experience sitting on a hot stove. For example, in response to a sensory stimulus, people's EEGs show pulses of electrical activity that are symmetrical across different sides of the brain. These pulses are called *event-related potentials* (ERPs). However, when people respond emotionally to these sensations, the ERPs appear more toward the right side of the brain.[48] The following sections also describe many more specific forms of evaluations that involve our anticipations of outcomes.

ECONOMIC MODELS OF THE EVALUATION PROCESS

Behavioral economists have proposed several models that describe the way people compute evaluations. This section describes those that are consistent with an economic model of efficacy. Table 3–1 displays these models to facilitate their comparison. The table first describes *multiattribute utility* models, which compute anticipations of value at a single point in time under conditions of certainty (when one is sure that the outcomes will occur). The table also illustrates several models that describe evaluations at a single point in time under conditions of uncertainty (when one is not sure if the outcomes will happen). These models include expected value, expected utility, and subjective expected utility.

Table 3-1 Efficacy Models

Economic Model	Model Components	Advantages and Disadvantages	Neurobiology	Pathology
Multiattribute utility MAU = SUM b_i o_i Weights (b) and outcomes (o)	Change in weights inferred from neural activities or induced by brain lesions	Estimates tradeoffs, which may not be apparent in conscious preferences Does not consider uncertainty	Reward-related activity during sex or drug films Subthalamic nucleus (STN) damage alters desire to work for different rewards	Changes in importance weights of drugs vs. sex in cocaine addicts Disabling STN changes food-cocaine tradeoffs
Expected value EV = SUM p_i x_i Probability (p) and amount of outcomes (x)	Net gains in gambling tasks	Using EV maximizes net gains Does consider probability but not risk attitude or values	Lower net gain in the Iowa Gambling Task for patients with PFC lesions	Diminished net gains in gamblers and addicts
Expected utility EU= SUM p_i u_i Probability (p) and utility (u) of outcomes, x Measures: Risk premium Decision quality Relative performance	Measures of risk aversion, "risk adjustment" and "decision quality" The "relative performance" (RP) measures the capacity of one's choices to satisfy his values, compared to the performance of a random decision rule	EU considers risk attitude but not subjective probability The RP measure can consider values ignored by net gain measures of performance	Amygdala, medial vs. lateral frontal and SSI cortex activity associated with risk attitude	Increased risk aversion in anxiety Decreased decision quality, risk adjustment in some addicts and in right VMPFC damage

(continued)

Table 3-1 (continued)

Economic Model	Model Components	Advantages and Disadvantages	Neurobiology	Pathology
Subjective expected utility SEU = SUM sp_i u_i Subjective probability (*sp*) and utility $u(x)$	Calibration awareness and quality Probability scoring rules Changes in probability estimates with new information	Quality calibration assesses distortions of subjective probability estimates Awareness calibration assesses over and under confidence in estimates Probability scoring rules can separate calibration, resolution, and variability/ difficulty in task Other methods can estimate bias, slope and scatter of estimates as well as assess how well one uses information to update estimates See Table 4-1 for disadvantages	Poor awareness calibration parietal/OF/DLPFC lesions Poor quality FC lesions Worst information use with parietal lesions Infrequent events represented more anteriorly in the VMPFC	Normal calibration for general events in anxiety Increased estimation of negative social events in phobics and of positive smoking-related outcomes in smokers

Not shown in Table 3–1 are more general models called "neural counters." Although similar in form to the models shown in Table 3–1, these "counters" can also consider the duration and frequency of repeated outcomes.[49] In addition, they include separate perceptual, timing, and evaluative channels. The perceptual channels represent the magnitude, location, and other salient features of the outcomes. The timing channels represent their anticipated time of availability, duration of delay, and rate of reward. Finally, the evaluative channels compute the reward values and guide the choice between options. Chapter 4 will introduce a few elementary aspects of such choices related to the timing of rewards. However, the present chapter considers only simple hypothetical choices similar to those used in economic analyses and gambling tasks.

For heuristic purposes, Figure 3–1 illustrates a simple model of the commonly occurring components of evaluation. These components include the inputs (outcomes and goals), comparators (which integrate information about outcomes and goals), and the outputs (the evaluations themselves).

Inputs

Outcomes

The inputs to the comparators in the economic efficacy model shown in Figure 3–1 include outcomes. Neuroeconomic experiments usually consider only specific measurable outcomes, such as winning or losing money in a gamble. But the word "outcome" can be used broadly to include also the acquisition of commodities, such as a car, or the occurrence of an event, such as marriage. These outcomes might include external rewards, such as the receipt of a paycheck, as well as more subjective life events, such as the stress of relocation, divorce, the loss of a family member or job, and failure to achieve other important goals.

In this chapter, the term "outcome" refers to an imagined event or state. When contemplating the risks of a business decision, for example, a person might imagine that he would feel unhappy if the proposed business plan failed and happy if it succeeded. Likewise, the term "outcome" could apply to a temporal sequence of events. Rewards and penalties often vary according

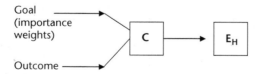

Figure 3–1 A comparator model of a multiattribute evaluation under conditions of certainty: If the importance weights of a job on two dimensions, such as free time and salary, are b_1 and b_2, and the outcomes are o_1 and o_2, then a simple additive model of the evaluation is $E_H = b_1 o_1 + b_2 o_2$.

to their consistency, quality, quantity, frequency, severity, and duration. They may occur at a single point in time, such as the World Trade Center bombing in New York on September 11, 2001. But other traumatic events, such as parental abuse, are often repeated, extending over many years.

Goals

A person's goals are the states that he is motivated by pleasure to seek and by fear to avoid. Goal pursuit is linked to many different psychological processes. These include the ability to sustain intention, to complete simple motor actions, or to perform hierarchically organized tasks. However, in the context of the evaluations discussed in this chapter, goals serve as the comparison standards against which outcomes are evaluated.

Goals are often arranged hierarchically. At the lowest level are concrete biological goals, such as maintaining nutrition, stabilizing chemicals, and sustaining fluids in the body. Intermediate-level goals may involve other survival-related or reproductive goals. Higher-order goals may arise from one's concept of the ideal self and vocation, such as the desire to become a nurse. Many representations of goals are enabled by circuits involving the *premotor and parietal cortex, caudate,* and *putamen,* as well as the PFC. As will be noted in chapter 4, dopamine signals in the PFC gate changes in goals. Parts of the *dorsolateral prefrontal cortex* (DLPFC) also help maintain intermediate goals in working memory as one implements plans to achieve one's objectives.

In addition, the "goals" depicted in Figure 3–1 may have different meanings. For example, goals may represent changing internal needs or representations of learned reward values, which generate expectancies (see chapter 4 for details).

The Comparators

Evaluations, such as pleasure or displeasure, result from the comparison of outcomes and goals, as illustrated in Figure 3–1. The comparisons between outcomes and goals depend on hardwired biology as well as learning-related biological changes. Regarding the former, many unconditioned stimuli—such as the perception of a snake—are compared with goals hardwired into the central nervous system, such as the desire to avoid danger or to fill bodily needs. Regarding the latter, conditioned stimuli, such as money acquired through gambling, are compared with learned reinforcement values, generated from plastic alterations in neural circuits.

Figure 3–2 shows a somewhat more refined model of the comparison process. In this model, the conditioned stimulus or outcome (O) is compared with information from long-term memory (LTM) about the category of the stimulus/outcome. This produces a short-term memory (STM) trace, which is in turn matched to the goal (G) and its information about the rewardingness of that type of outcome.

Although many brain regions participate in comparison processes, different elements of goals, outcomes, and comparisons may be represented separately.

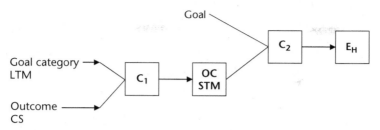

Figure 3–2 A more detailed comparator model of evaluation under uncertainty: A conditioned stimulus or imagined outcome (O) is interpreted by a preliminary comparator (C_1) with goal category information from long-term memory (LTM). This produces a short-term memory trace (STM), which indicates the stimulus/outcome category (OC) and may include information about the probability of the outcome. This trace, in turn, is matched to the goal system and its information about the rewardingness of that particular category of outcome, resulting in an evaluation of it (E_H) by a second comparator (C_2).

For example, in an incentive delay task, different regional activations correlated with goal-related values and outcomes.[50] The anterior cingulate cortex (ACC) and ventral striatum responded to the valenced, goal-related value of the rewards, whereas several cortical and subcortical regions responded to the magnitudes of the outcomes. In addition, interactions between outcome and goal (as well as probability) were found only in the ACC and the right tail of the caudate. Such interactions presumably reflected the comparison processes or results.

Output: Evaluations

The comparisons of outcomes and goals produce evaluations of the outcomes. The term "evaluation" will refer to the degree of subjective well-being experienced in response to a real or imagined outcome, such as the occurrence of an event or the acquisition of an object. For example, surveys have monitored measures of well-being after specific and life-defining events, such as marriage. They have asked: Does marriage have a happy outcome?[51]

The economic efficacy model appears to consider only one sense of "well-being," which it calls "utility." Accordingly, when the experienced outcomes match goals, one may feel elation or "happiness," and when they do not match goals, one may feel disappointment, or "unhappiness." In addition, however, other, more specific emotions can be associated with economic evaluations. When one imagines possible future outcomes and these outcomes match goals, one may experience optimism, hope, desire, pleasurable anticipation, or craving. When they do not, one may feel pessimism, hopelessness, dysphoria, or fear. More specific economic models clarify possible sources of these and other types of evaluations.

A MODEL OF EVALUATION UNDER CERTAINTY

Multiattribute Utility: The Evaluation of Tradeoffs

> Death should not be seen as the end, but as a very effective way to cut down expenses.
>
> Woody Allen[52]

A *multiattribute utility* (MAU) model can enable us to weigh tradeoffs between good and bad attributes of a choice—for example, money gained or life lost. Alternatively, in an economic decision analysis, one might ask: How much money am I willing to give up to obtain the color of car that I want? How much salary will I forego to get more free time in my job?

Figure 3–1 illustrates the evaluations of the job decision. According to this model, the person computes each job's MAU, a combination of the different benefits of each job expressed in a single numerical currency. In the simplest such model, the utility of each job is the sum of the different features of the job, each multiplied by their relative "importance weights." These weights express the values of each feature on a common scale. They resemble the "exchange rates" one might use to compute one's total wealth if one had a wallet full of currencies from different countries. After applying the appropriate weights (conversion rates) to the amount of each bill in one's wallet, one could compute their total value in terms of a single currency. In the case of MAU theory, that currency is called utility.

Many different methods exist to compute multiattribute utilities.[53] For example, in the selection of jobs differing in pay and free time, one may simply ask how important free time is relative to salary (assuming you would get the maximum of one vs. the minimum of the other). Suppose that the job seeker said that the salary was twice as important—that is, $b_1^* = 2b_2^*$, where b_1^* and b_2^* are crude measures of importance, which need not sum to one. From these crude measures, one can calculate the actual "importance weight" of salary, relative to the total importance of the other attributes, as: $b_1 = b_1^*/(b_1^* + b_2^*) = 2b_2^*/3b_2^* = .67$. Since these actual weights sum to one, the "importance" of free time would be $b_2 = .33$, roughly one half of the importance of salary.

Other MAU models can involve more complex valuation mechanisms, such as the multiplication, rather than addition, of attribute values. For example, suppose we want to describe how people value different health outcomes when medical treatment promises a higher quality of life but lower life expectancy, whereas surgery promises the opposite. To predict whether the patient will choose medical or surgical treatment, simply adding the adjusted values of duration and quality will not do. One values longevity not for its own sake but in proportion to the quality of life experienced. Thus, we require models that allow for interactions between the two factors—such as a "quality adjusted life years" model, which multiplies the quality of the health state by its duration.[54] Similar interactions may exist also in hedonic processes—for example, in which one has a choice between a longer duration of an unpleasant state or a shorter duration of a pleasant one. More complex models of such processes are described by the "anxiety" and "quality adjusted life minutes" (QALMs) models discussed in chapter 4.

Neurobiology of Tradeoffs

Tradeoffs may be particularly important in addictions. Neural adaptations from repeated drug use appear to make addicts more willing to give up, or trade off, alternative rewards for addictive substances. For example, in amphetamine addiction, the sensitivity of some dopamine receptors declines, making people less responsive to the actual experience of alternative rewards such as work, friends, and family. Likewise, cocaine addicts have abnormally high fMRI activity in reward-related regions of the brain when viewing films of drug use but low activity when viewing sexually arousing films.[55] Although few studies have directly estimated tradeoffs from such neural activity measures, one could evaluate their correlations with subjects' willingness to pay for the different rewards.

Likewise, one can determine implicit rather than conscious, explicit tradeoffs, as in the previously described job choice example. For example, the job choice evaluation asks the person how much reward (salary) she is willing to give up to do less work (get more free time). Animal experiments have, in effect, "asked" the subject how much extra work it is willing to do to get more reward (e.g., lever pressing to get a cocaine reward rather than a food reward).[56,57] Such experiments could enable us to estimate the relative importance of reward and work.

Similarly, such experiments can help evaluate the effects of neurologic lesions on the willingness to work for different types of rewards. For instance, the *subthalamic nucleus* (STN), a key structure in controlling outputs from the *basal ganglia*, appears to help modulate the magnitudes of tradeoffs for different types of rewards, such as food and cocaine.[58] Lesions to this area decrease the willingness of animals to work for cocaine while they increase the motivation to work for food rewards.

Furthermore, experiments can evaluate the effects of neurochemical changes on tradeoffs, determined by the willingness to "pay" different types of "costs"—such as the willingness to exert effort or endure delay.[59] For instance, in animal experiments, the blockade of brain dopamine with a drug called Haldol impairs both the willingness to exert effort and to endure delay. But a similar blockade of serotonin systems affects only the latter.

MODELS OF CHOICE UNDER UNCERTAINTY

Several other models can describe anticipatory evaluations when the outcomes are not certain but occur with varying probabilities. In all of these models, goals and outcomes may still be combined to produce evaluations, as shown in Figure 3–2, but with one further addition. The possible outcome (O) is compared not only with information from LTM about the category of the outcome, but also with information about its frequency. Such frequency may derive either from one's imagination, when possible outcomes are described, or from repetition of events, when outcomes are actually experienced.

Some research suggests that repetition of the events strengthens the STM trace that transmits information about both the likelihood and the category of the outcome. Ultimately, either form of frequency evaluation can be combined with information about goals to generate an evaluation.[60] Several economic efficacy models have been proposed to describe more specifically how such information is combined to produce evaluations.

The Expected Value Model

Some have suggested that people evaluate gambles as if they are computing their *expected values*: the sum of the amount of the outcomes (x_i), each multiplied by the chance that it will occur (p_i). For example, suppose that you set up a gambling experiment in which you offer the subject a choice between $3 for sure or an 80% (or $p = .8$) chance to win $4, otherwise nothing. The expected value of the gamble is SUM $p_i x_i = .8(\$4) + .2(0) = \$3.20$. That is more than the $3 the subject could have received for sure. So a subject following the expected value principle should choose the gamble.

But is it rational to choose gambles with the highest expected value? The answer is "yes, under some circumstances." If you know that you are going to repeatedly play the same gamble *ad infinitum*, then the average *net payoff* of the gamble would be its expected value (here, $3.20), which you would prefer to a sure $3 for each play.[61] So if you know the risks and possible payoffs in advance, play the same gambles long enough, and get the payoffs only after an experiment is over, then you will be rational if you maximize expected value. Also, to see how well one is following this strategy, one could measure the net gains, as has been done in the Iowa Gambling Task (IGT).

Neurobiology and Pathology

Let us for a moment take for granted the assumption commonly made in gambling experiments that the net gains are an adequate measure of performance. A series of experiments were conducted with the IGT, in which subjects repeatedly selected cards from one of four decks, with different probabilities of winning and losing as well as different ranges of amounts to win or lose. Subjects did not initially know the composition of the decks; however, two of the decks, termed advantageous ones, were more conservative, with less chance of a large gain but with a positive expected value ($25). The other two, termed disadvantageous decks, were riskier, with a greater chance of a large gain but with a negative expected value (−$25). The authors monitored both the net gains in the task as well as the SCRs before and after the outcomes of each card selection were announced. They found that the net gains—as well as anticipatory skin conductances—were reduced in the patients with bilateral lesions of the *amygdala* or VMPFC.[62]

From these and other data, the authors developed the "somatic marker theory." In this theory, the inability to make advantageous decisions seen in patients with these neurologic lesions is due to a defective emotional capacity to rapidly signal the possible consequences of a choice and thereby suggest what deck to select.

In this theory, the VMPFC acts in concert with the amygdala to produce the bodily sensation of anticipation (Figure 3–3). In essence, each plays a role in the comparisons of outcomes with goals or related states (e.g., representations of hedonic states associated with certain types of outcomes). However, the two structures play somewhat different roles. Patients with bilateral damage to

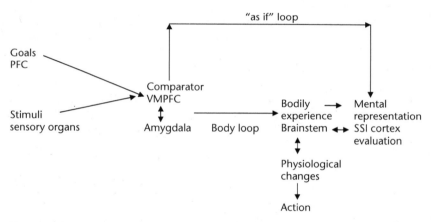

Figure 3–3 Body and "as if" loops underlying simulation. Illustrated are mechanisms underlying simulated evaluations according to the original theory of somatic markers. The visual input from a hypothetical gamble presented to a subject, as well as information about goals from the PFC, provide input to neural processors, which determine the anticipated rewardingness of a stimulus. When these neural circuits are activated, one can actually experience physiological changes in the body via a "body loop" through the brainstem to initiate physiological changes that prepare the body for action. Information about these bodily changes then travels back through the brainstem and then to the somatosensory/insular (SSI) cortex, which can enable the person to become aware of the feelings. An "as if" loop is also pictured in the diagram. This loop enables people to bypass the reexperiencing of somatic states, once one learns what feeling states result from the associations between particular outcomes and goals. One experiences the psychological component of emotions alone, "as if" the physical changes were really occurring. According to one theory, this weaker "as if" loop goes directly from the VMPFC and amygdala to the brainstem nuclei and SSI cortex. That theory holds that it may be involved more in processing known risks, whereas, the body loop may be involved in processing unknown or ambiguous ones.

the amygdala generated neither experienced nor anticipatory SCRs. Thus, the somatic marker theory held that the amygdala may help mediate experienced evaluations. In addition, it may enable learning through experience, which would guide anticipatory responses later.

By contrast, the VMPFC was thought to mediate anticipatory more than experienced evaluations, since VMPFC-damaged patients did not generate normal anticipatory SCRs but did generate normal experienced ones. In particular, the theory postulated that the VMPFC may help generate anticipatory responses through the induction of bodily changes. These changes then could be relayed to the somatosensory/insular (SSI) cortex, which enables an awareness of the somatic state associated with the anticipated outcome (see Figure 3–3).

In the somatic marker theory, moreover, the somatic states enable one to develop a "hunch" that certain gambles (certain decks of cards) are "good" or "bad," even prior to conscious awareness.[63] The "hunch" is in essence a memory trace, thought to be implicit in brainstem representations, which obtain bodily signals before relaying them to the SSI cortex. Also, connected with this "hunch" is a "somatic marker"—the sensation of "feeling" possible outcomes as if they were actually occurring.[64] Thus, if a rational subject's goals were to maximize net gains, this hunch would roughly indicate his best estimate of the gamble's expected value.

The somatic marker theory has stimulated a large body of related work, both supportive and contradictory. On the negative side, one experiment demonstrated that subjects have more conscious knowledge of the IGT than previously believed. It cast doubt on whether "unconscious hunches" necessarily played a role in their subjects' choices.[65] Another experiment found that patients with high cervical spinal cord lesions—who presumably had some somatic sensations blocked—performed the IGT normally despite an absence of SCRs.[66] However, the criticisms of the somatic marker theory have had their own problems.[67] For instance, other pathways—for example, neurochemical mechanisms—may relay sensory awareness, even in patients with cervical spinal cord lesions. Also, on the positive side, some experiments appear to provide support for the theory. For example, external augmentation of physiologic responses does affect decision making, as the somatic marker hypothesis would predict.[68]

In any case, if the somatic marker hypothesis is a useful one, then, like any good theory, it will undergo revisions. And already that appears to be occurring. For example, the VMPFC may not play a purely anticipatory role. In a task much simpler than the IGT, the medial PFC (mPFC) did not appear to be activated during anticipation, only during the experience of reward.[69] This task differed from the IGT in that the receipt of a reward or penalty depended on how quickly one responded, not merely how thoughtfully. Also, the study only had subjects anticipate either rewards or losses, not both as with the IGT. Possibly, then, the VMPFC may play less of a role in anticipation than in the experience of particular outcomes for purely positive or negative prospects, yet it could help subjects combine and anticipate information about multiple, mixed outcomes.

In addition, experiments also have identified other neural structures, such as the striatum and nucleus accumbens, that could help generate the representations of expected value originally addressed by the somatic marker theory. In one study that searched for brain regions that correlated best with expected value and its components, the subcortical NAc activated proportionally to the magnitude of anticipated gains; whereas a cortical structure, the mPFC, activated proportionally to their probabilities.[70] The authors suggested that the expected values then may be computed in an ascending, subcortical–cortical network, in which the subcortical structures compute the affective value of outcomes and the cortical structures represent their probabilities as well as possibly integrate the two—a function of the comparator, discussed earlier in this chapter.

The Adequacy of the Expected Value Theory and the "Net Gain" Criterion for Optimal Performance

The above evidence for the expected value and somatic marker theories represent important contributions to our knowledge. Nevertheless, they have limitations. For instance, the research showing correlations between neural activities and expected values did not seek to test specific predictions of the expected value theory or to compare it with alternative models. Like many other neuroeconomic studies, it was based on a search for neural activation patterns that appear consistent with the expected value theory; if you torture such data long enough, they will usually confess.

Also, the most common method used to test the validity of the somatic marker theory has its own limitations. Its measure of success is the "net monetary gains." That is, in the IGT, according to the "net gains" criterion, whoever wins more money is judged to perform better. Thus, when patients thought to have somatic marker impairments, due to neurologic lesions, have lower net gains, this presumably indicates an inability to make advantageous decisions. But the net gains are maximized in the long run only when people compute the expected values of gambles and use these values to make their choices. So one must ask: do people really seek to maximize expected values?

Many experiments have found that even apparently normal people do not seek to maximize expected values in gambling experiments similar to the IGT.[71] Neither do they do so in real life. Instead, they travel to Las Vegas or Monte Carlo just to have the opportunity to play gambles with negative expected values. They buy insurance policies, even though they are likely to pay out more than they gain. People often seem not to care if their gambles or insurance policies have negative expected values and promise lower net gains in the long term. In the oft-quoted words of economist John Maynard Keynes, "In the very long run, we are all dead." Perhaps in part to forestall that inevitability and promote our survival, we evolved brain mechanisms that consider factors other than expected value, such as risk.

Expected Utility: A Model That Can Consider Risk Attitude

A model called expected utility has the capacity to describe peoples' attitudes toward risk and to suggest factors other than "net gains" that may be pertinent to economic performance. As shown in Table 3–1, the expected utility model takes a form similar to expected value, except that the amount of an outcome, x, is replaced by its utility: $u(x)$. Thus, the expected utility of an outcome is the product of the utility of each outcome, multiplied by the chance that it will occur.

By adding the element of "utility" to the expected value model, the expected utility approach enables much more latitude in describing peoples' preferences for risk. How does one determine risk attitude? A person is "risk-averse" if she would rather have a payment equal to the expected value of the gamble instead of playing the gamble itself. For example, if a gamble yields $20 fifty percent of the time and $0 the other fifty percent of the time, the expected value is $10. A risk-averse person would prefer to have the certain $10 than to play the gamble. A risk-seeking individual would prefer the opposite.[72] Thus, by inquiring about such preferences, one can determine whether or not a person seeks risk.

Other questions can determine the extent to which a person seeks or avoids risk. For example, suppose that a risk-averse individual has a small but risky "investment" that now is equivalent to a 50/50 gamble to win or lose $10. We then ask how much the person would pay for an insurance company to assume responsibility for the gamble. Suppose that the individual says $1. That amount is called the *risk premium*; the higher it is, the more risk-averse she is. Given multiple questions like these about preferences between certain monetary amounts and gambles, one can eventually draw a graph of her utility as a function of monetary outcomes.

Given a measured utility function, one can also compute another measure of risk aversion—the ratio of the utility function's second and first derivatives (u''/u', termed the Arrow/Pratt measure). If the utility of a given amount of money, x, is an exponential function, $u(x) = 1 - e^{-bx}$, the risk aversion is its acceleration divided by its rate of change ($-u''/u' = b$). The constant, b, reflects the curvature of the utility function, and the person is said to be risk-averse if $b > 0$, risk-neutral if $b = 0$, and risk-seeking if $b < 0$. Note that though the constant, b, measures the degree of risk aversion in this simple example, such aversion may change with the decision-maker's level of wealth. That occurs, for example, when the person becomes less risk-averse the wealthier she becomes (i.e., $b(x) \neq b$). A neuroeconomic study might then assess changes in her risk aversion depending on factors related to her perceived initial level of "wealth" (e.g., where $x =$ the level of assets accrued in a gambling experiment).

In addition, neuroeconomic studies can look at how neural activities vary as a function of a gamble's expected value and variance, the latter of which is often used as a measure of risk. For example, if a gamble offers a chance, p, of winning x and $(1 - p)$ of winning y, then the expected value of the gamble $[px + (1 - p)y]$ increases as p rises. The variance of the gamble $[(x - y)^2 p(1 - p)]$ rises until the chances of winning rise to even ($p = .5$). As the chances rise beyond that, the variance actually decreases, since $p(1 - p)$ is maximal at $p = .5$. So neural activity correlated with this measure of risk should rise and then fall as the probability rises.

Neurobiology and Pathology

Neuroeconomic studies already have tried to sketch the correlates of expected utility functions from direct neural measures. For instance, one study suggested that neuron activities in the parietal cortex of monkeys may reflect the expected utility of juice rewards anticipated by monkeys in a visual discrimination task.[73] As the amount of a juice reward increased, so did the activities of the neurons, but perhaps with a declining rate, termed decreasing marginal utility.

To test whether preferences are sensitive to risk, other studies have offered gambles with equal expected value but different degrees of risk. In one such study, monkeys showed risk aversion when choosing between two uncertain options. Also, the activities of neurons in the posterior cingulate cortex varied with the degree of uncertainty.[74]

A similar study using the Rogers Decision Making Task found increased risk-seeking choices among drug users, in comparison with normal controls. This difference was attributed in part to decreased activation in the part of the ACC (the left pregenual ACC).[75] In yet another experiment, fMRI activities in parts of the cingulate uniquely associated with the riskiness of options.[76]

Other brain regions may also play a critical role in encoding attitudes toward risk. For example, using the Rogers Decision Making Task, subjects chose between different gambles with different amounts to win and probabilities of winning. One experiment also had subjects choose between certain gains or losses and risky options with the same expected value. The study showed that activity in the medial frontal cortex was associated with risk aversion and activity in the lateral frontal cortex was associated with risk-seeking choices.[77] In addition, various subcortical structures also appear to encode risk. In fact, they may separately encode the expected value and variance (or risk) of a gamble. Preuschoff et al. found that reward expectation correlated with initial activity in the ventral striatum, while reward variance correlated with delayed activity.[78]

Another study suggested distinct neural signature for perceived risk and return on investments. Since the level of acceptable risk, and perhaps perceived risk, may change with the expected value, the study correlated neural measures of risk perception with various corrected measures of "range," such as the coefficient of variation—the standard deviation (square root of the variance) divided by the expected value.[79] The authors found significant correlations between such a perceived risk measure and neural activities in the ACC and insula; whereas expected return correlated only with activity in the DLPFC.

In evaluating such studies of the neural correlates of risk, it is important to carefully note whether one is measuring risk, risk perception, risk acceptability or sensitivity to risk. It is also important to note whether some studies pertain to risk attitudes or to the quality of decisions. For instance, in the Rogers Decision Making Task, subjects make choices between multiple gambles, with differing probabilities and amounts to win or lose (see footnote for prototype study).[80] When the subject chooses between two gambles, the high gains are usually paired with low probabilities of winning and low gains with high probabilities. When the expected values of the two gambles are equal, and the person chooses the riskier ones, the person can then be said to exhibit risk-seeking choices. However, it is important not to confuse the above methods with another task used by Rogers that we can call the "Rogers Decision Quality Task." In this decision-quality assessment, subjects are offered gambles with a specified chance, p, of either winning or losing a fixed number of points. Subjects must first choose the type of bet they want—one with a high or low probability of winning—and then decide how many points to wager on the gamble. Given the structure of the study, it is always better to choose the gamble with the higher chances of winning.

For example, if you are offered a choice between a 60% chance to win $10 and a 40% chance to win $10 (otherwise zero), the first option probabilistically *dominates* the second. It offers a better chance for the preferred outcome—winning $10—and a lower chance for the nonpreferred outcome—winning nothing. So again, if you do not choose the first option, you are not seeking risk; rather, you are violating a basic principle of rational choice.[81] Rogers calls the frequency of similar violations a measure of *decision quality*.

A subtle feature of the Decision Quality task is that the gambles with the higher probability of winning ($>.5$) have positive expected values and those with the low probability ($p <.5$) have negative expected values. In one study, however, amphetamine abusers and patients with OFC damage often chose the dominated, negative expected value bets.[82] If, at this point, one were to measure the subjects' risk attitudes according to their willingness to increase wagers on bets, one could not meaningfully compare the above patient groups with the normal controls. The patients would be playing disadvantageous bets with negative expected values and the controls would be playing advantageous ones with positive expected values. Since risk attitudes often differ for gains and losses, any differences between subjects could be due to the type of bet and not due to their different risk attitudes.

Thus, the investigators did not make such comparisons but instead formulated measures of *risk adjustment*—sensitivity to changes in risk and the tendencies to wager more as the probability of winning increases.[83] The authors found such changes in choice due to changes in probability to be more conservative for the OFC-damaged patients compared with the normal controls. On the surface, this result might seem surprising, since the OFC-damaged patients often appear to be impulsive and risk-seeking. Possibly, they merely appear to be risk-seeking because they make poor quality choices and seemingly do not realize that a gamble with a higher probability of winning is more advantageous.[84] In any case, when this poor decision quality is not present, a more expected pattern seems to emerge. Patients with damage to the orbital and medial frontal cortex due to rupture of the anterior communicating artery (ACoA), who did not make poor quality choices—and therefore apparently recognized advantageous gambles— did have greater-than-normal risk adjustments.[85]

Pathological attitudes about gain, loss, and risk may also relate to other regions of the brain, as well as different biochemical systems. For example, activity in the ventral striatum appears to encode a signal specific to risk, as well as one specific to expected value.[86] Thus, the relative responsiveness of these signals could, in the future, clarify sources of risk-seeking, in disorders, such as mania and substance addictions.

Likewise, parts of the frontal cortex, as well as the amygdala, play a role in the suppression and development of fear conditioning, which may affect risk attitude.[87] In addition, the right insular cortex—part of the previously mentioned loop, which appeared to enable awareness of the bodily experience of risk—is more sensitive to punishment in anxious people who are more intent on avoiding harm.[88] In addition, some findings suggest that an area in posterior, ventral insula may specifically encode the degree of error or surprise in risk predictions.[89] And some of these structures may respond not only to risk but also to ambiguity (which is distinct from the variance of a gamble and is discussed in chapter 4).

A Measure of Utility Gain in Gambling Tasks

In the future, neuroeconomic measures could assess not merely changes in risk attitude, discrimination abilities, or net gains in gambling tasks; they could also summarize overall utility gains. Whereas the "net gains" in a gambling task does not consider peoples' abilities to make decisions consistent with their values, a neuroeconomic measure of relative performance (RP) provides more insight into these abilities.[90] Let us define the RP according to the utility gained if subjects follow their own preferences instead of selecting gambles to play at random.

More specifically,

$$RP = (EU_{avg} - EU_r)/(EU_I - EU_r)$$

where EU is the average expected utility actually obtained by the subject in his choices, EU_r is the average that would have been obtained had the subject made completely random selections, and EU_I is the ideal that could have been obtained.

The RP measure could derive from choices, subjective reports, or neural measures. It could derive either the anticipatory or the experienced utility of each outcome.[91] Let us illustrate the application of the RP measure using empirical data and a crude neural surrogate measure of utility—the skin conductance response—in subjects performing the IGT.

In one study using this task, the SCRs were measured before and after four different subject groups made choices between hypothetical gambles.[92] To measure the SCRs, Tranel et al. recorded the anticipatory responses prior to the individual's selection of a gamble as well as the experienced responses after the gamble.[93,94] To calculate the RP across multiple, sequential plays of the IGT, I used the reported frequencies of outcomes and average experienced SCRs as surrogate measures of the utility of each. I also used the reported frequencies of choosing the advantageous or disadvantageous decks. These values enable calculation of the average value actually obtained (EU_{avg}), the value that one would obtain if one made random selections of the decks (EU_r), and the ideal (EU_I).[95]

From these data, I found that the subjects without right-sided VMPFC damage performed better than those with such damage (RP = .15 vs. RP = −.14). In fact, the negative value of the RP for the patients with right-sided damage means that they perform even worse than a random rule in maximizing their own experienced values. That is, they would do better if they merely flipped a coin and then decided which deck to pick. Such worse-than-random performance is consistent with the findings of Rogers that the VMPFC-damaged patients often make poor quality (dominated) choices. In such cases, patients with VMPFC damage will not "rationally" maximize their experienced utilities, no matter what their risk attitudes are. Refined measures of outcome, such as the RP, may identify such cases and help determine if subjects' choices make them not only poorer but also less happy with the outcomes.

Subjectively Expected Utility Models and the Calibration of Probability

The previous section demonstrated how an expected utility model can consider the subjective utilities of outcomes rather than merely their objective values. Similarly, a subjectively expected utility (SEU) model can consider the subjective beliefs or opinions about the likelihood of events rather than merely their objective frequencies (as in the expected utility model shown in Table 3–1).

Such SEU models allow for the possibility that subjects might err in estimating the probability of winning or losing a gamble (a feature of diagnostic efficacy rather than management efficacy). For example, in the IGT, subjects do not initially know the chances of winning or losing with picks from the different decks of cards. In the course of an experiment, they may develop distorted beliefs and err in estimating the frequencies of different outcomes.

In fact, even if the objective probabilities of winning or losing are given explicitly, as in the Rogers Gambling Tasks, different subjects may have different interpretations of what the probabilities really mean. For example, if you were given numbers representing the brightness of two different candles, you might have only a very vague idea of what those numbers really mean. Similarly, people unfamiliar with probabilities may have trouble interpreting and using the numerical estimates.

METHODS FOR ASSESSING PREDICTION ABILITIES

Quality Calibration, Resolution, and Variability: Measures of Performance in Subjective Probability Estimation

One behavioral economic method used to evaluate the quality of subjective probability estimates is called a test of their calibration. One might ask a subject to estimate the chance of losing a gamble by picking a card from a deck in the IGT. Or one might ask a doctor to estimate the chance that a patient has pneumonia. Calibration measures the error of such estimates. For example, if the doctor's subjective estimates of pneumonia differ greatly from the actual frequencies of the outcome when particular estimates are made, then the doctor might be said to have poor calibration. By contrast, the doctor may be said to have perfect calibration when his or her subjective estimates equal the objective frequencies, for instance, for cases in which a perfectly calibrated physician predicts a 10% chance of pneumonia, the actual frequency of the illness also is 10%. Figure 3–4a provides sample computations of a calibration index (CI), which reflects this aspect of the quality of the estimates.

However, the quality of subjective probability judgment does not merely involve the calibration. For example, some computer programs presented with limited information about the characteristics of a patient may have better calibration than does a doctor who uses the same information. Yet the doctor who actually sees a patient may have access to more information about particular cases; so her estimates, though numerically less calibrated, may better discriminate between the cases that do or do not develop pneumonia.[96] Likewise, some patient groups with particular neurologic characteristics may have better discrimination, due to their perceptual or information processing skills, though others may have better calibration, due to their abilities to link event representations to their frequencies. Figure 3–4b provides an extreme example to illustrate how discrimination differs from calibration; and it also provides a sample computation of a discrimination index (DI), which reflects the subjective estimates' capacities to sort patients into different categories (higher values of DI reflect less error in discrimination).

Beyond the measures of calibration and discrimination, a probability score (PS) measures the overall error in judgment. One such score, called the Brier score, is the weighted average of squared differences between the estimated probability for each category and the estimate that would be made by a

(a)

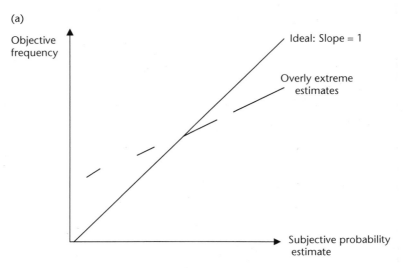

Figure 3–4 (a) Quality calibration of probability estimates. The horizontal axis is a doctor's subjective judgment of the probability that a person has pneumonia. The vertical axis is the objective frequency of cases of pneumonia when the doctor makes a particular probability judgment. The diagonal line indicates perfect quality calibration, wherein the subjective probability is the same as the actual frequency. The dotted line illustrates a case in which the doctor assigns too high a probability to frequent events and too low a probability to infrequent ones. (In the past, this tendency toward unjustifiably extreme estimates has sometimes been termed "overconfidence"; however, such overly extreme judgments should not be confused with the more common use of the term as reflecting a person's overconfidence in the accuracy of his own estimates. For a discussion of the latter, see the text discussion of "awareness calibration".) To compute a quality of "calibration index" (CI): suppose that, a doctor predicts the chance of pneumonia for 30 cases and uses only two different numerical estimates (10% to denote a low chance and 90% to denote a high one). When the doctor predicts a 10% chance of pneumonia, 20% of the cases actually have it (20 cases total); when the doctor predicts a 90% chance of pneumonia, 70% actually have it (10 cases); then, for each of the cases given a 10% subjective estimate, there is a miscalibration, measured as the squared error of the prediction = $(.1 - .2)^2 = .01$. For each case given a 90% subjective estimate, the miscalibration is $(.9 - .7)^2 = .04$. The total miscalibration then is the sum of these error terms across all the judgment categories, weighted by the proportion of such judgments in each, that is, CI = (20/30) (.01) + (10/30)(.04) = .02. A lower CI here is a sign of better probability judgments.

clairvoyant, who assigns a probability = 1 to all events that do occur and = 0 for all events that do not. Interestingly, this PS can be shown to include both the calibration and discrimination as well as a factor related to the inherent variability in the task outcomes.[97] That is, PS = CI − DI + VI, where VI is an index of the variability of discrimination, which is the average frequency of the predicted event times its complement.[98] This quantity is often related to

(b)

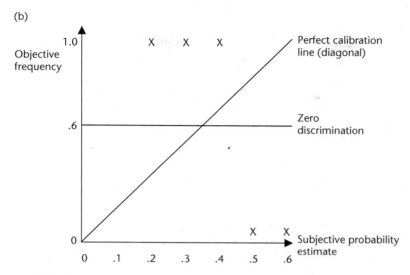

Figure 3–4 **(b)** Discrimination of probability estimates. The cases denoted by the symbol X do not lie close to the diagonal line, denoting perfect calibration. However, the subjective estimates corresponding to these cases reflect perfect discrimination— the ability to sort patients into different groups. That is, all the cases given a subjective probability of .2, .3, or .4 actually do turn out to have pneumonia, while all those given estimates of .5 or .6 do not develop it. By contrast, if the cases all fell along the horizontal line, corresponding to the average frequency of pneumonia (here =.6), then the subjective probabilities would provide no discrimination at all. To illustrate the measurement of a discrimination index (DI) in a less extreme example involving only two categories (e.g., denoting likely or unlikely events rather than the five sub-jective estimate categories shown in the figure), suppose that the average frequency of pneumonia when the doctor says that pneumonia is unlikely is .3 ($n = 6$ cases), and the average frequency when the doctor says pneumonia is likely is .6 ($n = 3$ cases). Then the DI is the squared difference between the average frequency for each category and the overall average frequency of pneumonia in the entire population, weighted by the proportion of cases. This average frequency is: $(6/9)(.3) + (3/9)(.6) = 0.4$. So the discrimination index is: $(6/9)(.3 - .4)^2 + (3/9)(.6 - .4)^2 = .02$. A similar method can apply to five subjective probability categories shown in the figure. A higher dis-crimination index indicates better separation of the distinct groups of patients.

the difficulty of the task. Hence, its value may tell us why the same types of subjects appear to have different probability scores in different experiments.

Yet other methods exist for decomposing the PS into other aspects of performance, such as the bias, the slope, and the scatter. The bias is the dif-ference between the average subjective probability judgments and the average frequency of events in the environment. Indicating the tendency to give overly high or low estimates, the bias may reflect tendencies to be more motivated to avoid one type of error than another. By contrast, the slope is the difference in the conditional mean probability judgments when the events do occur versus when they do not occur. It may reflect discrimination or labeling skills. Finally, the scatter is the inherent variability in the person's estimates. It may reflect the person's inconsistency or tendencies to attend to weakly predictive cues (see Yates for a more detailed discussion of these indices).[99]

Awareness Calibration: A Measure of the Awareness of Calibration Quality

In addition to assessing the quality of the subjective probability estimates, researchers also may wish to assess the person's awareness of the quality of her estimates. Is the person aware that he is making good estimates or poor ones? For example, to assess such awareness, researchers can ask the person to estimate her confidence regarding the estimates themselves—the chances that they are near the true values.

Awareness calibration can be applied to probability estimates (i.e., by asking people to estimate the chances that their likelihood estimates are within a given range of the true probabilities). However, such calibration questions may be less confusing when the estimates are other quantities. For instance, in one study, researchers asked normal controls and patients with various neurologic lesions to estimate the sales of consumer products during the next 4 months. Then the subjects were asked to estimate the chance that their predictions would match the actual sales (within a given range). This task depends in part on an awareness of their performances. In this case, people are considered *overconfident* in awareness if they give higher estimates than warranted, that is, if their subjective probabilities for being correct exceed the actual frequencies of correct predictions.

Abilities to Appraise and Use Information

The authors of the previously discussed calibration study also evaluated a third type of estimation ability: How well subjects appraise and use information to make estimates. The information involved advice from different experts, who themselves gave estimates of sales. The study tested the subjects' abilities to determine which experts were more accurate. It also tested their capacities to perform a more difficult task: combining and using opinions from multiple experts. The latter task tests subjects' abilities to retrieve the experts' past forecasts from LTM and then to hold them in working memory while making their own sales predictions.

Neurobiology and Pathology

A variety of brain regions, which appear to activate during choices involving uncertainty, are likely to play a role in different types of subjective probability estimates. These regions may include prefrontal and parietal cortices, as well as the striatum and ACC.[100] As such, damage to many different areas may affect the quality of probability estimates or the awareness of such quality.

For example, the previously mentioned study of probability calibration found that probability scoring rule measures were marginally better (lower) for controls than for patients with either orbitofrontal (OFC), dorsolateral (DLPFC), or parietal lobe damage (all predominantly right-sided).[101]

Yet, the same study suggested even more clearly that different neural structures mediate the quality of the estimates themselves and the awareness of their quality.[102] The groups with frontal lobe (OFC or DLPFC) damage had poorer estimation quality than did those with parietal lobe damage, whereas all the patient groups had impaired awareness of their own performance and demonstrated overconfidence in awareness (normal controls were not overconfident). So, though only frontal lobe deficits appeared to influence the quality of forecasts, a wide variety of lesions appeared to affect the awareness of one's predictive accuracy—a more cognitively complex ability.

Additional discriminations between different types of brain-damaged subjects were enabled by tests of the third set of abilities previously mentioned: how well subjects appraise and use information from others to make estimates. The OFC-damaged patients showed the greatest overall impairment in these tests. In addition to choosing the least qualified expert to guide their estimates, whatever advice they received they used poorly. Patients with DLPFC lesions had some capacity to assess the quality of different experts' advice, which indicates some learning abilities. Nevertheless, their failure to use this advice correctly suggests an impairment of working memory. The patients with parietal lobe lesions performed as well as the controls in assessing the advice; however, they were the least successful in using the advice. Thus, while the patients with frontal lobe lesions had the most severe and global deficits, those with parietal lesions had the most selective deficit of working memory, involving the most difficult decision-making tasks.

In the future, even more specific findings may emerge from more detailed analyses of the various estimation abilities, using the separate components of probability scoring rules. Such measures could help us determine whether neural activity measures, which reflect certain information processing capacities, relate to degree of impairment in the more difficult prediction tasks: those producing high *variability* scores. Do deficits in *discrimination* occur in patients with more severe information processing deficits—perhaps even those related to the preconscious "hunches" people may develop? Are deficits in *calibration* affected more by neurologic disconnections between circuits that affect the STM traces that encode event frequencies and therefore reflect the capacities required to assign numerical estimates to one's "gut feelings"? Ultimately, the answers to such questions may provide a more detailed understanding of different disturbances in rational choice.

Discounting and Time Preference

In some contexts, the previously discussed distortions of subjective probabilities might contribute to risky choices, even when the person has a conservative attitude toward most risks. For example, anxious people who avoid most risks might nevertheless be overconfident about the possible consequences of smoking and therefore choose to continue to smoke. Yet distortions of probability are not the only factors that may contribute to some risky choices, independently of the person's general risk attitudes. For example, smokers could also ignore future risks due to increased "time discounting." That is, the more delayed an outcome—such as the adverse health effects of smoking—is, the less importance people assign to it. Thus, smokers could discount deferred outcomes even more than other people do. When they look at the surgeon general's warning on a pack of cigarettes, they may not distort the probabilities—they may agree that "smoking may be dangerous to your health." They may simply care less about deferred heath risks than about the immediate pleasures of their habits.

In behavioral economic analyses, the relative preferences for immediate versus delayed rewards are captured by "discount rates," which are similar to the "discount rates" for money but also apply to psychological attitudes toward other deferred gains or penalties. Many purely economic analyses even assume that the same discount rates apply to nonmonetary as well as monetary outcomes, since they use money as a common currency to represent the worth of other goods.

Although time discounting is not, in itself, an axiom of the economic model of expected utility, economic analyses commonly assume that such discounting is necessary for rational choice. To better understand the argument, let us first consider the concept of discounting as it applies to money. When one "discounts" a $1,000 monetary reward that is to be paid in 10 years, one considers this reward less valuable than $1,000 obtained in the present. It makes sense to value the present reward more, since, as long as inflation continues, one can invest the money obtained today and gain additional interest from the investment in the future.

Models of Discounting

Discount rates reflect a person's tradeoffs, as do the MAU models. But instead of measuring tradeoffs, which assign different values to features of the same outcome, discount rates reflect tradeoffs between the "importance" of the outcome and its delay. Different models have described how the "importance" of the outcome changes over time (denoted $b(t)$ in Table 3–1).

First, classical economic models usually assume that people discount future outcomes—either financial or nonfinancial ones—at a constant rate. The value of a delayed reward decays over time exponentially, somewhat like the activity of a radioactive chemical. That is, the value of a reward x obtained at time t is

$$U(x, t) = xb(t) = x \exp(-KT)$$

where x is the value of the good obtained immediately, T is the delay and K is the *discount rate*, reflecting the tendency for a delayed good to have less value.

When neoclassical economists are asked how many *discount rates* they would like in their cup of utilitarian tea, many respond, "One will do fine, thank you." Most neoclassical economic analyses assume that the same discount rate applies across all time and to all goods and all people. However, such a restrictive formula is not everyone's "cup of tea." According to psychologists, if we measure discount rates from peoples' preferences, they often vary widely across different people, sometimes in systematic ways. For instance, more intelligent individuals seem better able to tolerate delays, even at very young ages. In an often-cited study, children were asked to decide whether they wanted one marshmallow immediately or two marshmallows in 2–5 min. Half of the children could not wait; the other half could. Years later, the ones who chose the delayed rewards were found to be more intelligent and successful. At age 18, they had higher SAT scores, and, at a later age, they had achieved much more.[103] In other studies, highly educated adults also have placed more emphasis on the future, which may explain their pursuit of advanced degree programs and other long-term goals. Less educated people, on the other hand, tend to seek more short-term pleasures, such as smoking or drinking, and have more trouble deliberating about the long-term dangers.[104]

Although one might argue that the educated people are more rational, because they have discount rates closer to that of the banks, another problem would still remain with the single-rate theory. Even if people did not differ in personality, impulsivity, or other factors that affect discount rates, these rates change over time, even when the bank rates do not.

How do we know that? One method that has been used to measure such differences in discount rates, or time preferences, is to ask people to choose between different monetary rewards that become available at different times. For example, let us say that the person prefers $1,000 now to $1,100 in 1 year. He prefers a shorter delay to a larger reward. But suppose we delay each of these outcomes by the same amount—say, 10 years—and then ask him if he prefers $1,000 in 10 years or $1,100 in 11 years. The further delay should not matter if the person has the same discount rate now and 10 years hence. He should still prefer the option with a shorter delay (now $1,000 in 10 years) to the option with the larger reward ($1,100 in 11 years). But in such cases, people often switch and say they prefer the option with the larger reward (see Figure 3–5).

Such behavior, which reflects changes over time in the discount rate, is not entirely hypothetical. It is reflected by peoples' preferences in the real world. For example, although their investment behaviors might suggest they use a 5% discount rate in choosing between investments that pay off at different times in the future, they often seem to use a much higher rate when an investment or other purchase produces more immediate effects. For instance, people discount the future by rates nearing 90% when choosing to buy a cheap air conditioner that would save immediately but lead to higher repair costs later.[105]

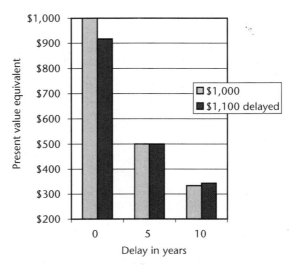

Figure 3–5 Illustration of temporal inconsistency and the hyperbolic discounting model. In this graph, the value of a delayed reward is $x(T) = xA/(1 + kT)$, where V is the present value of the delayed reward, T is the time of delay, and A and k are constants. The constant k reflects the degree of discounting. Illustrated are hypothetical values assuming a discount rate of 0.2 and plotted for three different choices: (a) a choice between $1,000 now and $1,100 a year later; (b) the same choices but with an additional 5-year delay for each; (c) the same alternatives with an additional 10-year delay. Note that the person places a higher value on the immediate $1,000 over the delayed $1,100 but prefers the $1,100 over the $1,000 when both options are delayed by an additional 10 years. This pattern is inconsistent with an economic model of exponential discounting with a constant rate. To see why, let us take the value of money to be its dollar amount, x, and T to be the delay in years. Then if the person is indifferent between $1,000 in 5 years and $1,100 in 6 years, as illustrated above, $1,000 \exp(-5K) = 1,100 \exp(-6K)$. However, dividing the above equation by $\exp(-5K)$, we find that $1,000 = 1,100 \exp(-K)$, meaning that the person should be indifferent between 1,000 now to 1,100 in 1 year, which is not consistent with the preference for the immediate reward shown in the graph. Note that, in the economic model, the one constant discount rate in all cases, must be $K = \log 1,100 - \log 1,000 = .041$ whether the delay $= 0$, 5, or 10 years.

Certain behavioral economic models can describe such changes in discount rates over time. One is called a *hyperbolic discounting* model. Although one can further refine this model, its simplest form takes the present utility of a delayed reward to be proportional to the actual size of the reward (x) divided by a function of the delay (T; see Figure 3–5). As noted in chapter 4, activities in some brain regions have been correlated with the values predicted by this model.

Another model, which describes such reversals of preference, has neural plausibility, and also predicts actual preferences is called a *hybrid* model. It considers the discount rates to involve two separate mechanisms: a discounting of future rewards, and a preference for present ones. In this model, the value of a reward, x, that is received at a delay, T, is equal to x when the reward is immediate ($T = 0$) and $\beta x \times \exp^{-KT}$ when it is delayed.[106] Note that the latter term is the same as the exponential discounting model, except that it is multiplied now by a parameter β. If β is lower, the importance of deferred rewards is lessened, relative to immediate gratification.

NEUROBIOLOGY OF DISCOUNTING AND RELATED PROCESSES

The hybrid model is consistent with recent neurobiologic findings that suggest shifts between two modes of processing, depending on whether the rewards are immediate or delayed.[107] In one study, choices that include immediate rewards were associated with more activation of dopamine systems in limbic regions, compared with choices that involve only gambles. In addition, the relative activation of different regions predicted what choices people actually made. Increased activation of lateral prefrontal and parietal areas (vs. limbic-related structures) predicted the choice of longer-term options.[108] Investigators speculate that the dopamine systems in limbic and paralimbic cortex may drive short-run impatience, while long-run patience is mediated to a greater extent by lateral prefrontal and lateral parietal cortices. So the latter regions could be involved in discounting calculations, as well as in combining information to estimate probabilities, as discussed in the section on calibration.

In addition to studying the brain regions that mediate discounting, it is important also to evaluate those that mediate additional abilities, which may appear to affect time preference. One of these involves the ability to think about consequences. For instance, VMPFC damage may not simply affect discounting, the standard measures of time preference. In one study, it was associated with an impaired time perspective—the ability to look into the future. Patients with such damage had trouble thinking into the future, and this trouble correlated with apathy, not impulsivity.[109] Elsewhere, investigators found that when children—who have immature VMPFCs—were asked to "think out loud" about the long- and short-term consequences of a criminal trial, they produced fewer long-term consequences than adults did.[110,111] These results raised questions about the children's competencies to stand trial.

The somatic marker theory is now being updated in an effort to consider how different brain regions enable one to think about future consequences. For example, VMPFC neurons are presumed now not merely to encode memories of somatic states but also to couple these memories with the person's representation of their timing. Lesion studies suggest that the representations of more immediate events recruit more posterior parts of the VMPFC, whereas those that are distant in time recruit more anterior regions.

PATHOLOGY OF TIME PREFERENCE

The impaired ability to appreciate future consequences due to VMPFC damage or other neurologic dysfunctions may often lead to impaired choices,
according to decision theory. This inability to appreciate future consequences
affects the "time horizon" for the analysis of a decision. The "time horizon"
resembles the point at which an economic model of a decision ceases to
consider possible future contingencies. Therefore, findings that apply to the
length of the "time horizon" in economic models may also apply to more
intuitive choices. For instance, more complex analyses, which extend further
into the future, may improve information processing in economic models
of complex problems.[112] Conversely, insufficient complexity in some problems may lead to declines in the measure of RP presented earlier in this
chapter.[113]

For intuitive decisions, then, one might question whether a low RP of
VMPFC-damaged patients, demonstrated earlier in this chapter, may be
related to their diminished abilities to see possible future events. In addition, patients with PTSD commonly report the sense of a foreshortened
future; and some of their poor decisions may result from this distorted view.
Interestingly, like the patients with VMPFC damage, they also commonly
become apathetic and lose interest in life. So do many patients with severe
depression. Thus, one might question whether their loss of interest is related
to an inability to conceptualize possible future rewards.

Yet another influence on temporal information processing—time
perception—also may be abnormal in similar, OFC-damaged patients.[114]
These patients felt more time had passed than actually had. A related phenomenon appears to occur in cigarette smokers during episodes of craving.
They overestimate the actual time duration and intensity of craving-related
discomfort.[115]

In addition, some pathologies in time preference may be related less to
an inability to consider the future and more to an increased motivation to
attend to the present. For instance, impulsive choices may be driven by temporal immediacy, such as seeing, smelling, or touching an object one wants.
Similarly, cues that trigger craving may give the illusion of immediacy by
driving limbic activation even when the rewards are not readily available.
Accordingly, cues that trigger craving among heroin addicts also trigger
more discounting of not only heroin but also money.[116] Perhaps for similar
reasons, higher discount rates have been found not only in heavy heroin
users but also in people with many other disorders, from alcoholism to
cocaine addiction and from withdrawal states to personality disorders.[117,118]

Such disorders may be related not only to higher discount rates but also
to rates that change over time, making some individuals more vulnerable to
earlier and more frequent preference reversals as outcomes are increasingly
delayed. For example, an alcoholic may plan to remain sober rather than to
drink at a wedding in 2 months. But as the time of the wedding arrives, he

may change his mind and go on a binge. Such choices depart from a narrow model of economic rationality in which discount rates do not change with time. However, they are consistent with the *hyperbolic and hybrid* models of discounting.

The sources of these temporal inconsistencies may sometimes be revealed more clearly by neural activity measures than by paper-and-pencil questions about preferences. Thus, in the future, in people with mental disorders, one might use neural activity measures to derive the parameters, β and K in the hybrid discounting model. We may then find, for example, that different mental disorders arise from different degrees and sources of reliance on present-oriented limbic processing relative to alternative, frontoparietal modes.

At the same time, to a lesser extent, even people with no mental disorders tend to place more weight on immediate outcomes than would be consistent with constant rate discounting. Thus, one may ask whether the bias is truly maladaptive in all situations. This bias could be maladaptive in stable environments, since it may prevent people from balancing present and future needs. But when an environment is rapidly changing, the "present reward" component of discounting may prevent individuals from becoming too fixed in their ways. It may help them choose the alternatives most closely associated with rewards and avoid those most closely associated with penalties.[119] And this tendency may sometimes be highly adaptive. If our evolutionary ancestors did not rapidly adjust to environmental change and avoid some penalties, they would not have survived long enough for future rewards to matter.

The Need for Complexity Versus Simplicity

This chapter has focused largely on parameters derived from the classical economic efficacy model, such as attitudes toward risks, tradeoffs, and delays as well as probability estimates. Although the last section also included some models of time preference outside the scope of usual economic analyses, most of the research presented in this chapter is entirely consistent with the theory. In fact, it may be viewed as a reaffirmation of the theory's appealing power, generality, and ability to reach across time and discipline. By no means have the neuroeconomic findings presented here produced what some have anticipated—a sign that the abstract economic theory will collapse under the weight of biological reality. On the contrary, the basic elements of the theory provide a framework that may help explain the neuroeconomic origins of a wide range of maladaptive behaviors, beyond those caused by neurologic lesions.

Yet even the findings presented so far do suggest needs for refinement in the simplest neoclassical economic methods. Sometimes, the economists identify one variable to explain a task but the neural evidence suggests two. The hybrid discounting model suggested two competing mechanisms for processing immediate and delayed outcomes; now the consideration of time representation in the brain is suggesting still others. The anxiety and QALMs models considered near the end of chapter 4 will consider additional factors, related to anticipatory emotion, which are not considered in the neoclassical economic theory. All of these variables may be important to consider in neuroeconomic concepts if they are found to have important real-world consequences.

In certain other contexts, the economic model may be more complex than required. For instance, it identifies two variables relevant to preference, such as the probability and delay of outcomes, yet the brain may not always see them as distinct. For instance, both of their values may depend on the relative recruitment of anterior versus posterior VMPFC processing. Likewise, the same brain regions may serve apparently different but correlated functions. Not only are the lateral prefrontal and parietal areas involved in calculating the value of delayed rewards, they may also be involved in other calculative tasks, such as combining advice from multiple experts. In addition, some common mechanisms may underlie discounting and risk attitude. Subjects who discount delayed outcomes also tend to select the disadvantageous, risky gambles in the IGT.[120] Also, lesions of the OFC increase the rates at which animals discount both delayed and uncertain outcomes (the latter being related to risk attitude).[121]

Two reasons have been suggested to explain this correlation. First, people often perceive future outcomes as uncertain and are therefore averse to the risk of waiting for them. Also, as the risk associated with a particular outcome changes, the expected delay before the outcome's occurrence will often change as well. Since the human brain has most likely developed mechanisms to handle such problems, it may often process risky and delayed prospects similarly.[122] When that is the case, neuroeconomic models may need to be simplified.

At the same time, risk attitude and discounting do sometimes diverge. For instance, attitude toward delay and risk have changed in different directions when the experimenters lengthened the duration of the waiting time or when they compared the discounting rates of smokers with those of nonsmokers. They also changed in different directions when the serotonergic brain circuits of animals were damaged. Likewise, though serotonin depletion does change a measure of risk adjustment, lesions in serotonin-mediated brain circuits do not always cause the discounting of delayed rewards.[123] Rather, the apparent association of serotonin deficits with impulsivity may derive, not from altered discounting, but from premature responding.[124]

Alterations of dopamine systems in the brain may also produce inconsistent effects on risk attitude and discounting. For example, animals with a selective impairment in a structure central to dopamine system—the NAc— may exhibit impairment in the ability to code delay, without an effect on risk attitude.[125] When this structure is damaged, the animals can no longer learn to encode delay and relate it to the magnitude of reward.[126] Therefore, they exhibit impulsive choices similar to those of some patients with attention deficit/hyperactivity disorder (AD/HD). Perhaps not coincidentally, stimulation by d-amphetamine—a common treatment for ADHD—also promotes performance in these animals, eventually leading to an increased tolerance for delayed reward.[127] Perhaps such stimulation increases the ability to learn to anticipate future rewards and therefore to persist toward them.[128,129] Other possible explanations are discussed in chapter 4.

In any case, the ability to learn the value of delayed rewards does involve capacities that extend beyond simple discounting. The simple neoclassical, economic efficacy model also does not identify many other important variables affecting decisions, nor does it account for many possible sources of inconsistency beyond the temporal consistency discussed in this chapter.

For instance, comparison of goals and outcomes in the economic efficacy model is assumed to generate expectations of future value; however, it also can generate inconsistent feelings of desire. A cocaine addict may expect little actual pleasure from a drug yet still desire to use it. Chapter 4 will discuss the different neural correlates of such desires, as well as a broader array of decision-making models, which may describe them.

4

The Effectiveness of Evaluation: What Other Psychological Abilities Affect Evaluation?

To this point, this book has primarily discussed models of the efficacy of decisions that are based largely upon a "neoclassical" view of economics. This view has had far-reaching applications. Also, its methods of analysis are not as narrow as its practical uses often suggest. As noted in chapter 3, these methods need not assume that peoples' evaluations of gambles change in direct proportion with the probability or that they discount delayed outcomes exponentially; they need not even ignore considerations of fairness.[130]

At the same time, however, many violations of the neoclassical theory's predictions have been noted in the past several decades. In fact, the study of these violations has given rise to a vast science of *behavioral economics*. This science has sought to strengthen economics by making its assumptions more psychologically realistic and more predictive of actual behavior. However, its use is not merely descriptive. For example, behavioral economic models may identify and correct biases in value estimates in health policy or clinical decision analyses.[131]

Likewise, as shown in subsequent sections, behavioral economic methods can identify the characteristics of the decision-maker more precisely, which may also have normative implications. That is, it may identify important parameters that predict decision-making impairments, defined by external criteria, such as the diagnosis of a mental disorder. In addition, it may suggest new forms of consistency in evaluation, which appear relevant to normative behavior but which the neoclassical model of economics does not address. Furthermore, unlike models from the neoclassical theory, they include not merely diagnostic and management elements but also the capacities to evaluate outcomes, as reflected in experienced evaluations. These models can transform the simpler ideas about economic efficacy into broader and more useful concepts of effectiveness.

THE MULTIPLE PERSPECTIVES OF EVALUATION

In economic models such as expected utility (EU), people are assumed to act rationally if they make choices that are consistent with each other and with a set of logical principles, or axioms. However, these axioms are often violated by otherwise normal individuals, and they do not adequately discriminate between normal and mentally disordered individuals. To provide a richer and potentially more discriminatory set of "consistency" tests, the present section discusses the consistency of our feelings across different temporal perspectives.

Ebenezer Scrooge may have been the best-known economic rationalist. He shunned gift-giving as a senseless exercise of human emotion. He reduced all goods to a common currency: money. And he assumed the unfailing accuracy of his own perceptions. However, one Christmas Eve, he was visited by three ghosts who showed him his life from three different angles—the past, present, and future. These new perspectives revealed some alarming inconsistencies. The past—seeing how his greed drove away the only woman who loved him—was not the life he remembered. The present—seeing how his own selfish wants caused his employees' families to despise him—did not give him pleasure. And the future—seeing the death of Tiny Tim—was not what he expected.

The present chapter shows how similar inconsistencies can arise in our evaluations, depending on the perspective: whether we are experiencing outcomes in the present, anticipating possible future events, or recalling past occurrences. The preceding model of economic efficacy does not address these inconsistencies. In addition, these inconsistencies run counter to the assumption of economist Jeremy Bentham that our past, present, and future evaluations should—and do—all agree.[132] The following section illustrates a few of the possible disagreements. It also discusses the neural correlates of the severe inconsistencies in people with "mental disorders" and perhaps even in Scrooge, whose decisions made him rich but not happy.

Why Different Forms of Evaluation Are Important

According to some pop psychology movements, Scrooge merely needed to purge the economist in his brain, stop calculating future costs and benefits, and just "live in the present moment" to achieve well-being. The pop psychology culture of the 1960s idealized the primitive, "on-line" evaluations of present experience and saw an exclusive focus on such experience as the only route to happiness. However, while some patients with mental disorders do dwell excessively on past failures or fears of the future, "living in the present"—even if it were possible for most of us—might not really be a panacea.

In *Descartes' Error*, Damasio describes a patient named David, who lived in the present moment to the exclusion of all else. When he engaged in activities, he would respond with statements such as, "Oh, this is terrific,"

"It's nice to be sitting here watching pictures with you guys," "Gosh, how terrible," and "This is my favorite kind."[133] Despite these reports of present happiness, however, David's life seemed profoundly strange and pathetic. He was so attuned to the present that he had no sense of the past or the future. Due to the destruction of large parts of his brain—the two temporal lobes and the hippocampus—he could not remember the past. In addition, extensive damage to the amygdala and to the medial cortices overlying the hippocampus prevented him from learning new facts. Thus, he could neither understand why he enjoyed a particular activity nor predict what he would like in the future. In David's case, his past and future evaluations did not accurately mirror the future because they were largely vacuous. His one-dimensional confabulations glittered with present experience but painted over a psychological void.

Yet, while we may question the sufficiency of an exclusive focus on the present, we also may question the sufficiency of an exclusive focus on the future. For example, in a very simplistic economic efficacy model, all we need to be rational is to make good *future evaluations*. Evaluations of the future involve our anticipation of events that might affect our future well-being. So in this model, Scrooge would be rational if he could make decisions that he expects to lead to good consequences, even if he never actually enjoys them. All he really needs to be economically rational are unlimited powers of computation and self-knowledge, as well as an ability to make consistent forecasts of his future feelings. It does not really matter if the old curmudgeon's forecasts of feelings are all very negative. In fact, the more negative they are, the more they may enable him to be consistent.

To be sure, these statements about the simplest form of the neoclassical economic model greatly oversimplify the broader economic perspective. They ignore much work in economics on social cooperation, which might help explain Scrooge's sorry state. Yet even that economic perspective does not account for some important problems with peoples' temporal evaluations. As shown in the following sections, people often have trouble predicting future feelings and do not accurately recall the past. So to better understand Scrooge's actual decision-making capacities, it may be important to examine his past and present evaluations, in addition to his future ones. The following sections will take you on a journey, somewhat like the one Scrooge took with the spirits. The journey will enable us to see how evaluations of the past, present, and future may conflict.

Disagreements Between Past and Present Evaluations: Myopia for the Past

> I always like to reminisce with people I don't even know.
>
> Steven Wright

In order to attain many future pleasures, we require a memory of past likes and dislikes. If experiences of the present, according to the economic efficacy model, resemble a response to the live television coverage of a sporting event, then evaluations of the past resemble our reaction to a rerun of the same event. In fact, an economist such as Bentham would have a simple method for us to rate the "rerun." The evaluation given to an episode in the past would be the sum of the person's "quality of life" in each time period of the episode multiplied by its duration.[134,135]

In fact, however, past evaluations are not simply ratings of reruns from old video tapes or DVDs. Rather, these evaluations, and the memories from which they derive, are actively created and edited and differ each time we retrieve them. Present circumstances, as well as our current goals and fears, tell us what is most essential to recall, thereby shaping our memories.[136]

In addition, our capacity to forge memories of the past has limits and our remembrance of the past is not simply an economic summation of previous experiences. Since memory is selective, its evaluation is often described by two moments: the "peak" or most salient periods, and the "end" or most recent events. In one experiment, for example, people were asked to rate their experiences at multiple points in time during a painful medical procedure called a colonoscopy.[137] Instead of reporting an evaluation resembling the sum of their experiences during the entire course of the procedure, they focused only on the amount of pain they felt at the worst point and at the very end of the ordeal. They did not even consider how long the procedure lasted.

This human tendency to ignore the duration of a painful state results in a paradox. Retrospective evaluations of a long procedure that gradually lessened the pain were, on average, less negative than evaluations of the same, but shorter, procedure that ended the pain abruptly. The patients did not care that the gradual process of completion lengthened the total duration of the pain.[138] The peak experiences of the two procedures were roughly the same and the only other differences the patients cared about were what they recalled—the final moments. In other contexts also, because subjects ignored the duration of pain, they often chose the longer experience when given a choice between that or a shorter procedure, which ended quickly.[139]

Neurobiology and Pathology

In cases of emotional rather than purely sensory pain, similar memory biases may exist. Also, we are beginning to understand their neural bases. Circuits involving the amygdala and the PFC may amplify emotional memories and thereby predispose us to remember peak experiences.[140] Although such amplification may help most individuals edit the past, patients with deficits in the amygdala often have trouble recalling emotional events. Patients with antisocial personality disorder also have diminished activity in the amygdala in response to social interactions, which may sometimes impair their emotional memories and capacities for moral learning.[141]

Pathological gamblers, who often are also antisocial, appear to have functional deficits in the PFC. As a result, they may not only write bad checks; they also may "forge" bogus memories by recalling past losses more positively than they actually were. When normal social gamblers were asked to recall past wins and losses, their remembrance of gains resulted in much greater skin conductance levels (SCLs) than did the memory of past losses. However, the SCLs of pathological gamblers who were asked to recall their past wins and losses were nearly equal.[142-144] Also, while normal controls reported more tension than excitement when they recalled losses, the opposite occurred in pathological gamblers, who often reported exhilaration over "near misses." If the gamblers did enjoy the wins much more than the losses when the events actually occurred, then the gamblers may have edited their memories to remove the painful recollections.

Other times, people may have not a deficient but an excessive memory of negative events. For instance, patients with major depression show heightened activity in the amygdala and recall the negative aspects of events too well.[145] Likewise, victims of childhood abuse have increased reactivity in circuits involving the amygdala and recall abuse-related events excessively. When they develop PTSD, they often experience intrusive memories of the trauma, which is one type of "peak event."[146]

Now, however, one may be able to rewrite some traumatic memory traces by changing the critical moments: the peak or most recent experiences. As noted earlier, a blood pressure medication called propanolol blocks neural receptors that contribute to arousal. It thereby reduces the effect of norepinephrine on the amygdala. This reduction may increase the bias to recall emotionally charged events—the peak experiences.[147] It reduces the risk of PTSD in patients who have just undergone a traumatic event.[148] To work, however, it must be given as a "morning after" pill, in the immediate aftermath of the trauma, suggesting a possible effect not only on the peak event but also on the "end" or most recent moment.

Peak and recent moments may also affect the recollection of drug side effects, which lead a patient to either adhere or not adhere to the doctor's recommendation to take it. For instance, in one experiment, subjects taking antidepressant medications were asked to recall their past side effects. While the mere presence or absence of side effects was not significantly correlated with discontinuation of the medicine, the worst side effect was. In fact, this "peak" effect was the best predictor. In addition, the general level of anxiety predicted discontinuation of medicine, and the use of benzodiazepine medicine, such as Valium, predicted its continued use.[149] Anxiety increases, and Valium decreases, activity in the amygdala, which may thereby modify the magnitude of peak effects. Moreover, Valium may not only diminish peak effects. It also impairs recent memory, thus affecting the most recent moments of an episode.

Future Evaluations and Their Disagreements
With Present Evaluations

> Hope is a good breakfast, but it is a bad supper.
>
> Sir Francis Bacon[150]

Like past and present evaluations, present and future evaluations often conflict with each other. While Bentham's economic theory would not assert that our future anticipations should always be correct, they should vary with the probabilities of the outcomes as well as our experiences of the outcomes when they actually occur. The following sections of the book describe more specific measures of such consistency. They also describe possible sources of inconsistency, which may be related to the different neural systems, which mediate present experience and future anticipation. The inconsistencies to be discussed can result from alterations in either present or future evaluations. The latter include the errors we make in anticipating events, predicting our own values, and estimating the probabilities of ambiguous events.

Inconsistent Responses to Uncertainty: Ambiguity and Emotion

As discussed in chapter 3, one way that probability judgments can cause our anticipations of the future to diverge from the actual experiences and frequencies of the outcomes is due to biases in our estimates of subjective probabilities. While such biases do not necessarily violate economic principles, other inconsistencies do. For example, people can make different choices when otherwise equivalent probabilities are known (called decision making under *risk*) and when they are not (called decision making under *ambiguity*).

To illustrate the concept of ambiguity, consider a scene from the movie *The Naked Gun*. The protagonist single-handedly breaks into a den of international drug dealers, only to find them waiting for him with a dozen machine guns. They greet him with a barrage of bullets. In the next scene, he lies in a hospital bed, bandaged from head to foot, looking glassy-eyed at the ceiling with his grief-stricken wife at his bedside. She overhears a medical discussion of the question she feared to ask: "What are his chances?" She hears an answer that is hardly reassuring: "His chances are 50:50...and there's only a 10% chance of that."

Such is the nature of ambiguity—uncertainty in the uncertainties. To be sure, the wife may not have appreciated a medical opinion indicating such unsureness, since people often are quite averse to ambiguity. In fact, a famous example called the "Ellsberg paradox" shows that people are more averse to ambiguity than the economic model of subjective EU allows.[151,152] Essentially, people prefer a risky gamble, where the probabilities of winning are known to be 50:50, to an ambiguous one, where the probabilities are unknown (and thus, the best estimate is still 50:50).

One possible interpretation of the Ellsberg paradox is that people underweigh probabilities more when the evidence is ambiguous or unfamiliar. So the attention given to winning additional money, as well as the attention given to keeping the same assets, may both be less than the probabilities suggest (the probability of winning and the probability of not winning are less than one, which is called "subcertainty"). Thus, the impact of a possible win is diluted when its occurrence is more ambiguous. Later sections of this chapter discuss probability weight functions in prospect theory, which have been used to model not merely known probabilities but also ambiguities.[153]

Other models used to capture tendencies to avoid ambiguous risks include measures of "belief" which also do not conform to the usual principles of subjective probability.[154] Dempster and Shafer have discussed "belief functions," which depend not merely on the direction the evidence points (e.g., toward the likelihood of a win or a loss in gambling experiments) but also on the quality of evidence and the amount of knowledge underlying it. These functions reduce to standard probability models when objective frequencies of the events are known.

Such models may be useful in expanding the concept of "predictability" currently used by many neurobiologists. For instance, when experiments refer to the "predictability" of rewards, they sometimes refer to low probabilities as indicating less predictability, other times taking the maximum "unpredictability" to occur when the probability is .5. In addition to being inconsistent, these alternative interpretations both ignore unpredictability due to ambiguity, which may result from insufficient knowledge (inability to formulate the components of a model for predicting the likelihood of events) or inadequate data (being certain of the model but uncertain about the sufficiency of the information used in the predictions).

In fact, such uncertainties about the nature and quality of expert opinion often are a prominent component of public risk perceptions of unpredictable dangers—from disease epidemics to stock market crashes to terrorism. While chapter 3 discussed how known statistics—the variance and expectation of a gamble—might affect risk perception, other research suggests that peoples' risk perceptions appear to be described by two more general factors: the uncertainty/ambiguity and dread of the risk.[155] The uncertainty involves factors such as the novelty and scientific uncertainty surrounding the risk. The dread, which is the strongest determinant of risk acceptability, relates in part to how involuntary and uncontrollable the risk is.

These perceptions partly explain why people often do not accept the facts that experts offer to reassure them that the statistical magnitude of a risk is low. They are guided by fears rather than facts. Slovic notes that, in particular, during states of strong affect, people may ignore statistical frequencies and catastrophize about events merely because of their severity. Slovic calls this the "affect heuristic"—the tagging of meaning to images of possible events rather than to parameters related to their frequencies.[156] For example, he postulates the learning of linkages between images (e.g., a tiger) and the somatic state that often follows the image (e.g., fear).

Neurobiology. Interestingly, the two dimensions of risk perception—uncertainty and dread—also correspond roughly to different evaluation systems in the brain. Some feelings of dread, which stimulate a desire to control outcomes, appear to activate neural structures (termed the "pain matrix") that are also activated in the actual physical experience of pain.[157] In particular, when people await the receipt of an electric shock, the degree of their dread is related to structures sensitive to the expected response to pain: the right primary sensory (S-I) and secondary sensory (S-II) cortex, the posterior mid-cingulate cortex and insula.[158] The neural correlates of uncertainty, as discussed next, differ from the correlates of dread.

In addition, the type of uncertainty matters. Responses to ambiguity do differ from responses to risk. Although the precise correlates do depend on the task, the striatum often has prominent activations in the presence of risk. As discussed later, the ventral striatum (VS) mediates evaluations of uncertainties in passive learning experiments, in which no action is required. The dorsal striatum (DS) mediates evaluations in active learning experiments, in which the person's action can potentially control the outcomes (see section on Learning models later in this chapter). By contrast, activations associated with ambiguity are more prominent in the OFC and amygdala.[159] In a sense, the OFC/amygdala activity is part of a system that stimulates vigilance and a desire to obtain more information due to the recognition of missing information and possible danger. And it attenuates the impact of expected values, and reward anticipation, coded in the VS. Thus, ambiguity aversion can make attractive gambles less valuable.

Note that the brain regions most prominently activated by ambiguity—the OFC and amygdala—have been associated with somatic marker systems. The authors of the somatic marker theory have suggested that ambiguity activates somatic markers early in the IGT, when the probabilities of winning or losing are unknown. When faced with such ambiguous gambles, subjects simulate the risks through a "body loop" which includes neurally induced bodily responses, which are then recorded in the cortex. Thus, subjects in the IGT had differential activity in the insular cortex, and increased anticipatory SCRs, reflecting the bodily response.[160] However, these SCRs were much less prominent in the Rogers Risk Attitude task, in which probabilities were specified and ambiguities minimal.

Bechara et al. suggest that, when probabilities are known, they are handled by a different mechanism. Early studies suggested they are processed by an "as if loop," contained solely within the brain and not requiring bodily responses (see Figure 3–3).[161] After repeated experiences, neural processes may simulate the possible future bodily states resulting from a decision, "as if" the physical changes were really occurring. This weaker "as if" loop may go directly from the VMPFC and amygdala to the brainstem nuclei and SSI cortex (see Figure 3–3). The authors later found that damage to the posterior, but not anterior, VMPFC affected performance in a task involving known probabilities. Only performance on the more ambiguous IGT was affected by anterior VMPFC damage, presumably because anterior lesions encode rare events, for which little experience is available.[162]

The authors note that these interpretations are speculative. Unlikely events are not necessarily ambiguous ones, just as the likely events are not always unambiguous.[163] Beyond this, performance on the IGT hinges on many factors beyond ambiguity (see the discussion of neuroepidemiology in chapter 5). Thus, even if we accept the use of expected values as a criterion for "good performance" on the IGT, we cannot be sure that poor performance indicates deficits in the use of ambiguous information.

Pathology.   Some authors have argued that OFC-damaged patients behave more like rational economists, in that they calculate expectations and do not consider ambiguity. In terms of the somatic marker theory, they rely on abstract thought that does not require bodily responses.[164]

Some evidence also suggests that other people who rely too much on one mechanism or the other—ambiguous or "as if" processing—may also develop problems. Paulus and his colleagues developed a Risky Gains task, which elicited attitudes toward ambiguous choices. He found increased insular activation increased not only as the level of risk rose but also as subjects exhibited more traits of neuroticism and harm avoidance. Thus, people with some mental disorders do exhibit a sensitivity to ambiguity.[165] Whether anxious patients respond less to risk than ambiguity is yet to be clearly determined. However, anxious patients do perform normally when asked to consciously estimate the probabilities of familiar risks.[166]

If people do alter responses to situations according to the familiarity or ambiguity of risks, neurochemical systems may play an important role in enabling them to adaptively change the responses.[167] For example, activity in systems mediated by acetylcholine appear (inversely) related to the subject's ability to recognize the degree of validity of predictive relationships. In a familiar and stable context, it would enable people to estimate well-defined risks from known associations. By contrast, activity in systems mediated by norepinephrine appears related to the subject's ability to recognize changes in context. Such activity lowers confidence in the predictive value of cues in an environment, where the contingencies may have changed. Perhaps not coincidentally, patients with borderline personalities often become more irritable and unstable when they take drugs that stimulate norepinephrine systems. Such stimulation could increase the sense that events in their world cannot be predicted.

One final disturbance in systems that mediate ambiguity might involve a paradoxical consistency in some impulsive individuals, including those with borderline personality disorder. One study measured differences in fMRI activity in parts of the brain which appear differentially activated in risky versus ambiguous gambles—the latter involving probabilities that were incompletely known.[168] For example, in nonimpulsive individuals, the inferior frontal cortex activated in response to ambiguity more than in response to risk. However, these differences between response to ambiguity and risk fell linearly as the degree of impulsivity, measured by an independent scale, rose. In a sense, these patients may have been overconfident in the ambiguous probabilities presented, much as found with the patients with frontal lobe damage discussed in the section on Calibration in chapter 3. To test such speculations, it would be useful to include potential losses, and not merely gains, in the experiment. We might find that the impulsive people whose brains did not discriminate risk and uncertainty also lacked the emotions correlated with the "uncertain" dimension of perceived risk. Whatever the cause, this apparent lack of difference between ambiguity and risk reflects a paradoxical consistency between responses, which normally are inconsistent.

Inconsistencies Between Predicted and Experienced Values

Anticipations and experiences can diverge not only when people have trouble interpreting uncertainty but also when they cannot predict their own future values—which Kahneman terms an error in *predictive utility*.[169] For instance, even normal individuals poorly predict their own well-being due to a future outcome. [170] They have trouble imagining how they will feel about marrying, moving, seeing the dentist, or having a baby.[171] They also often overestimate the pain they will experience in a dentist's office.[172] Conversely, pregnant women tend to underestimate the pain they will feel during childbirth, and their preferences for pain relief often change when they go into labor.[173]

While some of the difficulty people have looking into the future may arise from problems in accurately remembering the past, other troubles appear to arise from immediate emotions. For instance, peoples' preferences and values appear to change when they are in "hot" emotional states as opposed to "cold" unemotional states. For instance, either nonaddicts or addicts who are not currently craving drugs systematically underpredict their future desires for drugs.[174] Similarly, only 15% of high school students who smoked less than one cigarette a day predicted that they would still be smoking in 5 years; 43% actually were smoking when the 5 years elapsed.[175]

Some of the troubles people have in predicting future preferences may also arise from adaptations and cognitive biases. For example, when asked whether they would accept chemotherapy if it would extend their lives by 3 months, how many people said they would do so? No radiotherapists, only 6% of oncologists, and only 10% of healthy people said "yes."[176] Yet 42% of cancer patients say they would want to live. Many other studies have found similar changes in preference as one enters an illness state.

Several possible reasons have been suggested to explain such biases. One is that the people who have an illness adapt to it. Or they may have an unrealistically rosy view of their true state of well-being.[177] Another possible reason is that healthy people focus attention on a single attribute of their state—the condition of the illness—and they ignore many other dimensions of well-being—such as family, religious pursuits, and musical enjoyment.[178] Alternatively, healthy people could see the illness as a loss, whereas unhealthy ones might see the hope of recovery from it as a gain.[179] Whatever the reason, peoples' predictions of future feelings are not good.

Neurobiology of Predictive Utility. If people's conscious predictions of future feelings are so bad, how can they avoid the painful costs of their illusions? One possibility is that their nonconscious inclinations better predict the future consequences of their actions and better guide their actual choices. Could brain activation patterns that reflect these nonconscious inclinations, therefore, predict choice better than consciously stated preferences do?

Consider one neuroeconomic study that indirectly touches upon this question. The study suggests that, even when people's stated preferences do not predict stated satisfaction, neurobiologic measures sometimes do. In this study, people stated whether they preferred Coke or Pepsi before taking a drink, then indicated what (unknown) drink they actually preferred when actually tasting it. The prior, stated preferences did not correlate significantly with actual experience—their preferences after actually tasting the drink. By contrast, the difference in activity in the VMPFC when Coke or Pepsi were actually tasted did correlate very significantly with the experiential preferences.[180]

Upon close inspection, this study did not actually seek to demonstrate the predictive superiority of anticipatory neural measures over conscious preferences. It merely showed that experiential neural measures correlated more highly with the experienced taste test than did anticipatory preferences. To compare the predictive abilities of conscious and neural measures, therefore, one would need to compare "compatible" predictions: for example, to compare the predictive abilities of anticipatory preferences with anticipatory neural activities (e.g., prior to being told that they were to receive a bolus of Coke or Pepsi).

To draw clearer inferences about the predictive value of brain activation patterns, we also will need to consider other factors, such as the familiarity of the outcome to be predicted. We have long known that our unconscious inclinations are affected by familiar associations or labels. In the Coke–Pepsi study just cited, such familiarity appears to affect the patterns of brain activation. The study found that knowing the brand of the soft drink to be tasted had a significant effect on anticipatory preferences as well as on the experienced neural activity measures associated with the taste experience. When people were told the brand name of the drink, activation patterns shifted to the hippocampus, DLPFC, and midbrain rather than the VMPFC, which was silent. Since the report of the brand dramatically affected peoples' preferences as well as the brain activation, the authors suggested that these two separate circuits may bias preferences differently: the former based on cultural (i.e., brand-related) learning and the latter based on sensory information. Thus, one might find that the quality of peoples' predictions of their own likes and dislikes might depend on whether or not the brand is named (e.g., in predictions for the liking of ice cream).[181]

Pathology. Previous tests have not, to my knowledge, separately considered possible disorders of predictive utility in people with mental disorders.

Disorders of predictive utility do seem to occur in behavior-disordered adolescents, who may have immature VMPFCs. Some of them use drugs because they think that they will enjoy more popularity. Others might decide to have sex because they anticipate more enduring feelings of intimacy. In part, they take present risks because they have trouble predicting how they will feel about future outcomes and difficulty imagining how their present values will change.

Disorders of predictive utility seem evident in a variety of mental disorders. For instance, depressed patients often report an intense helplessness associated with the feeling that they will never be able to adjust to their predicament and that the depression will never end. Likewise, patients with panic disorder commonly have anticipatory anxiety, which is more disabling than the panic attacks themselves. Seemingly, they overpredict the intensity of future attacks. In addition, social phobics who avoid risky social encounters or giving public speeches often do not realize their abilities to adapt and to regulate negative affect should they fail. In one experiment, people were to participate in a dating game in which they would win or lose the competition and were asked to predict the dose of an (immediately acting) mood elevating drug that they would wish to take if they should lose. Those predicting the dose, however, chose much higher doses than those who had actually experienced the loss.[182] In such cases, there is an inconsistency between anticipation and experience that can lead anxious people to avoid all risks, resulting in empty and unrewarding lives.

Inconsistency Between Anticipatory and Experienced Feelings

> If the world looks dark to you, try cleaning your glasses.
>
> Garrison Keillor

Many other factors also may contribute to the inconsistencies between expectations and experience. First, the feelings one predicts often differ from those actually experienced. Also, the estimates of the likelihood of the outcomes may not be the same as their objective frequencies, as discussed in chapter 3. In addition, people may not combine values and probabilities in the way that Bentham may have imagined. People often do not simply compute the EU of a gamble. Contrary to economic theory, their choices do not coincide with the experienced utilities of the outcomes, multiplied by their probabilities.

One past approach to identifying the way that people do combine information in the process of anticipation has been to obtain peoples' verbal reports as they consider the possible outcomes and their probabilities (this procedure has been called process tracing). But conscious, declarative reports may not adequately tap the real determinants of some decisions.[183,184] For example, people avoid dreaded risks, such as air travel during threats of terrorism, even when they know consciously that the probability of harm is very small.[185] To an extent, people may also follow their "gut feelings" in making choices and may not be entirely aware of why they chose what they did.[186]

Conversely, some people may seem to reason about the future well, yet inadequately anticipate it in practice. Witness the behavior of patients with damage to the amygdala. In an experiment, they can learn to say when—and if—they will receive a shock, but their lack of SCRs in anticipation of the shock suggests that they may not actually anticipate it.[187] That possibility appears to be supported by observations of their behavior. They often appear unable to learn to fear real dangers in their environment. For instance, Damasio describes a female patient with bilateral damage to the amygdala. She easily made friends and formed romantic attachments; however, she was often taken advantage of by those whom she so easily befriended. Lacking the ability to experience fear, she could not learn to develop internal signals to identify dishonest and sometimes dangerous individuals.

Pathology. Some literature suggests that both patients with amygdala damage as well as those with damage to right VMPFC have deficits in anticipation relative to controls. However, Tranel et al. have reported that, unlike the patients with amygdala damage, the experienced SCRs of these VMPFC-damaged patients do not differ significantly from controls. Thus, one might speculate that they underanticipate outcomes.[188,189] If so, recall from chapter 3 that patients with such damage are overconfident in their judgments of probability (as if they assign more, rather than less, extreme probabilities to events). Such results could suggest a dissociation between conscious estimates of confidence and implicit measures of anticipation.[190] That is, while right-sided VMPFC-damaged subjects have great confidence in their estimates, they lack the anticipatory capacities that would justify such confidence. Possibly, they are unable to anticipate future outcomes but also unable to monitor their own performance well enough to realize their limitations (recall their performance monitoring deficits discussed in the section on Calibration in chapter 3).

In the future, however, to make more definitive conclusions, we will need measures of the agreement of the anticipatory with the experienced evaluations. For example, a person could appear to anticipate poorly relative to controls, yet his anticipations could be consistent with his values—he might just not care about the outcomes of the gambles. The opposite could also occur. So, ideally, the degree of anticipation we measure should be corrected, according the amount expected, based on the experienced evaluations. However, to make such corrections, one would also require a model that predicts the anticipatory SCRs from the measured ones. For example, chapter 3 discussed an EU model that could prescribe how a person should combine the probabilities of outcomes with their values, as might be reflected in the experienced SCRs. However, many other models seem to predict peoples' choices much better. In later sections of this chapter, we will review a number of possible candidates, including disappointment models, which also consider biases in attention to gains or losses as well as even more complex models, called rank-dependent utilities.

Experienced Utility

Another possible source of disagreement between anticipation and experience is the experience itself. Bechara et al. did acknowledge the possible role for the VMPFC in experience, and some experiments do suggest that its activity differs when individuals experience outcomes that do or do not provide rewards.[191] To help resolve the apparently conflicting opinions about the role of the VMPFC in mediating experienced evaluations, let us take a closer look at the experienced SCRs from the previously cited study of right VMPFC-damaged patients.

Figure 4–1 presents data on the experienced SCRs of the four different groups of subjects from the Tranel et al. study, and these data do suggest some differences between patients with and without right VMPFC damage.[192] While the shapes of the curves in Figure 4–1 appear similar across the groups, patients with right-sided VMPFC damage (R) seem less responsive than the normal ones to rewards or penalties. Just as they appear to underanticipate future outcomes, they also appear to underreact to experienced outcomes.[193,194] If so, the results would suggest that there may not be a complete dissociation between anticipation and experience in these patients, even though the former may be more impaired than the latter.

Additional insights may emerge from considering the general patterns of experienced reactions in more detail. First, some distortions of experience may involve the rate of increase in the SCRs as monetary gains rise. Note that as the amount to win increases, the actual SCR to a win increases in normal controls, but the magnitude of the increase gradually decreases. Although the data are too sparse to permit definitive conclusions, this adaptation is reminiscent of what economists term "marginally decreasing utility"—for instance, a gain from $1 to $2 would be valued more than an additional gain from $2 to $3.

Figure 4–1 also suggests that the response to gains may satiate more slowly in patients with right-sided VMPFC damage (verifying this finding would require analysis of the patterns of change within each subject); this suggests one reason why some patients with VMPFC damage, despite their impulsivity, have been found less sensitive to risk (i.e., they are more conservative in adjusting to more favorable gambles by increasing the sizes of their wagers).[195] For such patients, the joy of a large gain is not much greater than the pleasure of a small one.[196]

However, the same should not be true for losses. The patients with right-sided VMPFC damage do show a lower rate of change for losses. But in general, across all groups, the reactions to losses appear to differ from the reactions to gains. As losses increase, the change is nearly linear and does not adapt. Thus, if the SCR reflects the pain of a loss, then this pain continues to intensify at the same rate as the losses rise. Although one should not make too much of these sparse data, such linear changes for losses, as well as adaptations for gains, have previously been reported in experiments derived from peoples' (anticipatory) preferences.[197]

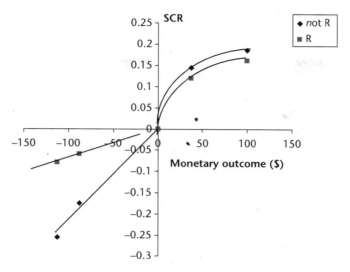

Figure 4–1 Experienced utility. Plotted are the experienced skin conductance responses (SCRs) as a function of the monetary outcomes of the gambles. The average SCRs are shown for patients with right VMPFC damage (denoted R, the patients with bilateral and unilateral damage) and for people without right-sided damage (denoted not-R, the patients with left-sided damage only, and the normal controls). Power functions analogous to those used by Kahneman and Tversky (see text) were used to describe the relationship between the SCR and monetary gains: $y^+(x) = Mx^m$. In the case of monetary losses, we can use a similar power function, $y^-(x) = -Nx^n$, but $n = 1$ approximately for both subject groups, suggesting a linear function to describe the relationship between the SCRs and monetary losses: $y^-(x) = -Nx$. If these functions were anticipatory utilities, they would both imply that the person is not uniformly loss averse [i.e., $-y^-(-x)/y^+(x)$ does not exceed 1 for all values of x]. The patients with no right-sided damage would be loss averse only for large values of x; and the patients with right-sided damage would never be loss averse in range of outcomes studied. In addition, the slope of the linear value function for losses is less for the patients with right-sided damage than it is for subjects without such damage ($N = .0009$ vs. $N = .0029$). Note that the curves drawn assign the values (0,0) to the status quo (no money gained or lost)—under the assumption that the effect of the baseline SCL has been removed, but would need to be redrawn in experiments that do not make this correction.

Let us emphasize here that the asymmetric responses to experienced gains and losses would not directly contradict the theory of EU, which involves only anticipatory evaluations. In the future, investigators should attempt to estimate the component of the anticipatory SCR attributable to a "utility function."[198] In addition, they may estimate "utility functions" derived from other neural measures.

Keep in mind, however, that measures such as fMRI responses to gambles (after a decision but before the outcome) are merely "difference measures." They reflect only a degree of anticipation of outcomes relative to some other standard. Utilities can be estimated from such difference measures.[199] For example, in an EU-like model, if a neural response after the choice in a 50:50 gamble between \$8 and \$4 exceeds the response to a 50:50 gamble between \$16 and \$0, then .5(8) + .5U(4) > .5U(16) + .5U(0). Thus, the utility difference between \$8 and \$0 exceeds the difference between \$16 and \$4 [i.e., U(8) − U(0) > U(16) − U(4)]. Miyamoto and Politser used multidimensional scaling methods to compress such difference estimates into a single "utility dimension"; similar methods could use neural measures rather than preferences.

At the same time, however, methods preferable to EU theory now exist to estimate such values. In addition, if we find an asymmetry between the utilities for gains and losses under conditions of uncertainty, similar to that shown in Figure 4–1, then that too could be a problem for EU. The EU theory considers the responses to gain or loss to be reflected not in two different, asymmetric functions but in a single function, from which one computes the value of a change in one's total assets. The next section considers alternative behavioral economic theories, consistent with asymmetric responses to gain and loss, which may differ depending on changes in reference points.

PROSPECT THEORY: A BEHAVIORAL ECONOMIC MODEL THAT COMPARES OUTCOMES WITH REFERENCE POINTS

Why must we consider reference points? In the earlier description of EU models, the economic theory assumes that people evaluate not the absolute value of gains or losses, but rather their total wealth after the outcomes of a gamble. However, even if a patient with brain damage could reliably report his net worth, and even when gambling tasks use real money, people do not recompute their total assets every time they win a dollar, as the EU theory assumes. Rather, they consider gains or losses in relations to a reference point, such as their current assets, as illustrated in Figure 4–1. To better understand this phenomenon, consider the case of Winona Ryder.

Wealthy, two-time Oscar nominee Winona Ryder, who played an impulsive patient with borderline personality disorder (BPD) in the movie *Girl, Interrupted*, went shopping in a posh store in Beverly Hills. In the dressing room, a security guard saw her cutting security tags off merchandise.[200] She was arrested and arraigned in court on charges of shoplifting \$4,800 worth of designer clothes.

Conceivably, such a theft might have had some rationale had Winona been penniless. If the clothes were fungible assets worth their retail value, the theft could have increased her net worth from nothing to \$4,800. But according to economic theory, such stealing would have appeared more improbable once Winona became a wealthy movie star. If she had, say, \$10 million in the bank, it would seemingly mean little to go from a net worth of \$10,000,000 to 10,004,800.[201] In fact, there was a risk not only that she would not succeed in enlarging her assets but also that she might go to jail.

Although most people will not take such extreme risks, they do often ignore their total wealth when making choices. For example, in a simpler gambling context, they would view a gamble that, in reality, has a 50:50 chance to increase their assets from $10,000,000 to $10,004,800 instead as a 50:50 chance to gain nothing or $4,800. That is, they mentally "edit" the gamble—in effect, subtracting or ignoring their $10,000,000 assets, before they evaluate it. So possibly, Winona lopped off her total assets from the decision-making equation while she was also cutting off the security tags.

The Editing Phase of Prospect Theory

Kahneman and Tversky developed a model called *prospect theory* which specifies the way that such editing and evaluation occurs (see Table 4–1). For instance, suppose the person is comparing a certain $10,000,000 versus a gamble with a .5 of chance of $10,000,000 and a .5 chance of $10,004,800.

In prospect theory, an initial editing mechanism could involve simplificat-ion, for example, rounding the gain of $4,800 to $5,000, so that the choice is between $10,000,000 versus a gamble with a .5 of chance of $10,000,000 and a .5 chance of $10,005,000.

Another editing mechanism, called segregation, would isolate the common irrelevant component of each gamble, resulting in a choice between a certain $10,000,000 versus a certain $10,000,000 + a gamble, where the gamble offers a .5 chance of no additional gain or a .5 chance of $5,000 more.

Then, another editing mechanism, called cancellation, removes the ele-ment common to both choices, resulting in a choice between $0 for sure versus a gamble with a .5 chance of $0 and a .5 chance of $5,000.

Thus, one's guaranteed assets of $10 million are edited from the prospect, leaving only the potential gains or losses. Here, the cancellation operation implies a reference point—our current assets of $10,000,000—and the gains and losses are now evaluated simply as changes from this. Other editing mechanisms also can simplify gambles; and one may use alternative pos-sible reference points, as discussed in the section on Changes in reference points.

Next to the selection of a reference point, the most fundamental edit-ing operations is the elimination of *dominated* alternatives. Such choices are no better and, depending on the outcome, could turn out to be worse than one of the other possible choices. Note that, in the edited choice just given, the edited gamble yields either $0 or $5,000, depending on whether one wins or loses. Thus, the certain outcome of $0 can be no better and may be worse than that of the gamble. Thus, the certain $0 is *dominated* by the gamble, and would be excluded from further consideration. If it were the only other option, the gamble would then be chosen, with no need to consider the person's values or attitudes toward risk. Although this is hardly a full description of Winona's choices, you could see why she might have been tempted by larceny.

In fact, however, if Winona considered more than just immediate monetary gains, we would have found that the safer choice of $0 for sure was not really dominated. For example, Winona's simplistic mental model would have disclosed yet another relevant outcome—jail. So if she lost the gamble of trying to steal, got a $0 payoff, and went to jail, that would definitely be worse than getting $0 and going back to her mansion in Beverly Hills. In this case, then, the gamble would not dominate the sure, safe alternative. So she should at least think before cutting off the security tags on the merchandise. That is, she should go on to the "evaluation phase" before deciding.

The Evaluation Phase of Prospect Theory

In prospect theory, when more than one nondominated option remains after the editing process, a second phase of evaluation begins. Such evaluation proceeds in a manner similar to that of EU theory—one combines elements of probability and value to estimate the gamble's worth. However, the computation differs from EU in several ways. First, the *value* of the outcomes differs from a *utility* and is not defined by one continuous curve describing the evaluation of total assets. Rather, the *value* is described by two different functions, which differ for gains and losses.[202] Second, the value is multiplied not by an objective probability based on statistics (as in the expected value (EV) or EU models), nor by a subjective probability based on personal beliefs (as in the SEU model, see Table 3–1). Rather, it is multiplied by a "decision weight," which represents the impact of probability on actual decisions.

More precisely, the combination rule resembles the formula for EU. For a gamble, g, that involves the prospect of only gains, x_i, with probabilities p_i, for $i = 1, 2, \ldots, n$, the value of the gamble (g) is

$$V(g) = \text{SUM}_i \pi\, (p_i) v_i(x_i)$$

A similar formula applies to gambles that have only losses, except that the value (v) and probability weight functions, π, differ.

Even this simple form of prospect theory can explain aspects of human behavior that give fits to EU theorists. For example, why do people fly to Las Vegas to gamble, then rent a car and buy extra insurance? Does their gambling tell us that they are risk-seeking? Or does their insurance purchase tell us that they are risk-averse? Can two parameters—probability and utility—explain these abrupt turns? Actually, it takes more than two to dance this tango. Prospect theory provided the first instructional video for getting us on the dance floor.

According to prospect theory, risk attitude is determined not only by prior editing mechanisms and the framing of decisions—for example, whether one sees the outcomes as losses or gains. Three factors in the evaluation phase also affect risk attitude: the shape of the probability weight function, the shape of the value function, and the degree of loss aversion.

Decision Weights: A Description of
Attention-Weighted Value

The "decision weight" in prospect theory can represent the attention given to gains or losses—hence, we have termed prospect theory an "attention-weighted value" model in Table 4–1 (see Figure 4–2 captions for more specific models of the weights). While subjective probabilities in SEU theory could be affected by attention, models such as prospect theory are more realistic and enable gains and losses to be weighted differently.

Figure 4–2a illustrates a common probability weight function, in which people underweigh high probabilities and overweigh small ones. With such overweighting of low probabilities, the visitor to Las Vegas who prefers a .001 chance to win $5,000 rather than to keep the $5 he has in his pocket will gamble. At the same time, the visitor may prefer to avoid a .001 chance to lose $5,000 over the loss of $5 from an insurance payment, and will therefore purchase additional insurance. Thus, his apparently conflicting risk attitudes may be determined in part by a consistent tendency to overweigh small probabilities.

Such probability weights also can explain people's preferences for certainty—the fact that, when one option promises a certain reward or penalty, it is often weighed more heavily than when it is just very likely. For instance, let us assume that one prefers $3,000 for sure to a gamble that offers a .8 chance to win $4,000, since the latter is a likely but not certain gain. Yet, now suppose that you are offered a choice between a .25 chance to win $3,000 and a .2 chance to win $4,000. In this case, many people prefer the latter gamble. Such preferences violate the *independence axiom* of the EU theory—which says essentially that your choice should not change if you add an independent, seemingly irrelevant event (e.g., if you would get to make the original choice only if it rains, which has a ¼ chance of occurring and makes the gain of $3,000 now not certain but merely possible).[203] Prospect theory explains the reversal—the preference for the $3,000 only when it is certain—as an example of the *certainty effect*: People value certain outcomes more than the theory would predict.[204]

The decision weights shown in Figure 4–2a illustrate a basis for the certainty effect. The weight given to a probability rises very rapidly as it increases from .99 to 1.0—meaning that the mere certainty of an occurrence makes it much more important than an extremely likely but still uncertain event. The same applies to a reduction in probability. Note that the weight function declines very rapidly as one goes from $p = .01$ to $p = 0$—meaning the outcome is then impossible. Such an *elimination* of risk is often viewed as far more important than a mere *reduction* in risk (e.g., from $p = .11$ to $p = .1$) Thus, people often are willing to pay more for treatments that can

Table 4-1 Effectiveness Models

Models	Model Components and Measures	Advantages and Drawbacks of Different Methods	Neurobiology	Pathology
Attention-weighted value (AWV) $= \Sigma\pi(p_i)v_i(x_i)$				
Prospect theory (PT) Probability weights $\pi(p_i)$ reflect the impact of uncertainty on choice; values $v_i(x_i)$ depend on a reference point	Editing phase: eliminate dominated alternatives Evaluation phase Probability weights: optimism-pessimism bias and sensitivity to probability Value function depends on declining marginal value and loss aversion coefficient	PT: values: change in reference points explains how evaluations vary with framing of the choice Different probability weights explain certainty preferences Weights on gain versus loss explain insurance purchase and gambling Risk aversion is a function of loss aversion, marginal value and probability weights Does not consider changes in attention with context	OFC/VMPFC lesions: impair editing, probability sensitivity and response to loss Cerebellar stroke: no loss aversion ACC activity related to probability weights Framing as loss or gain predicts choice through neural measures of affect and effort	Impaired editing of dominated choices in amphetamine abusers. Response to loss decreased in depression, increased in some drug abusers Lack of loss aversion in schizophrenia Altered probability weights with ACC disturbances/ADHD and mania
Complex disappointment (CD) model Probability weights $\pi(p_i) = h(p)$ values $v_i(x_i)$ depend on prior expectations	Biases in experience or anticipation can be measured as the difference between elation and disappointment coefficients $(e - d)$ and reactivity as their sum $(e + d)$. Attention biases are the ratio of attention weights to actual probabilities $[h(p)/p]$	CD models positive and negative deviations from expectations weighted differently Attention weight reflects over or under weighting of probabilities	Decreased attention to loss in RVMPFC damage	Decreased attention to loss in borderline personality disorder and some addictions Possible increased attention in anxiety

Context-dependent value (CDV) = $\sum w(p_i)v_i(x_1, x_2, \ldots, x_n)$

Cumulative Prospect theory *Security Potential/ Aspiration (SPA)*	Security/potential reflects the weight placed on obtained outcomes that are ranked better or worse than the outcomes, which might have occurred Aspiration considers the probability of attaining specified goals	CPT and SPA consider some aspects of the context of the choice SPA also may define goal-related craving or fears SPA thus distinguishes optimism and hope, pessimism and fear Neither model distinguishes separate fear and safety systems for loss	Striatal neurons respond to reward as a difference between actual and expected reward divided by the dispersion of possible outcomes SPA: security-potential affected by RVMPFC damage Expectation and goal-related components have distinct neural bases	Addicts may rescale rewards Rescaling in young people may improve learning but impair decision-making

Temporal models

Time perception, perspective, and preference Discounting	Time perception: subjective estimates of time duration during resting or craving Time perspective: The ability to list future outcomes, as well as the importance and probability of each	Time perception considers perceptual time distortions Time perspective considers the ability to formulate models of the future	Time perspective shortened by VMPFC or DLPFC damage without discounting changes Hybrid discounting: limbic activity may drive short-run impatience	Distorted time perception in craving Shortened time perspective in youth, PTSD, linked to apathy, not impulsivity Increased discount rate in substance/ personality-disorders

Discount models

Exponential $U(x, T) = b(T)x$ $b(T) = \exp(-KT)$ K = discount rate x = outcome T = delay *Hyperbolic model* $b(T) = K/T$	Discount rates inferred from choices between outcomes received at varying future times Neural correlates of discount rates predict future choices	Exponential discounting ensures temporal consistency (constant rate) Hyperbolic and hybrid model allow temporal inconsistency changes in rates according to delay	Lateral prefrontal and parietal cortex may mediate long-run patience	Increased time spent thinking about a substance in addiction or about a danger in anxiety

(continued)

Table 4–1 (continued)

Models	Model Components and Measures	Advantages and Drawbacks of Different Methods	Neurobiology	Pathology
Hybrid $b(T) = x$ for $T = 0$ $= \beta \exp(-KT)$ for $T > 0$ β = weighting on immediate vs. delayed outcomes *Anxiety model (AM)* $U(x, p; y) = EV +$ $G(t) h(p) (x - EV) +$ $L(t) (1 - h(p)) (EV - y)$	AM measures the quality of time spent thinking of future gains and losses, where the quality can vary as the time of the outcome nears Similar to the disappointment model but also considers, $h(p)$, the time spent thinking about the chances of x and the reaction to gain or loss can vary with time	Hybrid model reflects dual processing of immediate vs. delayed reward Exponential and hyperbolic models do not explain discount rate changes with outcome valence, size, and expectation as well as anticipatory emotions AM can model anticipatory emotions related to time and uncertainty	Fear and relief learning mediated by separate neural systems Dread activates pain-related brain areas Caudal ACC during pain may mirror pain expectations	Craving in drug use, dread in anxiety
QALMs Quality adjusted life minutes spent waiting $V(x, t) = $ constant + (costs of waiting due to dread) − (benefits of waiting due to discounting)	QALMs takes the value of a deferred reward to be the difference between the costs and benefits of waiting Distinguishes loss aversion $(L = d/b)$ and delay aversion $(D = e/c)$ parameters L and D can be measured from neural data or inferred from time preferences L and D define four different forms of the QALMs model	QALMs models Can consider the joint effects of discounting and anticipatory or mixed feelings Evaluates the magnitude and relative persistence of costs vs. benefits over time Unlike dual process models, with separate cognitive and affective systems, it enables analysis of interactions	Feedback effects suggested by delayed effects of serotonin agonists and altered effects with DA lesions	QALMs: Increased immediate aversion to negative consequences in high dreaders Increased immediate discounting in deprived smokers

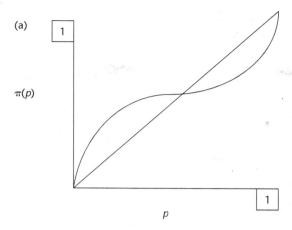

Figure 4–2 (a) The weight function of prospect theory $\pi(p)$. Pictured is the decision weight for a given probability of winning in a two-outcome gamble with a probability of winning, p. A similar weight function can describe the weight placed on a probability of losing; however, the shape may differ. The greater the degree of curvature, the lower the insensitivity to probability. To describe such weights, Kahneman and Tversky originally suggested using a function of the form: $w^+(P) = P^\gamma/[P^\gamma + (1 - P^\gamma)]^{1/\gamma}$. Here, γ is a parameter which, in experiments, usually reflects the general tendency to overweigh only very small probabilities of gain but underweigh most others. When $\gamma = 1$, the weight function is linear and is the diagonal line shown. However, in most studies, $.5 < \gamma < 1$, which produces an inverted-S-shaped curve. The function switches from over to underweighting of probabilities at some critical value of the objective probability (p). A similar but not necessarily identical weighting function for losses has been proposed. But in most studies, this function reflects a stronger tendency to overweigh most probabilities, perhaps reflecting a general pessimism.

cure a disease with a 1% mortality risk than for prevention programs that reduce the risk from 11% to 10%, even though risk reduction and the incremental gain in EU is the same.

Beyond clarifying responses to certainty versus uncertainty, the weight function in prospect theory also enables us to estimate two important parameters: *sensitivity* to changes in probability and *bias* or degree of optimism versus pessimism (see Figure 4–2). The more curvature the graph in Figure 4–2a has, the lower the sensitivity to probability. Such insensitivity occurs because, as the probability increases, the decision weight will rise rapidly to the midrange and then change little as the probability rises, reminiscent of the behavior of a child, who has little concept of probability. On the other hand, the extent to which the curve lies above or below the diagonal determines the degree of pessimism or optimism. When the bias term is high for gains, the curve lies largely above the diagonal and the person behaves in an optimistic way, reacting as if a win is more likely (see Figure 4–2b). When the bias term is low, the person is more

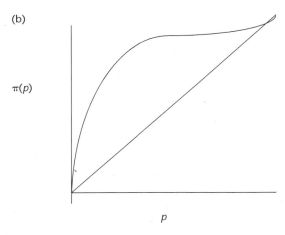

Figure 4–2 (b) An optimistic weighting function based on a refined model with two parameters. In the weighting function developed by Gonzalez and Wu[a]. $\pi(P) = \delta P^\gamma/[\delta P^\gamma + (1 - P^\gamma)]$ where γ controls the curvature (the sensitivity to probability) and δ reflects the elevation (the optimism or pessimism). Another two-parameter function that separately controls curvature and elevation was proposed by Prelec[b]. $\pi(P) = \exp(\delta[1 - \log(P)]^\gamma)$. The figure illustrates an optimistic weighting function that is largely above the diagonal. The weights exceed most probabilities, except for very high ones.

[a] Gonzalez, R., & Wu, G. (1999). On the shape of the probability weighting function. *Cognitive Psychology, 38,* 129–166.

[b] Prelec, D. (1998). The probability weighting function. *Econometrica, 66,* 497–527.

pessimistic and the curve lies largely under the diagonal. Such biases may explain some inconsistencies in choice due to the distortion of uncertainties. However, estimates of such biases derive implicitly from the actual choices that people make, whereas estimates of the calibration of probabilities, discussed in chapter 3, derive from consciously stated estimates.

Neurobiology and Pathology of Editing Operations and Decision Weights

Relatively few studies addressed the editing operations of prospect theory. A notable exception is the previously cited study by Rogers and his coauthors. They found that patients with VMPFC damage or dysfunction, due to amphetamine addiction, did fail to eliminate dominated alternatives.[205] Such a failure can explain what might seem to be risk-seeking behavior but which indicates a more fundamental disturbance.

A greater number of neurobiological studies have begun to clarify possible mechanisms underlying the certainty effect and other distortions of probability. For instance, very different brain regions are activated on positron emission tomography (PET) scans when people make choices that involve certain outcomes versus those that involve only risky choices.[206] In addition,

ACC activity is correlated with the probability weight function's curvature, which may create an overvaluation of certainty. Thus, the ACC, which is involved in monitoring the effects of action, does not relate simply to error rates and subjective probabilities—the belief that an outcome will occur. Rather it may mirror uncertainties related to actual choice, which is what the decision weights are.[207]

Several studies may also shed light on the two specific parameters of the weight function: sensitivity and bias. Although not specifically designed to measure probability weights, the risk sensitivity studied by Rogers could be related to the curvature of the probability weight function. In their study, patients with OFC damage and amphetamine abuse had little desire to increase their bets when the chances of winning rose.[208] They showed a child-like insensitivity to probability. Other studies found that intense emotion leads to changes in bias, which raises the weighting function above the diagonal and increases the tendency to overweigh small probabilities.[209] And some highly emotional individuals—patients with mania—not only have altered activity in the ACC but also have been found to be overly optimistic. [210,211] Thus, one would expect them to show probability weight distortions—perhaps even an optimistic bias represented by the curve in Figure 4–2b.

Note that the existence of probability weight distortions will, in general, bias estimates of value obtained by common EU methods. However, techniques are available now to estimate the parameters of the probability weighting function first, and then obtain "debiased" estimates of the values, which consider possible distortions in probability due to the weighting function.[212]

The Loss Aversion Coefficient and Declining Marginal Utility

Beyond the attention paid to the probabilities of wins or losses, prospect theory also identifies two other factors that contribute to risk aversion. First, people may be averse to risk because they have declining *marginal utility*: that is, they find the joy of a large gain to be not much greater than the pleasure of a moderate one (as previously illustrated in Figure 4–1). In addition, they may be *loss averse*. That is, they may avoid risk because they are more troubled by losses than they are made happy by equivalent gains. For instance, they could assign more significance to a $10 loss than a $10 gain. Kahneman and Tversky found such patterns in the values of experimental subjects. Their values were described roughly by an exponential function of the form $v(x) = x^{0.88}$ for possible gains and $v(x) = -2.25x^{0.88}$ for possible losses. One index of loss aversion (λ) divides the absolute value of losses by the value of equivalent gains: so $\lambda = 2.25(x)^{0.88}/x^{0.88} = 2.25$. This index suggests that the potential losses loom more than twice as large as potential gains.[213]

Neurobiology of Gain and Loss

Some studies have suggested that different neurochemical systems mediate the anticipation of loss or gain. For example, propanolol, a blocker of norepinephrine, impairs the ability to discriminate differences in the magnitude of punishments when the chances of loss are heightened—as when one is likely to be anxious about likely punishments. The opposite occurs with reboxetine, a stimulant of norepinephrine systems.[214] So propanolol diminishes and reboxetine increases stimulatory activation of stress response systems, which facilitates the simulation of possible future punishments.

By contrast, different systems appear to be involved for drugs or dietary changes that modify the *reward* systems. For instance, the depletion of tryptophan, a chemical needed to produce serotonin, impairs the ability to discriminate differences in the magnitude of possible future rewards.[215,216] The authors speculate that some antidepressant drugs that augment the effects of serotonin may have the opposite effects in depressed patients, restoring the ability to discriminate rewards.

In addition, many imaging studies have suggested that the active areas of the brain differ during gain or loss.[217] Activity is higher in the OFC when one is thinking about gains, whereas more activity occurs in inferior parietal and cerebellar (motor) areas when one is thinking about losses.[218] Likewise, activity in the PFC represents negatively valenced affect in the lateral regions and positively valenced affect in more frontal and medial sectors.[219] Beyond this, high levels of loss also lead to activity in other structures, including the hippocampus, which mediates the recall of past situations and the consequences of an action. Such memory, as well as the link to motor areas of the brain, may facilitate the corrective actions that often follow new experiences of loss.[220]

At the same time, other research suggests that some of the same regions of the brain may encode both gains and losses when people make choices that involve the possibility of both small monetary gains or losses. For instance, losses and gains appear to act antagonistically in some single-neuron recordings from the dorsal ACC as well as eye-movement-related areas (the supplemental eye fields, SEF).[221] Likewise, when people were presented with choices between gambles that involved both gains and losses, no regions were found that increased with losses.[222] Rather, the NAc activity rose in proportion to the possible gains and fell in proportion to the losses.

At first glance, one might question whether the seemingly very different results in various studies relate to the different experimental methods and assumptions. Some of the studies showing asymmetries in gains and losses involve experienced utilities and do not involve mixed gambles. Conceivably, in the experiments involving mixed gambles, prior editing mechanisms could have transformed gambles involving both gains and losses into ones perceived only as possible gains.[223] For instance, if subjects evaluate each gamble individually, through the editing mechanisms of prospect theory, the initial payment to subjects of a $30 fee could, in theory, transform a 50:50 chance to gain $12 or lose $14 into a 50:50 chance to gain $42 or $16 total. However, the study involving the mixed gambles did show impressive abilities of the neural activity measures to predict behavioral measures of loss aversion and preference. So, for particular types of decisions, at least, the same neural machinery could encode both losses and gains.

In addition, the above decisions involving mixed gambles with small monetary amounts may relate more directly to the expectancy-related utilities that determine more calculative decisions (called decision utilities). The experienced utilities measured in some other experiments may have more separable neural correlates. Likewise, more goal-related utilities that strongly stimulate automatic approach or avoidance behaviors may have very different and more separable neural correlates. The section on Changes in reference points will discuss these in more detail.

Pathology

The finding in the above studies of increased neural activity with gains and diminished activity with losses may suggest why people with relatively unresponsive physiological systems engage in sensation seeking.[224] For instance, underreactive sociopaths may appear to take risks because they feel there is little to lose, and they derive satisfaction only from very strong rewards.

At the same time, the absence of loss aversion in experienced utilities also may have important consequences. For instance, studies have found an impairment of response to punishments after a stroke that damages the cerebellum.[225] Accordingly, patients with cerebellar damage often display an apparent "flattening" of affect, which may reflect the loss of asymmetry in both experience and anticipation. The same may be true for schizophrenics with "flat affect," who also display abnormalities in cerebellar activity in PET scans.[226]

In fact, in many other mental disorders, experiments have noted an asymmetry of responses to gain and loss. Some substance users show increased responses to rewards and decreased responses to penalties—a response pattern similar to that seen in patients with amygdalar damage.[227] Conversely, depressed patients show different patterns of neural activation in response to happy words and sad words. In some brain regions there is an underresponse to the former and an overresponse to the latter, compared with normal controls.[228] Likewise, patients with BPD have more extensive activation, particularly in the cerebellum, when viewing negative as opposed to positive stimuli, possibly contributing to their overreactions to minor losses.[229]

ALTERNATIVE POINTS AND MODELS

The previous discussion of prospect theory has shown how it may be useful in estimating some of the parameters of evaluation. To perform such evaluations, however, one must establish the reference point—a basis against which possible outcomes can be compared or evaluated.

Suppose you just bought a used car. To determine your feelings about the purchase, you might compare the new car to your old one—the status quo. Or you might compare it to your neighbor's car, thus making a social comparison. Likewise, after choosing the car and later breaking down on the road, you might compare this outcome to "what might have been" had you chosen a different make or model. Alternatively, you might compare the outcome with your initial expectations—what the used car salesman led you to believe about the condition of the vehicle. Let us discuss each of these comparisons in turn.

Comparisons With the Status Quo

People often compare the possible outcomes of a choice to their current state— the status quo. Hence, the perception of current assets often influences evaluations. For example, when people actually possess an item, such as a coffee mug, they perceive the status quo as "having the mug." They are generally averse to losing it and, if asked to sell it, usually charge more than the price in a store. But if people do not initially possess the item and perceives the status quo as "not having the mug," then they are often unwilling to pay the store's price. Indeed, experiments have shown that the amount one must be paid to give up a possession greatly exceeds the amount one is willing to pay to acquire the same item. Economic theory, on the other hand, asserts that the evaluation of the item's worth should be identical in both cases.[230] According to economists, this reflects a bias toward preserving the status quo—either having or not having the mug—and is termed the "endowment effect."[231] It illustrates one of many types of inconsistencies that may arise from variations in the reference point.

Other types of inconsistencies arise from what have been termed "framing effects." For example, prospect theory stipulates that people have different attitudes toward risk that depend on whether one sees the outcomes as gains or losses in relation to the status quo. Thus, one's apparent risk attitude can be manipulated by "framing" the status quo in different ways. For instance, scientists gave subjects a hypothetical choice between conservative medical treatment or surgery for lung cancer. When the experimenters described the outcomes in terms of life years expected to be gained—the status quo being their current longevity—most people were risk-averse and chose medical treatment. When they described the outcomes in terms of life years to be lost from their prior life expectancy—a different status quo—most people were risk-seeking and chose surgery.[232] In its earliest form, prospect theory concluded that when individuals choose between potential gains, they are generally risk-averse and that when they choose between potential losses, they tend to be risk-seeking.

Neurobiology

Neural responses underlying aversive and uncertain states could explain risk-seeking after the status quo declines.[233] For example, since the IGT commonly begins with lower losses in the disadvantageous decks, many people initially pick these decks and sustain financial losses. For instance, if someone has lost $200 and feels disheartened, he might accept a 50:50 gamble to either win back the $200 or nothing over an offer of $100 for sure.

Only if he selects the gamble can he entirely remove the negative affective state. So he may select the gamble, even if he would normally prefer a sure $100. Similar mechanisms may explain why race-track betters wager more on long-shots toward the end of the day in order to recoup their losses.

The "somatic marker" hypothesis of risk-seeking implies that external influences could also affect risk attitude. Other factors being equal, influences which make the experienced somatic state less negative after a loss should make people avoid risk. Thus, right-sided VMPFC lesions that make the experienced state less negative should make the lesioned patients avoid risk more than controls do.

In addition, according to Bechara and Damasio, the gamble lessens the negative response not merely due to the escape from a negative status quo to an uncertain but possibly more positive state. It also does so partly due to its uncertainty. Uncertain losses appear to be mediated by more anterior portions of the VMPFC, whereas "certain losses" trigger representations in the posterior VMPFC, which produces stronger somatic markers. So if the person sees the certain gain really as a $100 net loss, after losing $200 earlier, the certain $100 loss will trigger a stronger somatic response than does a gamble.

The effort of thinking, as well as the intensity of feeling, also may explain inconsistencies due to the way different choices are framed.[234] Changes in preference commonly occur when gambles are framed as gains versus losses, as illustrated previously for the gain or loss of life years in a medical versus surgical decision. In one study, subjects who preferred the gamble in the gain frame had increased activation in the DLPFC, which plays a role in working memory. Presumably, subjects needed such memory to hold in mind the values of the probabilities and outcomes while calculating the expected value of the gamble. The investigators speculated that it was to avoid such effort that most people chose the certain option in the gain frame. However, when affective intensity became more important—as when subjects made choices in the loss frame—effort reduction became less important, so many subjects chose the risky options.

Many of the above neurobiologic hypotheses have not yet been adequately studied. Also, to understand many decision-making disturbances, experiments must consider more than framing, mood, and effort. For instance, they may tell us how feelings in biased frames make people think more about gains or losses.[235] However, these studies do not tell us how the person actually constructs a frame of reference; many of the difficulties of some irrational individuals may stem from an inflexible tendency to see problems in either a positive or negative light. Thus, future research should examine the neural correlates of choices in problems that could be viewed as either a gain or a loss, depending on the person's perspective.

Comparison With the Outcomes of Other Choices: Regret

Note that people do not merely compare their current assets with prior ones but also with a variety of other reference points, including each other's assets, what they expected, and what might have been. For example, if the outcome is bad and an alternative choice could have avoided it, they commonly experience regret.

Mellers has proposed a model, "decision affect theory," for assessing the contributions of regret to experience and anticipation. To illustrate, suppose that a person chooses one of two gambles and then plays both. The value of the obtained outcome is u_a. The value of the outcome that would have occurred for the alternative choice is u_c. Then the regret would be the difference between the outcome that occurred and the one that could have been obtained, multiplied by a term that reflects how surprising the results were (i.e., the chance that both outcomes would not have occurred together). Thus the regret $R = r(u_a - u_c)(1 - s_a s_c)$, where s_a is the subjective probability that one would have obtained outcome, a in the chosen gamble and s_c is the subjective probability for outcome, c in the unchosen alternative.

Neurobiology

What happens in the brain when people experience such regret? More specific models, related to Mellers's decision affect theory, are just beginning to be used in neurobiologic investigation.[236] However, the correlates of regret in the brain are becoming a bit clearer. For instance, in experiments that reward people for making particular choices, brain activity depends on whether or not a reward is received, but the specific distribution of brain activity also appears to depend upon whether or not one acted to obtain the reward.[237] Thus, the value of a bad outcome could be experienced more negatively, with regret, if it resulted from one's action. Other experiments have also tied regret to action systems in the brain. For example, in one experiment, people chose fastest after regret experience and also made more risk-seeking choices.[238] The authors concluded that regret may signal to the person that he has chosen poorly and could motivate him to change his decision strategies.

In addition, some evidence suggests a role for the OFC in mediating regret. Patients with damage to this area consider regret in their choices less often than do normal controls or patients with damage to other regions.[239] In one experiment, when control group subjects received feedback not only about the outcome of a chosen gamble but also the outcome of an unchosen one, they did not simply respond to the outcome they received. The outcome of the unchosen gamble also affected their SCRs and the received outcome's subjective value. The unchosen outcome, by contrast, did not affect the evaluations of the OFC-damaged patients. The authors concluded that the OFC helps represent the value of the outcomes obtained from one's choices relative to those that could have been obtained from a different selection.

Pathology

Although clearly people experience regret at times, whether or not the fear of regret guides their choices, in general, has not been clearly determined.[240]

However, refined regret models suggest that people do consider anticipatory regret when they receive feedback about foregone alternatives that may affect their self-esteem.[241] Accordingly, one might expect regret to be most salient when self-esteem is most vulnerable, as in depression. And, indeed, depressed patients often do blame themselves for every bad outcome, even when they really could have done little to prevent it. Such regrets could not only influence their decisions but also undermine their motivation to act.

Comparison With Expectations: Elation and Disappointment

While regret appears to be a component of evaluation that signals a deviation from the best outcome of alternative actions, other components of evaluation signal a deviation from prior expectations. While a positive deviation is said to produce elation, a negative deviation is often said to produce disappointment.

Mellers proposed a model of disappointment, similar to her previously discussed model of regret. The disappointment is proportional to the difference between the value of the outcome one obtained and the one that could have occurred but did not ($u_a - u_b$). This difference in values is again multiplied by a term that reflects the surprise of the outcome (the probability that the outcome would not have occurred, $1 - s_a$). This product is added to the "economic" value of the outcome itself, u_a. Hence, the disappointment, $D = u_a + d(u_a - u_b)(1 - s_a)$. Mellers hypothesizes that a person's overall anticipatory rating of an outcome is the sum of the expected disappointment and regret. From experimental data, she and her colleagues have then estimated the contribution of disappointment (d), relative to the regret (r).

Somewhat more complex models allow us to assign different weights to better-than-expected deviations and worse-than-expected ones, as well as to consider the effects of attention on probabilities. In David Bell's disappointment model, the value one derives from a reward depends on the extent to which it deviates from initial expectations.[242]

For example, suppose a person plays a gamble with a probability, denoted by p, to yield an amount, x, and a probability denoted by $1 - p$, to yield an amount, y. Then, according to Bell's model, the elation experienced when obtaining the larger amount, say x, is proportional to the amount obtained (x) minus the amount expected (E). That is,

$$\text{The elation due to a reward} = e(x - E)$$

where e is a constant called the "elation coefficient."

Similarly, the amount of negatively valued disappointment experienced when obtaining the smaller amount, y, is proportional to the expectation (E) minus the amount obtained, times a positive constant, d, which is termed the "disappointment coefficient." That is, the disappointment due to an unexpected punishment = $-d(E - y)$.

To illustrate, suppose a gamble offers a 9/10 chance of paying $37.50 and a 1/10 chance of losing $87.50. The expected value of that gamble is (.9)$37.5 − (.1)$87.5 = +$25 (this gamble represents the average win and loss outcomes and probabilities in the advantageous decks in the IGT). If one wins the gamble, he receives $37.50 − $25 = $12.50 in unexpected reward. According to Bell, then, the total amount of elation one receives is proportional to this amount. Similarly, if someone loses the gamble, then he receives $25 − to −$87.50) = $112.50 in unexpected loss; and the total amount of disappointment is proportional to this amount, but the constant of proportionality differs: this constant is d, the disappointment coefficient.

Finally, the anticipated value of a risky prospect is the sum of the gamble's expectation (E) and the total elation and disappointment calculated above, each multiplied by their respective probabilities (p and $1 − p$). In the simple disappointment model, this value simplifies to $V = E + (e − d)(x − y)$ $p(1 − p)$—the sum of the monetary expected value of the gamble (E) plus its "psychological value" $[(e − d)p(1 − p)(x − y)]$. Thus, the value is affected by a cognitive assessment of the expectation of the gamble as well as by a term reflecting the relative importance of incentive or aversive responses— the "anticipatory bias" ($e − d$). According to this model, then, the subjects who are best at maximizing their own satisfaction in a gambling task might not be those who maximize their net gains—which is in general best done by considering only the expected values. Rather, if the task has known probabilities and outcomes, the decision-makers who best seek satisfaction would also consider the "psychological value" of the gamble, as reflecting in the elation and disappointment it may provide.

In a more complex disappointment model, the original disappointment and elation coefficients (e and d) can also change according to the probability of winning, p_i. This model expresses the original disappointment and elation coefficients as the product of value and the "weight" given to the chances of winning or losing (since $e^* = h(p)e$ and $d^* = [1 − h(p)]d$, where $h(p)$ is a weight reflecting the relative attention given to the prospect of a win).[243,244]

Neurobiology of Disappointment and Elation

Some evidence suggests that a comparison between actual and expected outcomes—similar to that expressed in the disappointment model—is also reflected in the activity of dopamine systems in VS.[245] In this view, dopamine neurons encode a reward prediction error—the deviation of the reward from one's prior expectations—rather than a reward per se.[246]

In one well-known experiment, for example, rats were taught to expect a juice after a light appeared. While they consistently showed a surge of dopamine release immediately upon the appearance of light, dopamine release did not rise when the reward finally came. The reward was fully expected after the flash of light and there was no prediction error. On the other hand, there was a prediction error when the reward was expected and the rats did not receive the juice. In that case, the amount of dopamine release actually declined.[247] Also, the results changed when the reward was not expected. Then, if the reward was received, the error of prediction was larger and the unexpected reward led to proportionately greater dopamine neuron activity. Hence, as in Bell's model, prior expectations appeared to influence the way that outcomes were experienced.

The attention given to the chances of gains versus losses could also affect anticipatory values, and they could differ from the actual probabilities, as in the more complex disappointment model with decision weights. Also, there is reason to believe in some separation of these cognitive, attentional processes (as reflected in the decision weights) from incentive, motivational ones (as reflected in the elation or disappointment). For example, one structure thought to be involved in both cognitive and motivational aspects of attention is the ACC, which has two major subdivisions—a dorsal cognitive section and a rostroventral emotional section.[248] In the future, one could test whether the influences of these divisions are reflected, respectively, in the probability weights and motivational constants (elation and disappointment).

Finally, the disappointment model may enable us to clarify some neurobiological components not only of evaluation but also learning. First, as noted earlier, the anticipatory value of a gamble is the sum of an expectation or monetary component (E) and a psychological component $[\Psi = (e - d) p(1 - p)(x - y)]$. Note that Ψ is proportional to $p(1 - p)$, which reaches a maximum when $p = .5$—that is, when there is, in one sense, maximum uncertainty about whether or not a reward will occur. In a crude way, this psychological component depends on the amount of uncertainty and the potential to reduce it through learning.

Recent neurobiologic findings suggest that this interpretation is not entirely hypothetical. First, they confirm the existence and distinctness of the two components of anticipation, such as the monetary and the psychological components. First, the magnitude of some neural signals rise as monetary expectations—$[E = px + (1 - p)y]$—increase. These rising expectations are reflected in a brief, phasic response in the dopamine neurons when a conditioned stimulus (CS), such as a gamble, is presented.

Second, other neurons encode signals that are related to the uncertainty of the reward and may roughly correspond to the psychological component of anticipation. One aspect of uncertainty is greatest when the probability of winning the gamble $p = .5$. As the probability of reward approaches the point of maximal uncertainty at $p = .5$, the dopamine neurons show an increased anticipatory response. This slower response outlasts the reward's expectation component and continues from the CS to the delivery of the reward.[249] It enables us to attend to the stimuli that teach us about potential future rewards.[250] Also, since the sustained component is associated with uncertainty, it is also associated with the psychological value of the gamble, which is a "teaching signal" that may be crucial to learning.

In addition, when the probabilities of outcomes are not initially known, this "teaching signal" has anticipatory value that may influence choices between gambles. Consequently, a person might not always choose the gamble that appears to have the highest expected value. In the initial stages of the IGT, for example, suppose one has selected a particular deck multiple times and feels that its expected value is greater than that of a second deck, from which one has selected fewer times. Despite the expectation of a lower reward from the second deck, he might still sample it as a "test" selection. In that way, he could discover whether or not it could provide even greater rewards than the first deck in the future. If the gamble's outcome is highly uncertain, it seems to offer not only the value of its expectation in a single selection but also a chance to learn and profit from future choices.[251]

Evolutionary theorists have observed such "sampling" behavior in birds that must choose between large and small worms. They select the worms predicted by a simple value-maximizing model about 85% of the time (curiously similar to the 87% frequency reported for humans who make choices consistent with EU theory).[252] Their periodic "sampling" of the small worms has been explained as an adaptation to environments in which the reward value of prey may change over time.[253] However, whereas in most evolutionary models, the criterion to be optimized relates to organism's efficiency in obtaining food,[254] it is related directly to hedonic experience in the disappointment model.

Pathology

The disappointment model also may enable us to help separate components of maladaptive choice due to incentive or aversive processes (elation vs. disappointment weights) as well as the relative importance of attentional or motivational factors.

For instance, one experiment found attention biases in patients with BPD.[255] When such patients chose between hypothetical gambles involving money, they paid less attention to potential losses than did normal controls. This conclusion is based on measurements of the patients' eye fixations on wins and losses during the choice process.[256] However, one could also examine the attention weights of a complex disappointment model.

The examination of attention weights could be important, since borderline patients who did not attend to losses had greater impulsivity (measured by other scales). Such inattention could foster impulsivity, which often has been explained in terms of other neuroeconomic factors, such as risk-seeking and discounting. The inattention might even explain the impulsive behavior of the BPD patient that Winona Ryder portrayed in a movie—as well as the impulsive kleptomaniac that she became in real life. Such inattention would reflect not the previously discussed problems in editing gambles but rather trouble in evaluating them.

Similarly, the separate estimation of incentive, aversive, and attentional processes in the disappointment model appears useful in the study of attention-deficit hyperactivity disorder (ADHD). During a gambling task, compared with controls, ADHD patients showed less activation in regions mediating cognitive and emotional processes mediating attention, including the hippocampus and the ACC.[257] Also, while both major divisions of the ACC, corresponding to cognitive and motivational processes, were more active in controls, only a more caudal area of the right ACC showed more activation in ADHD subjects.

Likewise, the parameters of a disappointment-like model, which reflect the relative importance of psychological and monetary elements, may vary among different age groups. For instance, adolescents with behavior disorders chose the lower expected value decks in the IGT more often than did the healthy adolescents or adults.[258,259] Since the PFC is one of the last regions of the brain to mature, these adolescents' poor choices could be related to their immature circuitry.[260] At the same time, however, unlike many patients with VMPFC lesions, the adolescents made more errors only initially, and later learned to choose from the advantageous decks. Could the initial bias of adolescents to sample the disadvantageous decks have been due to a greater appetite for the psychological satisfaction of learning than for the maximization of expected gains? That is, did these adolescents exhibit a bias toward one of the components of value in the disappointment model (the psychological satisfaction of learning) at the expense of the other component (expectation)?

Such a fascination with novel learning experiences exists even in normal adolescents and may be enabled by the configuration of children's brains.[261] Increased cortical interconnectivity and neuroplasticity bias the child toward choices with high "psychological," learning value, while interfering with the ability to make choices that maximize "expected value." Children become less able to remember, store, and process the information needed to make predictions. Accordingly, cortical interconnectivity declines in adolescence in order to facilitate a shift toward more effective decision making, which is guided more by expected value than learning considerations.[262]

This developmental shift toward the "calculation" of expectations can be reversed or prevented, however, in some cases of mental disorder. The developmental shift may not have occurred properly in the behaviorally disturbed adolescents. A similar, but episodic, deficit may occur in manic patients. When these patients solve problems, the brain structures normally involved in calculating expectation show less activation and those possibly related to novel, learning experiences show more.[263]

Similar deficits may occur due to drug use. For instance, in one experiment, as the expected value of a gamble increased, the neural structures activated in normal controls were not activated in methamphetamine-dependent individuals. In these patients, by contrast, the activation related to the prospect's uncertainty.[264] Methamphetamine, like cocaine, stimulates the same dopamine systems that produce uncertainty-related learning signals. Methamphetamine abusers, therefore, learn to pay increased attention to drug-related rewards. A similar mechanism may also explain why stimulants such as methamphetamine or methylphenidate (Ritalin) are useful in treating ADHD.[265] The

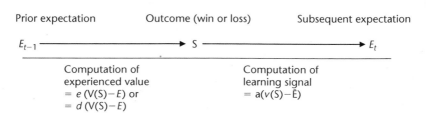

Prior expectation   Outcome (win or loss)   Subsequent expectation

E_{t-1} ⟶ S ⟶ E_t

Computation of   Computation of
experienced value   learning signal
$= e\,(V(S)-E)$ or $= a(v(S)-\bar{E})$
$= d\,(V(S)-E)$

Figure 4–3 Illustration of two stages addressed by the disappointment model and the TD-EV learning model. Pictured is a numeric scale which shows how the disappointment model computes experienced value and how the TD-EV model computes the learning signal. The scale notes the prior expectation, E_{t-1}, the outcome or state experienced during the interval (S), and the subsequent expectation, E_t. The disappointment model takes the value of the experience of S to be a monetary amount. If the amount exceeds the prior expectation, then the unexpected component is valued proportionately to an elation coefficient, e; or if it is less than the expectation, proportionality to a disappointment coefficient, d. The original form of this model takes the expectation of the gamble to be determined by the win and loss amounts and probabilities. Note the similarities of this model of hedonic experience to the learning component of the TD-EV model. The learning signal is the value of the outcome $v(S)$ minus the discounted expectation of reward during the interval from $t-1$ to t, $a(v(S) - \bar{E})$. At a particular time, t, $\bar{E}_{t-1} = E_{t-1} - \gamma E_t$ in a more general TD model of learning. The learning signal is multiplied by a single learning coefficient, a, in order to determine the degree of change in subsequent expectation, $E_t - E_{t-1}$.

drugs may improve an ADHD patient's attention to tasks that offer a reward, making their pursuit appear to have additional learning value. In fact, Ritalin increases the effects of monetary incentives in children with ADHD when they tackle math problems.[266] PET studies suggested that the increased interest in such educational tasks is due to Ritalin's effects in increasing dopamine system activity.

At the same time, we must note that the disappointment model concerns only the ability to generate learning signals and not the ability to profit from their use (see Figure 4–3). Furthermore, a strict interpretation of the model takes the outcomes and their probabilities to be known in advance. Such an assumption applies to certain neuroeconomic studies, such as some done by Rogers.[267] However, in the IGT, the probabilities are not known initially. As such, they can change with experience and also thereby change the expectations of the gamble.[268] Fortunately, more recent, dynamic models of serial choices over time have enabled us to investigate the capacity to learn to change expectations over time. The following section illustrates such investigations as well as models of other changes in reference points.

CHANGES IN REFERENCE POINTS

As illustrated in the previous section, different reference points may alter evaluations, adding other possible sources of inconsistency in choice, although not all such changes are maladaptive. Particularly, changes in the reference points themselves sometimes occur and facilitate adaptation.

Changes in Expectations: Models of Learning

One common adaptive mechanism involves learning, which may produce changes in expectations and even reversal of previously learned contingencies (see Table 4–1). To illustrate, let us return to the earlier example of a terminally ill patient and consider a highly oversimplified explanation of his behavior. After the initial disappointment of his diagnosis, his expectations can change in an adaptive manner. The disappointment is encoded as a neurochemically mediated "learning signal" that signifies that prior expectations were too high. This signal may cause expectations to fall, thereby enabling more positive evaluations of subsequent events.

Busemeyer and Stout developed the expectancy-valence (EV) model to identify three main factors involved in learning that changes expectations:[269]

1. The value (V) of a stimulus (S), which is determined by the weight placed on penalties relative to rewards [and denoted V(S)];
2. The rate at which expectations change (called the learning coefficient, a)
3. The consistency of choice (θ), which is maximal when the person relies entirely upon expectations and is minimal if the person chooses at random.

For example, they applied this model using data from the IGT.[270] They estimated the rate at which the individual learns to distinguish between a "good" deck providing higher expectations of reward and a "bad" deck providing lower expectations. More specifically, they took the change in expectation (ΔE_t) after an outcome, S, to be the difference between the received value of the outcome, V(S), and the prior expectation of the outcome (E_{t-1}), multiplied by the learning coefficient, a; that is

$$\Delta E_t = E_t - E_{t-1} = a(v(S) - E_{t-1}).$$

Since the outcomes of gambles in the IGT can have mixed elements of reward [R(S)] and penalty [P(S)], the total value of the reward, V(S), was assumed to be the sum of these elements multiplied by weights: w for penalties and $1 - w$ for rewards. A type of "loss aversion" occurs when the weight of a given monetary penalty exceeds that of an equivalent monetary reward.

When one considers the value of future rewards, the authors' model takes essentially the same form as widely used models, called temporal discounting (TD). For example, since the reward of choosing a deck of cards in the IGT derives not only from direct rewards ($v(s)$) but also from knowledge that can guide future choices. So one has an improved future expectation (valued at γE_t, with the discounting parameter, γ, reflecting the value placed on the future relative to the present).

Thus, the change in expectation is

$$\Delta E_t = \text{Learning rate} \times \text{Learning signal} = a[v(s) + (\gamma E_t) - E_{t-1}] = a\delta$$

where δ is called the "learning signal" in the usual terminology of TD models. The similarity of the expectation change to the experienced evaluation in the simple disappointment model are discussed in Figure 4–3 and the following note.[271]

The TD-EV model takes the likelihood of choosing a deck to increase as its expectation relative to that of other decks rises. The degree to which subjects are guided by the learned expectation is measured by a "consistency" parameter, θ. So when the consistency of choice, $\sigma\pi$, is zero, choice is random and one is as likely to choose one alternative as the next. As θ becomes very large, the most advantageous deck is chosen with near certainty.[272,273]

Thus, in this model, one could make apparently impulsive choices due to a tendency to underweigh future outcomes (high discount rate, γ) or an increased weight placed on penalties versus rewards (w).[274] Additionally, when the learning rate is extremely high (e.g., $a = 1$), one may be guided by recent rewards only and not prior expectations. Also, when the consistency parameter is low, one may not be guided by "rational expectations" but rather make choices at random.

Neurobiology of Temporal Discounting and Learning

Previous studies have suggested some possible neurobiologic foundations of learning that underlie the temporal discounting (TD) model. For heuristic purposes, let us first consider an overly simple but influential model of the learning process. In this model, learned associations enable the recomputation of expected values through connections between the cortex and striatum. Early in learning, when a cue signals a reward and the reward is experienced, a dopamine signal appears. If the memory trace from the cue persists long enough to overlap with the reward, then an association between the cue and the reward is gradually established. As learning progresses, if the cue reliably predicts the reward, then the dopamine signal occurs immediately after the cue and not with the actual arrival of the reward.

In this formulation, the immediate dopamine response to the cue is mediated by a fast-acting *subthalamic* loop connecting to dopamine neurons in the striatum.[275] This excitatory signal produces the expectation component of the predicted reward (E_{t-1} in Figure 4–4). In addition, however, another signal is transmitted more directly through slow-acting inhibitory projections to the dopamine neurons ($-E_{t-1}$).

Once the reward (v) arrives, it induces an excitatory response, often through connections to the lateral *hypothalamus*. However, the inhibitory signal diminishes the extent of excitation and determines how much the

Learning to change expectations

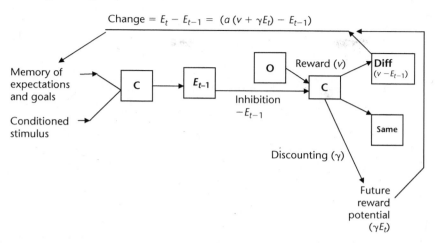

$$\text{Change} = E_t - E_{t-1} = (a(v + \gamma E_t) - E_{t-1})$$

Figure 4–4 Learning and changes in expectations. In a greatly simplified model, when a stimulus is presented at a particular time, $t - 1$, an expectation (E_{t-1}) is generated. This effect may produce an immediate reward signal through a fast-acting subthalamic loop that connects with dopamine neurons. It also generates a slow-acting inhibitory signal to dopamine neurons ($-E_{t-1}$). Then, when an outcome (O) produces a reward (v), it combines with the inhibitory impulse. This process generates an error signal when the outcome differs from expectations (abbreviated as "diff" in the figure; if there is no error signal, this is denoted "same"). If there is an error signal, the difference ($v - E_{t-1}$) then combines with the information about future reward potential (γE_t) to produce a learning signal ($v + (\gamma E_t) - E_{t-1}$). This signal is multiplied by the learning rate (a) to produce changes in expectations ($E_t - E_{t-1}$), which are reflected by changes in neural connections.

pleasure of the reward is reduced.[276] If the reward is perfectly predictable, the two signals cancel each other, and there is no dopamine release at the time of the reward. Thus, there is no learning signal. If the reward is not predictable, however, the delayed inhibitory feedback from the expectations is weaker and the signal is stronger.

The learning signal determines subsequent changes in expectations by modifying the connectivity between neurons. In the striatum, the learning signal changes expectations in part by altering the strength of the connections between nerve cells in the *ventral tegmental area* (VTA), the NAc and the PFC.[277]

Pathology

Before considering more complex neurobiolgic models of learning, let us examine some empirical results from the EV model (without the TD-EV refinements). This model provided a good fit to data from the IGT and has been tested in several populations. In one study, patients with Huntington's disease (HD) had higher values of the learning coefficient. They relied less on past expectations and more on recent experience, in comparison with normal controls and patients with Parkinson's disease (PD).[278] One possible explanation is that the HD patients had poor memories, forgot their prior expectations, and therefore changed them very rapidly. However, as Figure 4–3 indicates, they may fail to generate inhibitory signals or they may not use these signals to diminish current reward values.

While HD patients may have appeared to act impulsively due to these rapid changes in expectation, other patients may have done so for other reasons. For example, severe cocaine abusers and patients with OFC damage had normal learning parameters but made more inconsistent choices unrelated to their expectations. Possibly, then, they were able to generate learning signals and change expectations, but they did not exploit these changes in their actual choices.

In addition, however, the cocaine abusers and OFC-damaged patients had abnormal motivational measures.[279] Thus, they may appear impulsive because they place less weight on losses and more on gains.[280]

In the future, it may be useful to refine the learning models so that they also consider multiple elements of anticipatory evaluation: such as risk attitude, attention biases, and even differential learning rates for rewards and penalties.[281] Such asymmetries in the learning rates for rewards and penalties could relate to a variety of mental disorders. For example, some depressed individuals with reduced serotonin levels may have more trouble learning from wins than losses, even after the magnitude of the learning signal is considered.[282-284] Perhaps cocaine addicts have more trouble learning from penalties than rewards. Such an impairment could hurt discrimination between the values of alternative gambles and make their choices more inconsistent. Possibly, more complex variants of the TD models—called average reward models—would help consider such asymmetries in the learning from rewards and penalties. These models describe learning signals as the result of opponent interactions between avoidance signals derived from the serotonin system and approach signals from dopamine systems.[285,286]

However, some other questions would still remain. For instance, we do not know to what extent the learning signals derive from prior expectations or counterfactual outcomes, such as those that might have occurred but did not. Even regret over the outcomes could have played a role. Such counterfactual comparisons have been found to be reflected in the learning signals, when they are measured from activities in the VS.[287] A later section of this chapter will discuss "rank-dependent" behavioral economic models, which suggest how one might begin to model the effects of unobtained outcomes.

Only future research will enable us to determine whether adding such complexities to the TD models is worth the loss in parsimony. The authors of the TD-EV model did already examine a large array of alternative models, including some economic decision theoretic ones; they found that by incorporating psychological knowledge about learning their model fit the data much better. So, perhaps other psychological models of decision making will provide similar, worthwhile advances.

We will also need to assess different forms of learning capacity, such as the abilities to learn and unlearn associations. In the IGT, if the gains associated with disadvantageous decks or the losses associated with advantageous ones appear early in a deck, the subject then must unlearn previous associations. Although the previously cited studies found no differences in the learning coefficient in VMPFC-damaged patients versus controls, some studies have found that such damage impairs the process of unlearning. In addition, one study found that, when cards were shuffled, eliminating the reversal from early gains to later losses in the IGT, the VMPFC-damaged patients performed normally.[288] Conceivably, then, the patients with VMPFC damage may have a one-way (reversal) impairment in learning; a single learning coefficient across the entire study might hide these impairments.[289]

Yet other differences in learning may also be important to consider in some contexts. For instance, we appear to have neurally distinct short- and long-term memories for different types of associations.[290] The *frontomedian cortex* (FMC) appears to mediate associations that develop over a long period of time, whereas the DLPFC and parietal cortex appear to mediate those that develop over a short period. Thus, depending on the time scale, one could find different results, depending on the types of neural dysfunction being studied.

Changes in the Status Quo: The Environmental Cues Model

To adequately understand the hedonic responses that give rise to learning signals, we may also need to consider changes in other reference points to which the rewards are compared. For instance, some drugs may cause long-term adaptations in reference points, such as the perceived status quo. Such changes could help us understand why cocaine addicts are unresponsive to expectations.

How do such changes in status quo occur? Studies suggest that both drug use and the drug-related cues that induce expectations have a dual effect. They may begin to oppose the effects of subsequent reward. In addition, however, they can lead to more lasting physiological changes underlying the evaluation of the status quo—the average sense of well-being. The reduction of both drug effects and the status quo have been attributed to "opponent processes."[291]

For example, when an addict withdraws from a substance, he often experiences a new status quo—a dysphoria that is worse than his baseline state. Likewise, cues of drug availability—the mere sight or smell of alcohol or cigarettes—also can trigger preparatory or compensatory physiological responses that intensify the state of deficiency. In addition, such compensatory changes can reduce well-being after the administration of the drug. That is, when an addict sees needles or other people using drugs, he will experience physiological changes that oppose the effect of the drug when it is actually given.[292] An addict may then increase the dose of the drug to compensate. But when the opposing effects are absent—when animal or human drug users lack the familiar cues that enable them to anticipate the effects of the drug—the effects of the drug become larger. In fact, heroin overdoses are more common in such cases.[293]

Laibson developed an *environmental cues model* of drug consumption based on opponent processes.[294] In the model, a variable, x, summarizes the status quo—the current state of a physiological process affected by the cue and repeated drug use (see Figure 4–5).[295]

Laibson's model proposes a utility function that depends on the status quo—the extent of neural or physiological change. According to the model, the degree of "wanting" in an addict is the difference in utility between consuming or not consuming the drug at a particular level of the status quo.[296] When a person becomes addicted, the opponent processes decrease

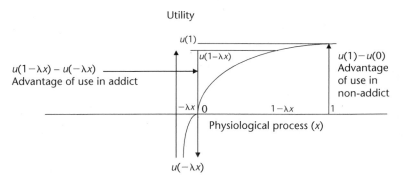

Utility of reward

Figure 4–5 Change in incremental utility of use depending on the presence of a cue. Note that the amount of utility to be gained in the absence of addiction (arrow from $u(0)$ to $u(1)$) is less than the amount of utility to be gained in the presence of addiction [arrow from $u(-\lambda x)$ to $u(1 - \lambda x)$]. The opposite is true for the total utility. That is, the total utility of use, $u(1)$, in the absence of the addiction is greater than the total utility in its presence $(1 - \lambda x)$. Although this reversal of inequalities is illustrated under the standard economic assumption of a concave utility function, it would also hold under the prospect theory assumption of a utility function that is concave for gains and convex for losses, where losses loom larger than equivalent gains. Laibson also allows value to be given to an alternative activity and the same conclusions apply.

the utility of both consumption and nonconsumption but not in equal amounts.[297] According to standard economic (or prospect theory) assumptions about the shape of the utility function, the utility of use is affected less than the utility of nonuse (Figure 4–5). As a result, the difference between the two actually increases. That is, in spite of the decline in overall pleasure with increased use, the "incremental," or comparative amount to be gained, actually increases. Thus, according to this theory, addicts continue to want to use drugs even when they enjoy the drugs less.[298]

Neurobiology

A variety of neurobiologic processes may contribute to the opponent effects. For example, some addictions may cause changes in gene expression in the NAc, which reduce a drug's effects when it is given. Also, there is a decrease in the number of available dopamine receptors. In addition, negative feedback mechanisms decrease dopamine activity and cause a blunted response to dopamine stimulants.[299,300] During withdrawal, there is also an increase of corticotrophin-releasing factor (CRF) and norepinephrine, which are associated with anxiety as well as dynorphin, which "turns off" reward mechanisms and produces dysphoria.[301–304]

Changes in Goals

Drugs may also induce changes in a different kind of "reference point"— the person's goals or aspiration levels. In most economic models, such goals are assumed to be stable and, in some theories, even to predict experience when the doctrine of utilitarianism began to take hold during the early 19th century, economists assumed that our "wants" predict our "likes": that we do what gives us pleasure and avoid what gives us pain.[305] Jeremy Bentham (1894) took this assumption a step further when he asserted that motivated actions merely reflect the state we are experiencing.[306] If we act to prolong a particular state, for example, then we are experiencing pleasure. If we act to terminate it, we are experiencing displeasure.

But current neurobiologic research seriously questions these economic assumptions. For example, as just illustrated in the environmental cues model, a profound wanting can motivate drug consumption even when the drugs no longer produce the expected euphoria.[307] In one experiment, heroin addicts who were given low doses of morphine continued the morphine even though they did not like it.[308] Similarly, cocaine addicts chose low doses of cocaine rather than a fake drug—a salt solution—even when they no longer experienced a cardiovascular response to the cocaine.[309] Thus, while the drug appeared to have no experienced value, people continued to seek it.[310]

Conversely, drugs that antagonize dopamine systems do not change the appetitive value of rewards—an animal placed near the rewards will still consume them. Yet the same drugs can change motivational systems, so that the animal placed at a distance from the rewards will not make the effort to approach them.[311] So just as "wants"—the desire to achieve goals—can directly trigger actions to obtain what is not liked, drugs that block such wants can prevent the implementation of goals to obtain what is liked.

Some neurobiologic evidence also suggests that expectations and wants may derive from separable neural systems.[312] In learning experiments, the "learning signal" that drives changes in expectations is found in two different brain regions. It can appear by itself in the VS, one region which helps change expectations based on prior outcomes. It also can appear in the DS, but—according to some studies—only when an action is initiated.[313] In fact, according to an "actor-critic" model, both the goal-related and expectancy-related utilities derive from the same learning signal but put it to different uses. A critic updates the expectations of reward and reevaluates policies according to experience—computing what we call "expectancy-related utilities"—which may be related to learning signals encoded in dopamine neurons. Then an "actor" binds the dopamine-mediated predictions of the hedonic value of stimuli to the sequences of acts needed to obtain them.[314,315] The binding elements are what we call here the goal-related utilities.[316,317]

In addition, the same signal is input to the PFC, which can lead to changes in goals. The PFC maintains a representation of current goals, and is resistant to changing the representation until it receives a dopamine signal, which indicates that a larger reward is obtainable elsewhere. That signal opens a gate, which enables the PFC to change its goal representation. The gate appears to involve structures in the basal ganglia that are interconnected with the PFC in recurrent loops.[318]

Additional information about the functions of different regions derives from experiments that examined different statistical aspects of the dopamine signal.[319] In one study, PFC activity varied with a transient error-related prediction signal, increased with reward expectation. The VS activity covaried with a sustained signal, peaking when the probability of reward was maximally uncertain. The latter was thought to be related to sustained attention and the expected value from obtaining more information about the environment.

Further questions about the sources of expectations and goals derives from studies involving neurotransmitters other than dopamine. In one experiment, dopamine-deficient mice were still able to learn, so long as they have a cup of caffeine to start their days.[320] In fact, they are even able to enjoy rewards. Berridge suggests that dopamine thus may have more to do with producing the goal-related sensation of wanting than the ability to learn expectations in some cases.[321] In addition, the role of dopamine in aversive (as opposed to appetitive) learning has been hotly debated, and serotonin systems may play an important role in the latter.[322]

Neural Systems That Integrate Goals, Expectations, and Habits

The preceding review suggests an emerging complex picture that involves different hedonic and action control systems. While the precise details of this picture may not yet be entirely clear, the picture certainly will not match the simple economic model, which takes evaluations to be the result of a simple comparison of outcomes with goals. We will require—among other things—a more detailed model that separates expectations, goals, and experience.

To illustrate the need to refine the economic model, let us roughly sketch a model of the multiple interlocking comparison systems for a system that causes us to want and like salt.

Figure 4–6 illustrates a physiologic system that helps us maintain balanced salt levels within the body, which is a requirement for our survival. Salt constituents help regulate the transmission of neural impulses within vital organs such as the brain and heart. To enable such regulation and maintain salt balance, our bodies have neural monitors that initially compare the levels of salt ingredients in the blood with the thermostat-like settings that indicate the "ideal" value of sodium.[323] The level of sodium in the blood is a type of internal "outcome," and the "ideal levels" represent one primitive type of biological "goal." However, this comparison produces a stimulus (E_1) that elevates the importance of a more overt, behavioral goal—satisfying a need for salt (G_2).

The memory of past experiences, together with the biological need for salt, is first compared with an imagined outcome—the salt content of a particular food (O_2). To illustrate the process heuristically, let's say you imagine a salty sausage that you recently saw in the window of a deli. One product of this comparison is the opinion of a food "critic" in your brain who looks at the reward value of the deli's sausages in your hedonic memory—what you might regard as the neural equivalent of the Michelin guide to restaurants. The critic then reports the rating of the food or the expected satisfaction (termed here the *expectancy-related* utility, E_2). Such expectancies are generated by prior learning signals, which associate that food with a reward (and compile the Michelin guide). Also, they are what Kahneman terms "predicted utility"—a prediction of the value of future outcomes.[324]

In addition, the expectancy rating of the deli's food soon gets out and spreads metaphorically through neural cross talk from the VS to the DS, where an unemployed, starving, very hungry "actor" resides.[325] He reports a high degree of "wanting" for the "part"—involving a voluminous con- sumption of food—that is called here the *goal-related* utility (E_3). Unlike the expectancy-related utility, which is the critical rating—a prediction of reward or punishment—the goal-related utility reflects the current motiva- tion toward action. Under the direction of the critic's expectancies, the actor uses his high-voltage goal-related energies to try to get the part.

Finally, both the expectancy-related and goal-related utility also are input to a comparator (C_4) that determines the experienced utility, which resembles an "audience reaction" to the "actor's" play (E_4 in Figure 4–6). More concretely, this utility is the "liking" of the food or drink when it is consumed. Such liking can be increased by the goal-related utility (e.g., wanting).[326] However, increased   expectancy-related   utility   (e.g.,   expectation)   will   commonly

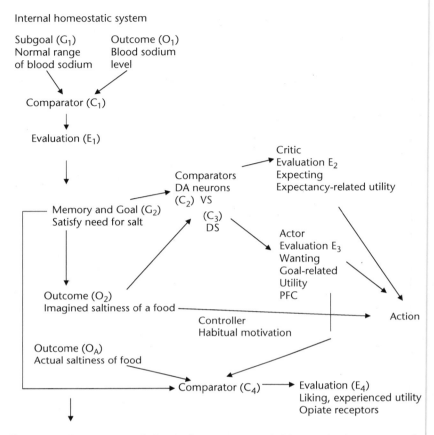

Figure 4–6 Systems underlying the wanting and liking of salt. See text for description. DS = dorsal striatum, VS = ventral striatum, PFC = prefrontal cortex.

decrease the experienced reward. The economic models, which assume that preferences and values are stable, do not adequately explain such changes of likes and dislikes.

The economic models also do not explain a part of the system that does not even care about such likes and dislikes. A habitual "automatic pilot" system competes with the actor and critic systems for control. While the actor tries to satisfy the audience of bodily needs, the habitual system drives action independently of the experienced pleasure or the learned expectancies. For example, if it has repeatedly received satisfaction from sausage consumption in the past, it may later seek it almost automatically, at the mere sight of a salami, even if one now is dismayed by the fattening habit and derives little pleasure from it. So the actor and critic are in a race with a fat yet deceptively quick opponent who may get to the director before the hungry "actor" even has his audition.

How do such reward-independent habits develop? When subjects are exposed to changes in contingencies—for instance, if a stimulus that had repeatedly provided rewards suddenly changed and became highly penalizing—the cells in the lateral DS that modulate action can be quite resistant to adaptation to these changes.[327] Thus, subjects can persist in pursuing stimuli that no longer provide pleasure or ones that are ineffective in one's current motivational state. In such cases, direct associations may form between actions and outcomes, independently of expectancies and changes in motivations. The habitual choices appear to be mediated though circuits involving the DS, amygdala, and cerebellum together with their connections to the midbrain, brainstem motor nuclei, and sensory motor cortex.

To a limited extent, however, habitual choices can respond to changing motivations by altering the rate of certain actions in particular motivational states. The frequency of habit-related activity depends on changes in "drive," even if these changes are insensitive to changes in the value of rewards.[328] For example, when animals are more motivated, they engage in reward-ir-relevant as well as reward-related activity. Some studies have attributed such indiscriminate activity to the effect of a general "drive" or "vigor" variable related to sustained dopamine levels.[329–331]

Pathologies

> I'm not the laziest person around. But most of those who are lazier are dead.
>
> Mark Twain

Motivational pathologies may sometimes impede adaptive goal changes. Some people lack the motivation to change goals. Pathological gamblers appear reluctant to abandon the goal of regaining prior losses.[332] Addicts often cling to seemingly unattainable long-term goals, such as quitting drinking forever.[333] Since dopamine signals to the PFC help prompt the actor to change goals, PFC dysfunctions in addicts may partly explain their maladaptive inflexibility. In addition, since many drug abusers and patients with personality disorders also develop action responses that do not depend on rewards, such responses could partly be explained by altered drive.[334] Since cocaine is a potent dopamine stimulant, its general effects on drive could increase the vigor of drug-seeking activity, independently of learned expectation.

Habit learning clearly differs from the learning explained by dopamine-mediated actor-critic systems. In fact, animals given cocaine intermittently show surprisingly little dopamine response in the NAc, despite escalating motivations to use. The escalation of use appears to be separate from the rewarding effects of the substance. In fact, while dopamine-dependent learning signals may at first drive learned responses, they may gradually lead to persistent cellular changes that do not require dopamine. In such cases, glutamate may play a role since the administration of a drug that antagonizes glutamate will prevent repeated administration despite the lack of any reinforcing effects.[335]

COMBINATIONS OF GOAL, EXPECTANCY, AND EXPERIENCE MODELS

The SPA Model

Behavioral decision theory has suggested alternatives to current actor-critic models for combining expectations and goals. One alternative model, which combines expectancy- and goal-related utilities, is Lopes' security-potential/aspiration (SPA) model (see context-dependent value models in Table 4–1). A goal-related aspiration level—which might vary with changes in set point—considers the probability of attaining specified goals. Unlike previously discussed reference points, it is a critical level that triggers a hedonic change only if it is achieved. The model also considers a non-goal-related security/potential component. This component does not involve an all-or-none response depending on whether goals are achieved. Rather, it involves a measured response according the prospect of maximizing expectancy-related outcomes—that is, obtaining as many rewards and as few penalties as possible.[336] Thus, while the goal-seeking may coincide with feelings of "wanting," the security-potential may reflect feelings of "expecting."

Also, the security-potential component varies with the context, which gives rise to inconsistent choices in different settings (see Table 4–1). Like "cumulative" prospect theory—a revision of the original theory—the SPA model does not evaluate the outcomes in isolation; rather, it ranks the desirability of each outcome and then evaluates it relative to the others, hence, the term "rank-dependent utility (RDU)."[337] As a result, more favorable but unobtained outcomes of a gamble can lower the value of those obtained.

As in the original prospect theory, the adjusted values of outcomes are multiplied by decision weights and then summed (see Table 4–1). But the SPA theory acknowledges that people can attend disproportionately to the best and worst outcomes in a complex gamble. Thus, in fear, the weights emphasize the worst of the rank-ordered outcomes, and in hope, they emphasize the best.[338,339]

In general, RDU models such as SPA better fit experimental data than do simpler EU and prospect theory models. However, generalizations of SPA theory have suggested the use of multiple aspiration points, such as survival thresholds or peer group standards. Also, lower-level goals, such as survival, could be given greater importance than higher-level ones, like peer group acceptance. However, in such models, the salience of risks and rewards could also change their importance.[340] Models that capture such changes could lead to a better understanding of behaviors previously called "risk-seeking." For instance, an adolescent might not show risk-seeking tendencies in simple gambling tasks, when the goal is simply to win money. However, he may put his most basic goal of survival at risk by taking drugs, driving recklessly, or resorting to violence in a context in which the goal of peer acceptance becomes much more salient. Additional model refinements are also needed to explain some habitual actions—like drug use—that are no longer responsive to learning.

Neurobiology

Some neurobiologic research now directly illustrates how context influences value. In one experiment, animals received a series of different rewards while experimenters monitored signal neuron recordings in the striatum. The neurons responded more when the animals received grenadine than when they received orange juice and more when they received orange than when they received black currant juice. However, the response to the grenadine was higher when the most inferior option—black currant—was the alternative reward than when an intermediate option—orange—was the other possible outcome. Thus, the neuronal activities were said to reflect relative rather than absolute rewards. Also, the reward contrast declined after damage to the VS.[341]

In another experiment, experimenters recorded striatal neuron activity after providing different quantities of reward with different probabilities. The neurons responded as if the expectation of the reward value (which had been coded earlier as a transient response to the cue signaling reward) was subtracted from the actual reward. However, this difference also was divided by a measure of the dispersion of the outcomes (which had been reflected by a sustained anticipatory neural response earlier).[342] This dispersion reflected one feature of the task context—the range of the possible rewards and their associated probabilities.[343]

One recent experiment has failed to replicate the context-dependent preferences found in the above studies. Using a different experimental design, the study found that OFC neurons reported the value of the rewards independently of the menu of offered choices.[344] So perhaps the presence of context effects may depend on the context in which they are studied.

In any case, if it is necessary to use the more complex RDU models that consider context effects, it will be useful also to examine the neuroeconomic consequences of the conclusions reached by Shultz and his colleagues—that rescaling the "learning signal" enables better discrimination of rewards and learning about their reward values. If so, the results suggest that we may need to modify the previously discussed learning models to consider values that depend not only on expectations but also the alternative outcomes.

Pathology

Even if rescaling the learning signal to magnify small differences facilitates learning, it may impair decision making. For instance, if you are driving by one gas station that sells gas at $3.00 per gallon (including taxes) but you could go a total of 10 miles further and get a 60c/gallon discount (2.40 per gallon), you might take the trip. If you buy 10 gallons, it will save you $6.00 total. But if you are near a store where you can buy a TV set for $2,070, would you forego purchasing it to save the same amount? That is, if you knew that you could travel 10 miles out of your way and buy it for $2,064, would you go? If not, your preferences would resemble those of many consumers who may forego even larger savings on big-ticket items, which seem to be a small percentage of the total cost.[345] Similar phenomena may underlie consumers' willingness to buy items on credit, even when they would be unwilling to pay cash for the same items. On credit, the items seem to cost only a small percent of the monthly bill. In cash, the items seem to cost a much larger percent of out-of-pocket expenses.

Patients with mental disorders may have an even harder time resisting the seduction of other context effects. For instance, to addicts, a rescaled reward such as "social interaction" may seem little in comparison to an alternative outcome from drug use. Social interaction is likely to have a high dispersion in the values obtained, thereby lowering the value of obtained rewards. By contrast, a drug reward that has little variation could make its pleasure signal proportionately much larger.

Context effects also suggest research questions. For instance, do individuals who magnify error signals function better in learning and poorer in decision making? Do they resemble young people, who learn well but choose poorly?[346] If so, a more rational individual may need to balance the value of learning against the needs for good short-term decisions.

MODELS THAT ASSIGN VALUE TO ANTICIPATORY FEELINGS

The Anxiety Model

Yet another model that combines goal and expectancy-related values is the anxiety model, proposed by George Wu. It is a disappointment-like model that considers a gamble's expected monetary value and a "psychological" value, which does not simply value outcomes but also anticipatory feelings. It may provide a more flexible description of anomalies in time preferences, which are not adequately handled by existing discounting models. Also, it may explain some goal-related desires that are inconsistent with expectations or experience (see discounting models in Table 4–1).

In Wu's anxiety model, people can weigh the expected value of a gamble with deferred outcomes against the often uncomfortable anticipatory feelings about waiting for uncertainties to be resolved.[347] For example, an expectant couple might seek "peace of mind" and opt to have an amniocentesis to discover whether or not their unborn child is impaired. Even though this information would not change the expected outcomes of their actions, their goal-related anticipatory feelings also guide choice. They prefer to know now rather than wait to learn about possible defects in the child. Likewise, a person with a brain aneurism, who fears he has a "time bomb" in his head, might choose immediate surgery to end the uncertainty. He might do so even when a more conservative "watching and waiting" strategy promises somewhat better end-outcomes. Pure expectancy models prescribe choices that produce the best end-outcomes but ignore these psychological effects—the discomfort of waiting.

The formula for the anxiety model takes the same form as the complex disappointment model, which included a probability weight reflecting attention.

The model assumes that the psychological value of a win is equal to [the importance assigned to winning an above-expected return at time t, that is, $G(t)$] times [the time spent thinking the probability of winning, p, that is, $h(p)$] times [the amount to be won (x) in excess of expectations, EV, that is, $(x - \text{EV})$].

Similarly, the psychological value of a loss of y is equal to [the importance $L(t)$ assigned to losing a below-expected return y] times [the time spent thinking about losing, $(1 - h(p))$] times [the amount to be lost compared with expectations, $(\text{EV} - y)$].

So the anticipated utility of the gamble in Wu's model is

$$U(x, p; y, 1 - p) = \text{(monetary expected value)} + \text{(psychological value)}$$
$$= (\text{EV}) + \{G(t)\, h(p)\, (x - \text{EV}) + L(t)\, [1 - h(p)]\, (\text{EV} - y)\}.\text{[348]}$$

Note that in Wu's model, the quantity $G(t)\, h(p)$ is similar to the elation coefficient in the simple or complex disappointment models. However, while $h(p)$ is merely the attention to the probability, p, of an end-outcome in the latter, it is a time-related measure in the anxiety model. Specifically, it reflects the proportion of time spent thinking about the possibility of an outcome. In addition, the importance given to gains and losses now can change with time. Anxiety may decay, persist, or even increase during a period of waiting for a resolution of the uncertainty, as the time for the resolution comes nearer. Such patterns of change are described by the function $G(t)$ for changes in the anticipation of gains over time and $L(t)$ for changes in the anticipation of losses. Given these parameters, the positive psychological component of the gamble is the product of the value of anticipating a reward, $G(t)$, and the proportion of time spent thinking about reward [$h(p)$]—a kind of "quality adjusted" time period (see Appendix).[349] The negative component is defined similarly, and the total value of anticipation is a sum of the positive and negative components.[350]

The anxiety model identifies several factors that may promote immediate choices and avoid uncertainties. For example, if one spends too much time thinking about possible negative events [$1 - h(p) > 1 - p$], then she will try to reduce the worry associated with the period of waiting for the uncertainty to be resolved. Hence, she may choose a certain immediate option over a gamble with delayed outcomes that has the same expected value. She may also do so if potential losses loom larger than gains or when losses decay less rapidly [$-L(t) > G(t)$]. For instance, anxious people catastrophize about the severity of possible losses and their worries are difficult to extinguish.[351]

Although Wu intended his model to describe immediate choices in response to anxiety, his model also may explain some "impulsive" choices in response to the excitement of future risks. Similarities exist between the avoidance systems that mediate anticipatory fears and the incentive systems that mediate anticipatory wanting. For instance, lesions of the central amygdala, which dissociate anticipatory fear from experienced pain, also dissociate anticipatory wanting from experienced pleasure. That is, such lesions abolish fear in animals with a normal pain response and also prevent the wanting and seeking of a salt solution in animals who do like salt.[352] Berridge suggests that different dopamine systems involving the NAc and amygdala might mediate these partly overlapping incentive and aversive responses.[353]

In fact, some types of craving for future gains may be the mirror image of the fear of possible future losses (see Figure 4–7). Fear may drive a person to favor the positive immediate experience of his current state over the discomfort of waiting for a resolution of a gamble. By contrast, craving may drive the person to avoid the continuing discomfort of his present state in favor of a gamble that promises relief.

Likewise, the factors that involve craving are the mirror image of those involving anxiety. For example, a person who gives more thought to gains than losses [$h(p) > p$] will choose a gamble over a continuing state of craving

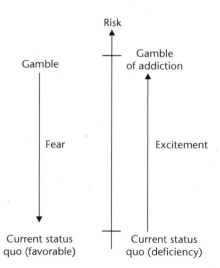

Figure 4–7 Responses to different types of goal-related utility. Fear may drive a person to favor a certain status quo now and reject a gamble with deferred outcomes. Excitement, by contrast, may drive the person to reject a certain state of deficiency now and accept a gamble with possible delayed consequences (e.g., drug use).

with equivalent expected value. That may occur when addicts pay undue attention to drug-related rewards or fail to attend to possible losses. Likewise, the person will do so when unexpected gains loom larger than losses $[e^* = G(t) > d^* = -L(t)]$. Accordingly, addicts who crave future rewards may think much less about deferred penalties.

This model might apply to impulsive choices made in cases other than addiction, including impulsive people with personality disorders or neurologic lesions. For instance, patients with right VMPFC damage, in the previously cited study by Tranel et al., may not spend as much time thinking about deferred losses as they do about gains. Such biases could make them seek risks when they must wait for outcomes, even when these patients are not risk-seeking for the gambles they play immediately. Inattention to possible losses also could explain why patients with BPD—who also have VMPFC dysfunction—are impatient and tend to plunge rapidly into risky endeavors. They act more quickly when they do not attend to information about losses.[354]

The QALMs Model

Methods similar to the anxiety model may also augment the exponential or hyperbolic discounting models discussed in chapter 3 (and reviewed in Table 3–1).[355] To be sure, the single-rate exponential models are economical. Hyperbolic models are not only tractable but also explain observed changes in discount rates over time. In addition, if one seeks to maximize the rate of reward over time, then one will value delayed outcomes according to a hyperbolic model.[356] Likewise, single exponential or hyperbolic discount rates often have *appeared* to fit the data in a wide range of studies. In fact, single-rate hyperbolic discounting models do even fit data from single-neuron recordings in the PFC-equivalent of pigeons adequately, at least better than single-rate exponential models.[357]

The single-rate discounting models resemble expectancy-related value theories. Thus, they may approximate very well the learned expected value of deferred rewards that people report in some experiments. They may even predict well the choices in some learning contexts, wherein subjects base their choices on the recollection of the rate of reward.

At the same time, however, Kahneman's work discussed earlier in the section on remembered utility suggests other factors affecting recollection, which pay little heed to rates over time. Also, the experiments using single rate models have typically used a restricted range of stimuli. And many other studies have shown that the so-called "single rates" of discounting often do not adequately capture a single "discount rate" characteristic of an individual. Rather, the rates often change widely with the context; for example, when rewards are larger or smaller, when the outcomes are rewards or penalties, and when prior expectations or other reference points vary.[358] In addition, the single rate models may not adequately account for the online, goal-related, anticipatory feelings that often drive people to stop waiting or act "impulsively." For example, the single-rate discounting models typically assume that a rational person expects delayed rewards to be less valuable, but people often want to wait for a kiss due to the pleasure of anticipation. Likewise, the models assume that people expect delayed penalties to be less aversive, but people often prefer an immediate over a delayed electric shock due to their "qualms" about waiting to receive it.[359]

To account for such emotions, one must consider the anticipatory value of waiting times—here termed QALMs or Quality Adjusted Life Minutes. This concept is reminiscent of the models of Quality Adjusted Life Years (QALYs). But QALMs represent the value of the waiting time prior to an outcome, while QALYs represent the value of time spent during and after an outcome when the effects of that outcome are prolonged (e.g., disability after a medical illness). In general then, the more time one spends anticipating life outcomes and the more that such anticipations affect quality of life, the more important that QALMs will be.

QALMs are also reminiscent of the anxiety model that takes the psychological value of a waiting period to be the amount of time multiplied by the quality of the time spent in a state, except that the anticipation derives from thinking about a certain (rather than possible) gain or loss. For example, if one anticipates an electric shock, two components could exist: The cost of delay could involve the dread of anticipating a shock, increasing the longer one waits. The benefit could involve the relief of avoiding the shock for as long as possible.

That is, if x is an outcome,

$$V(x,t) = \text{A Constant} + (\text{Benefits of waiting}) - (\text{Costs of waiting})$$

where the constant may be related to a reference point, such as the value of an immediate small penalty or one's prior expectations.[360]

Neurobiology

The two-component model above is similar not only to the anxiety model but also to models of excitation and inhibition in multiple interconnected neural networks, such as those that could modulate time preference.[361] For instance, experiments using the hybrid model discussed in chapter 3 suggested that two different circuits—limbic/paralimbic and lateral PFC/parietal systems— switch in activity depending on whether one attends to immediate or delayed rewards.[362]

When such multiple interconnected networks also involve feedback, a single-rate discounting model can easily fail to predict the value of waiting, integrated over its actual experience. Why? Assuming a single rate is like assuming that, a half hour after a person takes a drug, its effective blood concentration over time depends only on its current concentration and elimination rate, as depicted in Figure 4–8a. If human physiology were really this simple, the blood concentration of a drug would fall at roughly a single exponential rate of decay. But considering only the elimination rate of a drug would ignore its rate of absorption from the GI tract into the blood, as well as its distribution between different states. Many drugs are not only absorbed and eliminated, they may be present either free in the blood or bound to protein. The concentrations in these different forms constitute different "compartments," and there are interactions: the concentration in one affects the other (see Figure 4–8b).

Studies have modeled the processes of excitation and inhibition in neural systems through similar compartmental models.[363] In fact, highly simplified models of neural activities or membrane potentials, which capture the essential features, have been used to clarify the processes of excitation and inhibition.[364] For heuristic purposes, then, suppose that the firing rates of particular neurons parallel the experience of anticipation according to compartmental models of neural activation (enabling others to encode delayed reward values).[363,364] If the activities of these neurons merely "leak" over time, as well as self-stimulate, their activity could follow a single exponential, or hyperbolic, rate of decline (as shown in Figure 4–8c).

However, as shown in Figure 4–8d, most models of neural activation also have inputs, from cues and pharmacologic changes. For instance, when drugs such as d-amphetamine are given, their effects on preferences for delayed rewards can depend on their dose.[365]

Interactions between different neural systems, such as serotonin and dopamine, also affect time preferences.[366] Such interactions could in theory

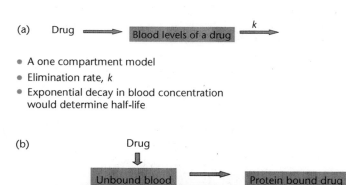

- Blood levels, in general, do not change exponentially at a single rate

Figure 4–8 (a) Exponential discounting of blood levels of a drug. (b) A simplified two-compartment model.

(c)

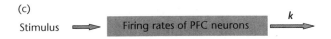

- Elimination rate, *k*, determines the "leakage" rate from a neural compartment
- Activity proportional to $V = A \exp(-k_t)$
- Hyperbolic model involves a rate, *k*, that changes with time

(d)

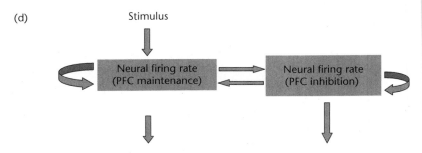

- Two exponential terms reflect
  - *Decay due to "Leakage" vs. self-stimulation*
  - *Inputs*
  - *Interactions*

Figure 4–8 (c) Exponential decline in neural activities related to delayed reward. (d) A simplified model of neural activation. Environmental or neural stimuli (e.g., cues or drugs).

explain some reversals in drug effects due to delayed feedback interactions.[367] For example, the effects of 5HT1a agonists on preferences for delayed reward change early and later in the experiment, after the feedback effects may have intensified.[368] Also, the effects of serotonin agonists change when dopamine systems are altered—for instance, when rats are given lesions to dopamine neurons in the NAc that normally may stimulate delayed reward representations in the PFC.[369,370]

If two neural systems interact, as shown in Figure 4–8d, and the activity in the first compartment roughly represents the online anticipatory experience of delay, then the simplest approximation of activity would derive from the solution of two differential equations.[371] The integral of this activity over a given delay takes exactly the same form as the previously discussed behavioral model of QALMs—a double exponential form:

$V(x_1, t) = \text{Constant} + \text{Benefits} - \text{Costs} = a + (b/c)\,[1 - \exp(-ct)] - (d/e)\,\exp[-et]$

In this context, the first exponential term may reflect factors that increase activation related to the value of delayed reward and the latter ones that decrease it. Perhaps not coincidentally, the double exponential form of this model is similar to a behavioral economic model of deferred value developed by Lowenstein.[372] It also resembles previously developed two-attribute, exponential economic models of QALYs, which multiply the duration of time in a state by its value and assume both good and bad features to the state.[373] In addition, a similar, double exponential model outperformed the single-rate discounting methods in explaining animals' preferences for juices.[374] And a related, two-component model was also necessary to model preferences for a deferred penalty—an electric shock. The model considered not only its discounted future experience but also the dread people had from waiting for it.[375]

Components of QALMs and Time Preference Patterns

A two-exponent QALMs model separates the benefits and costs of waiting for a penalty. It also identifies other distinct aspects of time preference (see Figure 4–9). To illustrate how, note that the cost component, the total amount of dread prior to a deferred penalty, is like the total distance that a car travels before stopping in order to avoid a collision with the vehicle in front of it—that is, the integral or area above the curve in Figure 4–9a. This distance is determined by the initial value or "speed" [d in the above formula for $V(x,t)$] and by the "quality of the brakes"—reflected in the rate of curvature or decline in speed. Behaviorally, an extremely high persistence of costs (related to $1/e$ in the formula) may reflect an inability to dampen one's dread, while an extremely low persistence may reflect very rapid inhibition or present-orientation.

Likewise, one can interpret the benefit component of the formula for $V(x,t)$—which is similar to the discounted value of a future penalty—as the total distance that a car in front of you travels before stopping—that is, the integral or area below the curve in Figure 4–9b.

To avoid a collision, you would prefer to increase this area—to have the car in front of you stop as slowly as possible. In Figure 4–9b, this area is again determined by the initial speed and the capacity to put on the brakes. Behaviorally, if the penalty is an electric shock, the speed may reflect the initial magnitude of your relief when an experimenter delays administering the shock (b), and the curvature may reflect the persistence of such relief ($1/c$).

Unlike the single-rate discount models, which only include the benefits but not the costs of delaying a penalty, two-exponent models consider both factors. Furthermore, their separation enables us to define two useful indices that compare different aspects of the response to costs versus benefits. One factor called the Aversion to Consequences (AC) is the initial sensitivity to costs (d)—divided by the sensitivity to the benefit (b). So AC = d/b. It is like the initial velocity of your anticipatory dread in comparison with the speed

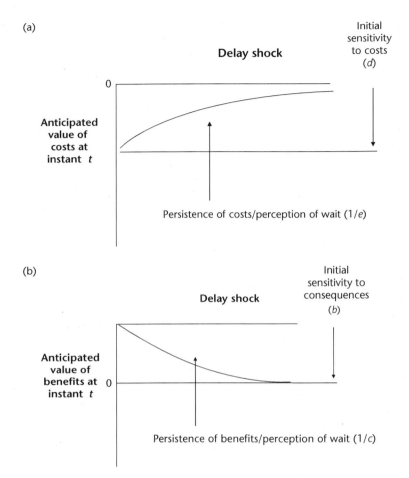

Figure 4–9 (a) Costs of delay; (b) benefits of delay.

of relief, related to economic discounting. Similarly, the Aversion to Delay (AD) considers the brakes—or (the persistence of the dread, $1/e$) divided by (the persistence of the relief, $1/c$). So AD = c/e.

Given these parameters, the QALMs model is simply a constant plus the sum of the areas under the two curves (the instantaneous costs or benefits integrated over their durations).[376]

As illustrated in Figure 4–10, depending on whether or not the person is averse to consequences (AC > 1) and/or averse to delay (AD > 1), the net QALMs take one of four specific forms (see note for proof).[377] In case 1, it is single peaked (as when one prefers an ideal delay for a kiss). In case 2, it is monotone increasing, which motivates delay seeking for rewards or discounting for penalties. In case 3, it is monotone decreasing, which promotes discounting for rewards and dread or delay avoidance for penalties. In case 4, it is single dipped, which may explain conflict (see Figure 4–10).

Empirical Results and Pathology

Reanalyses of published data from a study of penalty discounting enable us to illustrate the use of the double exponential QALMs model. In this study, human subjects received different voltages of shocks at different delays and then stated their preferences. For instance, they would be asked: do you want 10 V now or 90 V in 5 min?

Although the reanalyses are intended merely to illustrate use of the method, it is interesting to note that the single-rate exponential and hyperbolic models fit the data poorly—the average $r^2_{adj} = .74$; while $r^2_{adj} = .99$ for the two-exponent QALMs model. One reason why the single-rate discounting models performed poorly in these reanalyses is that they assume people

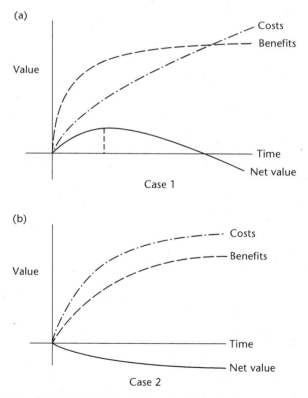

Figure 4–10 (a) Case 1, ideal delay (AC < 1, AD > 1): low consequence and high delay sensitivity. (b) Case 2, high consequence and delay aversion (AC > 1, AD > 1).

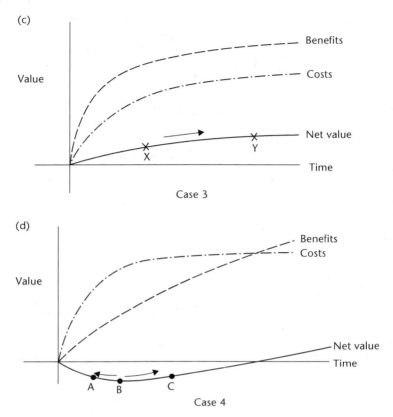

Figure 4–10 (*continued*) (c) Case 3, procrastination (AC < 1, AD < 1). (d) Case 4, high aversion to consequence and low aversion to delay (AC > 1, AD < 1).

have only one discount rate. Yet, as Figure 4–11 slide shows, people had much higher discount rates when the shocks were larger. Somewhat more complex hyperbolic models can partly account for the size of such shocks but only by adding parameters.[378]

In addition, even the more complex hyperbolic models would not account for other group differences. A group defined in the published study as "mild dreaders" had an essentially neutral aversion to consequences (AC ≈ 1) but a moderate aversion to delay (AD > 1), whereas a group labeled as "high dreaders" had a very high aversion to consequences (AC > 1) yet a lack of aversion to delay (AD < 1). Why? Possibly, the extremely high initial dread— reflected in the stimulation of many of the same areas of the brain activated during physical pain, including the caudal ACC and the insula—may have resulted in a higher level of negative feedback to oppose such activation. The endurance of dread (hence the AD) is related to the degree of delayed inhibition from competing systems in the previously discussed neural network

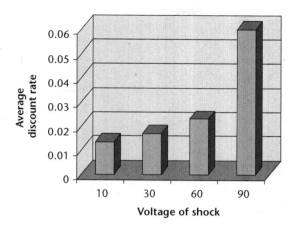

Figure 4–11 Changes in discount rate with voltage.

model. Possible sources of such inhibition are those involved in cognitive re-appraisals of highly negative emotions, such as the dorsal ACC and PFC systems, as well as circuits in PFC or the striatum that mediate the pleasurable feelings of relief that oppose the dread of deferring a shock.[379]

The values of AC and AD were also computed from a published study of smokers presented with choices between a certain small reward versus a delayed monetary gain.[380] Smokers not recently deprived of their cigarettes exhibited a mild aversion to consequences and delay (AC > 1, AD > 1); whereas deprived smokers showed the same pattern as the high dreaders—an extremely high consequence but low delay aversion (AC > 1, AD < 1). Importantly, however, when the outcome is actually a monetary reward instead of an electrical penalty, the interpretations of the indices, AC and AD, differ. In this case, the costs of waiting more closely resemble expectancy-related discounting; while the benefits may involve the goal-related, pleasurable anticipation of a larger gain. If so, the extremely high AC of deprived smokers would be consistent with previous findings suggesting that they have higher initial discount rates for any delay at all.[381]

In addition, the somewhat low AD suggests that the discounting is far more immediate and less time sensitive than the goal-related anticipation of reward. This low but increased persistence of reward anticipation with time could reflect cigarette smokers' diminished serotonin function, which may decrease inhibition of striatal-frontal dopamine circuits.[382]

While the above analyses merely illustrate the use of the method based on published aggregate data, they do show how an analysis of QALMs separates some previously lumped dimensions of time preference. While the single rate discounting models may suffice in describing many empirical data, the more complex analyses may enable us to identify distinct disorders of time preference in a way that single-rate models do not. These single-rate models have reported high rates in a wide variety of mental disorders—from attention-deficit disorder to antisocial or borderline personality to mania and many drug, cigarette, and alcohol addictions.[383,384] But the discount rates do little to discriminate between them.

Ultimately, QALMs models may link axiomatic models of utility (similar to QALYs) with the formally identical biophysical models illustrated in Figure 4–8, as well as with the behavioral models of value developed by Loewenstein and Wu.

Thus, the additional parameters in QALMs models may enable some discriminations that the single-rate models do not as well as provide a richer neural and theoretical interpretation. However, one might question whether the QALMs models may be too complex. When we add variables to simpler discounting models, collinearity and model misspecification can harm parameter estimates. In yet another sense, though, one might also argue that the QALMs models illustrated are actually too simple. For example, the parameters in the model could vary with time.[385] Such methods may also apply when we more accurately describe physiological systems, using not only time varying parameters but also more than two compartments and when the cost and benefit functions are not simple exponentials.[386] Also, many more complex models of cortical activations in response to a dopamine stimulus still can be defined by the solution of a set of two differential equations. They show how DA modulates cortical activation and consider interactions with glutamate, effects of NMDA and AMPA receptors, receptor affinities, and tissue responses and are compatible with a multitude of other more detailed observations.[387] In the future, then, one challenge in creating neural models of time preference is to make them as simple as is necessary, given the limitations of our data, but not to make them any simpler than that.[388]

5

Conclusion: Future Directions for the New Science

This book has presented the developing science of neuroeconomics as a realistic and logical blend of neurobiology, economics, and multiple branches of psychology. The field of economics provided a clear and testable theory, while neurobiology enabled detailed empirical research. Behavioral economics also provided many new methods that can broaden the psychological spectrum of neuroeconomic variables. Likewise, the clinical neurosciences enlarged the scope of the real-world disorders linked to neuroeconomic deficits.

The book also outlined a framework to enable a more unified understanding of the different concepts, models, and methods of the many related disciplines. In chapter 2, the framework categorized the types of mental capacities that neuroeconomics can study. It defined two general levels of capacities, termed efficacy and effectiveness.

The "efficacy" concepts derive from neoclassical economic models. These functions correspond to the abilities to "diagnose" opportunities or threats, to act based on these beliefs, and to benefit from the actions. Chapter 3 presented more specific models of anticipatory evaluations at the diagnostic and management levels that are consistent with neoclassical economic models. As one descends the list in Table 3–1, each successive model describes an additional complexity, including elements of diagnostic efficacy (the calibration of subjective probability estimates) and elements of management efficacy (the anticipated value of multiattribute outcomes, risky prospects, and delayed outcomes).[389] The neurobiologic studies of these parameters clarified what brain circuits mediate different decisional functions. They also suggested how people perform some diagnostic, management, and evaluative functions. Finally, the discussion clarified the potential importance of these capacities. It described not only the neural correlates of poor economic importance in the lab but also the actual behavioral correlates of these impairments in real life. In some cases, the neurobiologic and mental health correlates of these parameters appeared to strengthen the fabric of the existing economic theory by demonstrating a reasonable fit between some neural activities and economic variables, such as expected value or utility. They also clarified how the violation of basic economic principles correlates with poor adaptation in the real world. For example, some very maladapted subjects, including amphetamine users and OFC-lesioned patients, do not follow the economic principle of eliminating clearly inferior options, called *dominated alternatives*. The results question whether a basic violation of economic principles, rather than risk preference or discounting, could explain many of their poor choices. In other cases, neuroeconomic results clarified possible sources of violations of the economic principles and shed light on the models used to explain them. Chapter 4 considered in detail the alternative, behavioral economic models of evaluation. As shown in Table 4–1, these models included diagnostic elements (differences in response to risk vs. ambiguity, attention to the chances of a positive or negative event, sensitivity to changes in probability as well as optimism or pessimism). They also included elements related to management (expectancy-related and goal-related utilities) as well as outcome evaluations (disappointment, elation, and regret, as well as the experienced disutility of waiting for outcomes to occur). In addition, they considered other factors that can change evaluations, such as learning and context.

The investigation of the neural correlates of these behavioral economic parameters of choice clarified why some irrational violations of the axioms may occur or even be justified. For instance, according to the "independence" axiom, if one prefers a reward obtained with certainty over a gamble, one should still prefer the first option when additional uncertainty is added to all of the possible outcomes of a choice.[390] However, the violation of this principle often occurs and appears related to the degree of activation in the DLPFC, which plays a role in working memory and mental effort.[391] Hence, some subjects may choose the certain option to reduce mental effort, which may not be entirely irrational: The reduction of effort may be worth the price of a slightly suboptimal choice.

In addition, the chapter describes other forms of inconsistency in evaluation, beyond mere inconsistency with the economic axioms. These included conflicts between remembered, experienced, predictive, expectancy-related, and goal-related utility. The concepts may enlarge the scope of narrower economic consistency tests.

Beyond this, chapter 4 considered how some of the elements of effectiveness refined the neoclassical economic concepts, such as risk aversion. For instance, in prospect theory, risk aversion was determined by multiple elements of the value function (loss aversion and decreasing marginal value) as well as the probability weights (sensitivity to probability and optimism vs. pessimism).

Finally, the discussion provided a basis for testing between alternative behavioral economic models of evaluation. For instance, some neuroeconomic studies suggest that a two-component model, such as Lopes's SPA theory, corresponds better with neurobiologic findings than do simpler models. In the latter, goals are important only in so far as they generate expectancies, which guide choice. But in SPA theory, goal-related aspirations and expectancies each influence preference independently. Hence, one might expect discrete neural circuits that mediate these two influences.

One experiment, in fact, did report such evidence favoring the SPA model. It found that VMPFC damage affected the security potential component of the model.[392] Yet, the ACC and its surrounding structures may independently mediate the goal-related aspiration component. An ACC lesion does not impair the ability to learn the contingencies between stimuli and outcomes, as reflected in expectancies or "security/potential" values.[393] But such a lesion does affect the ability to associate outcomes with motivated actions, as reflected in goal-related aspirations. Furthermore, the ACC activates primarily when outcomes do not achieve the intended goal and not when they overachieve. Thus, in a sense, we may have partly independent mechanisms that mediate the expectations and "downside risk" of a choice. Such findings—as well as the considerable literature separating expectancy and goal-related incentive salience—may support Lopes's idea that at least two separate components predict choice.[394,395]

These neurobiologic findings may seem to cast a dark cloud over axiomatic theories of choice. But this cloud may have a silver lining if it motivates research on new axiom systems that explain the neural computations.[396,397] Recall that computations called expected utility preceded and motivated later efforts to uncover their axiomatic foundations.

Now we see this process beginning to repeat itself. Through empirical research, some investigators found a formula related to the degree of cortical activation by dopaminergic (DA) neurons, which—like economic calculators—also help determine the expectancy-related values of possible rewards.[398] This discovery then motivated the development of an axiomatic approach to derive the formula from seven more basic assumptions. These assumptions were unlike any that an economist would ordinarily use. For instance, according to one such principle, the likelihood of neuron activity is proportional to the concentration of a neurotransmitter multiplied by the number of available receptors.[399] However, although this work did not seek to derive a set of assumptions underlying expected utility computations, such an effort may not be far off. As noted earlier, the QALMs model demonstrated other possible points of contact between neurophysiologic computations, behavioral, and economic models of time preference with known axiomatic foundations. Such insights suggested not only biologic interpretations of economic variables but also behavioral interpretations of neurophysiologic parameters. Further work of this nature may ultimately move us nearer to a unified neuroeconomic explanation of seemingly disparate concepts.

ADDITIONAL ELEMENTS OF THE STRUCTURE: TOWARD
A BROADER VIEW OF FUNCTION

Perhaps we are still far away from understanding the similarities between models used in different fields. In many cases, explicit models do not yet exist. Thus, we still must rely heavily on studies that apply findings from one field to models in another—for instance, examining the neural correlates of the parameters in existing economic models. In the future, we may find that these existing models attract substantial support from neurobiologic findings. We may even show that some theories need only minor modifications. However, the natural inclination is to simply rearrange the furniture around contradictory facts. And, in the end, we may need considerable "remodeling" of our ideas about the sources of choice.

For instance, since a multiplicity of neural systems underlie many human capacities, we may need models showing how one switches between operations at different stages of decision making or between alternative systems at the same stage. A rational human may need not only to use a particular system well but also to know when to switch between different systems in different contexts. This is not a new idea. For example, decision-making researchers have investigated possible considerations for "deciding how to decide."[400] Likewise, many philosophers and psychologists have speculated about "dual process" theories of rational choice. Some have also noted that far more than two systems may be needed to describe the multiple processes in choice. In addition, however, neurobiologic evidence suggests that many of these processes may not be separate but interact. One of the most basic initial choices is the method we use to make sense of the world, as exemplified by the deductive and inductive reasoning methods in the fields of economics and neuroscience. In a sense, while the economist in our brain uses cues as evidence to deduce the correct choices, the experimental neurobiologist in our heads uses cues to signal a search for causation. Unsurprisingly, different neural mechanisms exist for optimizing cue use and evaluating causality. In split brain patients with severed connections between cortices, the right side of the brain may help more to deduce optimal choices, the left side to seek patterns.[401]

Another early element of deciding involves setting an agenda—that is, selecting a problem for analysis and choosing the alternatives to be considered. Although behavioral decision theorists have done some research on agenda setting, such research has yet to be integrated with neurobiologic knowledge. Yet such knowledge is now emerging. For instance, before the brain makes a final decision, the superior frontal gyrus—in a premotor area of the brain— selects a set of possible motor actions rather than a single choice.[402]

One of the next stages in choice is estimating the uncertainties. Economic decision theorists are clear about how this should be done: There should be no difference in choice, regardless of whether the uncertainties are known or ambiguous. However, evolutionary psychologists argue that some biases in the use of probability information can be adaptive when the organism responds to ambiguous events or engages in social communication. However, both academic camps may be right in different circumstances. On the one hand, people with OFC lesions, who oblige the economic theory by losing the ability to distinguish ambiguity and risk, do make many bad choices in real life as they do in the lab. In fact, the ability to distinguish risk from ambiguity may serve some useful purposes when environmental contingencies change. Then, we often need to reevaluate our choices by responding to ambiguity in the altered task. Perhaps to enable such reevaluation, we may have evolved different brain mechanisms for handling ambiguity and risk. Choices under risk activate the striatum more, whereas those under ambiguity activate the OFC and amygdala.[403]

Hence, while a distinction between ambiguity and risk may lead to some economically irrational choices, it may also be adaptive. Both social/emotional and analytic/cognitive systems operate in the brain. One system—which is discussed by cognitive psychologists—revises probability estimates correctly according to learned relationships between cues and outcomes. The other system—which is emphasized by evolutionary psychologists—treats the cues as ambiguous, initiating a reevaluation of their possible significance. The former may be mediated by acetylcholine and the latter by norepinephrine systems in the brain.[404] Wise choices may then involve the ability to switch between these systems according to the context. When the environment is rapidly changing, one should treat cues as ambiguous and reevaluate their significance. When the environment is stable, one should use the learned values of the cues.[405]

Similar neurochemical systems and switching mechanisms may pertain to recently developed dual process models of choice in which emotional and cognitive systems interact.[406] In one model, a cognitive system follows an expected utility approach—as one might follow when making a reasoned choice in a stable environment. An emotional system produces some behaviors predicted by prospect theory: It is loss-averse and more sensitive to value than probability. In the model, increasing affective stimulation exaggerates the shape of the probability weighting function, making people less sensitive to probability. Since increasing affective stimulation relates in part to heightened arousal and norepinephrine system activity, perhaps the insensitivity to probability is partly an insensitivity to learned probability cues and a tendency to treat the environment as if it is changing.

In any case, a failure to switch appropriately from one mode to another in different environments may produce pathology. For instance, patients with BPD often have great uncertainty about their relationships and values. Hyper-aroused by increased norepinephrine system activity, they appear to interpret their environments as more unstable than they really are. They act as if environmental cues cannot be trusted. In fact, they often behave even more erratically when they take noradrenergic stimulant medications.[407]

In addition, we may also need to consider different types of emotional systems that mediate goal-related evaluations. For example, different fear and safety systems may both affect anxiety and risk attitude. While people associate some cues with danger, they associate others with safety. Not only do these associations rely on partly different neural systems, but safety learning itself appears to activate two separate systems. One attenuates conditioned fear responses in the lateral nucleus of the amygdala. The other enhances pleasure responses in the striatum, presumably associated with feelings of "relief."[408] If these two systems also affect attitudes toward risk differently, we may need to augment current measures of risk aversion, decision weights, and loss aversion. In addition to "loss aversion," we may also need to consider a measure of "relief response."[409]

Beyond the competition of different emotional systems with each other and with cognitive systems, we may need to consider a similar competition between expectancy-related and habitual actions. That is, the brain circuits must select a processing mechanism that tells them whether to act based on habit or expectation. Separate neural circuits mediate the two systems. The expectation system is plastic and is guided by previously discussed learning signals, which vary with the outcomes. The habit system is hardwired and is engaged by repeated rewards. Once such engagement occurs, then, even if the same actions cause repeated punishment, the cells in the dorsal striatum that modulate action often resist adaptation to the changes. The choice whether to act by habit or expectation depends partly on the consequences of systematic error and the need for precision in control. For example, habits can be precise, reliable, and economical choice mechanisms. Yet, they are prone to bias. They may guide behaviors appropriately in one context but not in another. Daw, Div, and Dayan have argued that updated expectations can guide actions better when the environment is changing but can introduce unnecessary variability when the environment is stable.[410] Recall that, in the TD model of learning discussed in chapter 4, expectations derive in part from prior expectations. These, in turn, derive from even earlier expectations, and so forth. So any errors in earlier expectations may propagate during learning and lead our actions astray. The person may pay undue attention to random fluctuations in reward and penalty and appear quite fickle.

Conceivably, neural structures involved in cognitive control or in responses to cues could select either habitual or expectation mechanisms. For example, in one model, depending on the presence or absence of addictive cues, people enter one of two states: a "hot node" in which they automatically decide to act based on habit, or a "cold node" in which their decisions are guided by rational expectations.[411] To such models, based on the earlier discussions of ambiguity, one might add yet other nodes that permit one to ignore either expectations or habit and discover new relationships, when the environment is extremely unfamiliar or changes very quickly.

In adaptive behavior, the choice whether to act by habit or expectation also may be determined by many of the same factors involved in deciding whether to perform an economic analysis. The relevant factors include the importance or likely benefit of a considered choice, the feasibility of acquiring sufficient information to guide it, and the degree of effort likely to be needed for deciding.[412] In chapter 2, this topic is considered as the "cost-effectiveness" of a decision.

Where in the brain is such cost-effectiveness determined? Some have suggested that the NAc may compute the opportunity cost of time and the ACC may integrate this with immediate costs and benefits.[413] In particular, the ACC may resolve conflicts between different choices by doing a cost-benefit analysis, which considers the effort needed to obtain a reward. ACC lesions cause animals to prefer small, low effort rewards to the larger, higher effort rewards preferred by those without lesions; and they appear to foster more habitual modes of responding.

In some cases, the expectation systems for decision making may also compete with moral ones, which some philosophers see as preferable. Moral philosophers sometimes advocate a conscientious deontological system driven by moral principle over a shamelessly depraved consequential system driven by economic expectations. Since the writings of Immanuel Kant, they have often presumed that the moral judgments derive from conscientious reasoning.[414] However, neuroeconomic research now questions that assumption. Some moral judgments activate circuits that generate social/emotional responses, which depend less on reasoning systems.[415] In one experiment, deontological judgments activated the posterior cingulate cortex as well as superior temporal and medial prefrontal areas. Consequential judgments, by contrast, activated circuits more commonly associated with working memory and reasoned judgments—the DLPFC and inferior parietal cortex.[416]

Despite the ongoing combat between moral philosophers and economists about which system is more rational, both systems clearly play important roles in guiding choice. A failure to switch to moral evaluation mechanisms in patients with antisocial personality disorder often leads to ostracism or imprisonment. Yet, an inflexible adherence to rigid moral rules in other personality disordered individuals can prevent access to normal pleasures. In the future, therefore, it may be useful to develop models that can account for switches or tradeoffs between the two systems. Toward this end, some context-dependent value systems have already begun to combine individual gain expectations and moral social welfare considerations.[417]

One mechanism people commonly use for switching between social and individual perspectives is to change the frame of their decisions. Thus, we need to develop neuroeconomic models that clarify how people manage different reference points. Such models would be important not only because they may alter information processing but also since the altered perspectives can make people feel better or worse. For instance, after a raise in salary that was less than that of coworkers, some people who make a social comparison bemoan the inequity. Others may note that their individual salary level is still much higher or that the raise itself was much more than they had expected. For the most part, deviations in such reference points have been seen as undesirable sources of inconsistency in evaluations. However, the ability to modulate reference points may itself be important to adaptation.[418]

The management of reference points may also be important in social conflicts. In fact, some neural structures may actually help people combine different reference points. These structures may enable people to reconcile gains from the status quo with losses from social comparisons. More specifically, when subjects receive unfair but rewarding offers in economic games, they have increases in DLPFC activation, reflecting the possible monetary gain in relation to the status quo. However, they also make a social comparison and consider the amount that the competitor would keep for himself. In proportion to the unfairness they perceive, insular cortex activity rises, reflecting the disgust associated with an unfair offer. They also have increased activation of the ACC, which has been interpreted as reflecting the effort to resolve the conflict between wanting more money than one currently has (DLPFC) and the disgust from receiving less than the competitor (insula).

TOWARD A NEUROEPIDEMIOLOGY OF DECISION MAKING: THE STUDY OF NEUROECONOMIC STUDIES

One important obstacle to the development of more complex neuroeconomic models, however, is the lack of a systematic framework for designing and interpreting experiments. Not only do many studies use different designs, subject populations, and stimuli, they differ in many other ways. Some derive from behavioral decision models with empirical support; others derive from ad hoc models with an unclear relation to peoples' actual preferences. Some are based on largely exploratory analyses that search for data to support a given model; others provide more rigorous attempts to falsify a proposed model. They also provide different levels of evidence, which are often hard to compare. Such differences can obscure the reasons for different findings and slow the cultivation of scientific knowledge.

While the fields of neuroscience and psychology already have had much to say in identifying differences between studies, so does the neuroeconomic framework presented in this book. This framework does not merely help us understand rational functions; it also helps us understand the methods for studying these functions. Somewhat as the field of epidemiology categorizes medical investigations of disease rates or medical treatments, the framework in this text identifies different types of neuroeconomic studies. In so doing, lays the foundation for a broader field that we might term the "neuroepidemiology" of decision making.

Variations in the Level of Evaluation

First, epidemiology distinguished different levels of endpoints in outcome measures (e.g., at a diagnostic level, disease; at a management level, changes in patient behavior or physician practices; at an evaluation level, discomfort, disability, or death). Similarly, neuroepidemiology can distinguish criteria for measuring the human decisional capacities that different studies provide. These levels correspond in part to the levels of human performance outlined in chapter 2: diagnostic, management, and outcome efficacy (see Figure 5–1). At a diagnostic level, calibration or "scoring rules" have assessed peoples' estimates of the probability of uncertain events. At a management level; the percent of "optimal" selections has considered the accuracy of choice. At an outcome level, the net monetary gains have reported the overall economic outcomes. The relative performance measure illustrated in chapter 4 can also summarize the net utility gain.

Each type of analysis has its own value and limitations in this framework. For instance, a test of a lower level of decision-making capacity may better identify specific dysfunctions, but it tells us little about global performance. A test of a higher level gives a global impression of overall functioning, but multiple factors often contribute to such functions.

To illustrate how the higher level tests involve all of the levels of efficacy, let us consider performance measures commonly reported in the IGT. First,

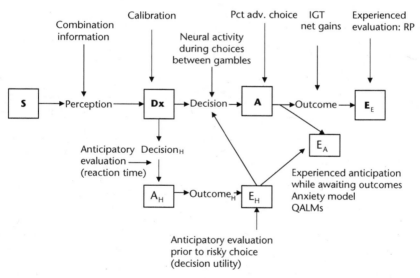

Figure 5–1 Levels of neuroeconomic evidence: Diagnostic efficacy includes the stages of perception and diagnosis (Dx); Management efficacy includes the stages of decision and action (A), as well as the intermediate steps pictured: Outcome efficacy includes the stages of outcome and evaluation (E). The evaluations that are based on hypothetical imagination of decision outcomes, anticipation of results, or experience outcomes are denoted with subscripts H, A, and E. A similar diagram can be constructed for outcomes that are delayed or involve multiple attributes without risk. IGT denotes the Iowa Gambling Task; SCR is the skin conductance response.

performance depends on elements of diagnostic efficacy: the ability to perceive outcomes. As such, it may involve factors such as the perception of ambiguity in the chances of winning or losing the gambles. In the IGT, there is also uncertainty about the amount of money to be gained or lost.

In addition, performance in the IGT depends on elements of management efficacy: the ability to make good choices. The person must hold the diagnostic information in memory, estimate the value of a choice, compare it to the alternatives, and then decide. As such, our choices will depend not merely on our beliefs or hunches about the likeliness of outcomes but also on our abilities to anticipate and simulate them in order to gauge our preferences for different gambles.

Furthermore, performance on the IGT depends on a nonevaluative aspect of outcome efficacy: the nature of the task. For example, people often will have surprisingly low net gains, even on later trials of the IGT, because the early trials give them better results when they choose disadvantageous gambles. Thus, though they may appear to lack outcome efficacy, this deficiency may not be simply due to poor diagnostic or management skills. Rather, the difficult task misleads these impaired subjects. In fact, when the task is altered, some VMPFC-damaged patients gain as much money as controls. As noted earlier, one trouble they originally had may have been due to an inability to unlearn the expectations formed from earlier trials.[419]

Beyond this, performance on the IGT likely depends also on the ability to evaluate—or react to—the outcomes themselves. For example, addicts or gamblers may experience gains more strongly than losses. Accordingly, they may not wish to maximize monetary gains but rather to maximize their own satisfaction with the outcomes.

Finally, all the levels of the efficacy—as well as some components of effectiveness—affect the overall value of the outcomes received. Thus, measures such as the net gains may assess global function in poor performers, such as those with right VMPFC damage. But they reveal little about the specific causes of the underperformance. From the measures of net gains alone, one cannot say whether those who perform poorly on the IGT lack the capacity to make choices due to the perception of ambiguity in probabilities, a lack of knowledge of outcomes, different preferences for ambiguous outcomes, or a distorted experience of the outcomes.

So what does one do if the intent is not to measure global performance but to measure specific dysfunctions? One possibility is to narrow the focus of an experiment to management efficacy. For example, in experiments offering choices between gambles with known probabilities and outcomes, one can assess the accuracy of choices. One can measure the percent of choices with a higher expected value. In such cases, the overall performance depends merely on whether one chose the higher EV gamble and not on how much better the choice was, relative to others.

However, accuracy may have limited or unclear value, depending on the criterion used to judge it. For example, defining "accuracy" as the selection of higher EV gambles may be misleading if people are not seeking to maximize EV but rather the utility of their choices.[420] In addition, with measures of management efficacy, such as accuracy, the ultimate choices made may depend on the prior level of diagnostic efficacy—the ability to perceive or edit the gambles and assign subjective meaning to the displayed probabilities and outcomes. For example, one person may frame the gambles as opportunities to gain; another may see them as opportunities to lose. This may have more to do with their perception and attention than with their capacities to choose.

Another option is to further narrow the focus of a study to diagnostic efficacy. One can focus more specifically on peoples' perceptions of their chances to win a gamble or to forecast an outcome accurately. For example, one study discussed in chapter 3 had subjects make sales predictions in a marketing problem, then measured the calibration of their confidence in the forecasts. Such calibration summarizes the ability to maintain and integrate performance information. It does not involve management or outcome efficacy. So, when patients with right-sided frontal lobe damage performed poorly, they demonstrated specific diagnostic difficulties.

The main drawback of narrowing the focus to diagnostic efficacy, however, is that it tells us much less about performance. If patients perform well at this level, they may still make poor management decisions or not experience better outcomes. For instance, one study found some anxious patients to be as well calibrated as normal controls,[421] yet these patients still make some very bad choices in life. Thus, they differ from controls at a higher level of management or outcome efficacy. In fact, one study found that anxious patients showed functional abnormalities in the rostral-ventral ACC, which is ssociated with an aspect of management efficacy—the processes of cognitive and emotional integration.[422] Hence, each level of evaluation—diagnostic, management, or outcome—has advantages and disadvantages. While diagnostic studies better clarify specific dysfunctions, outcome studies better summarize performance.

Tests Within and Between Levels

The previous discussions have considered overall performance at each level of the hierarchy. However, one can also test specific performance components within each level of the hierarchy. For example, rather than simply measure the overall calibration of peoples' probability estimates, one can ask how well people combine information to change probability estimates. The calibration study discussed in chapter 3 gave subjects information about the opinions of experts and then examined how this affected their own estimates.

Likewise, one can look at how information at one level affects the next. Some studies have changed the diagnostic information—the probabilities, as well as rewards and penalties, in different gambles—then examined how often these increases change choices. They have found that neither tryptophan depletion nor propanolol administration change choice patterns in response to altered probabilities. However, tryptophan—which affects serotonin systems—decreases the effects of altered rewards on choice.[423] Propanolol—which affects norepinephrine systems—decreases the effects of altered penalties, but only when the chances of penalty are high.[424]

Tests of Effectiveness

In addition to the levels of efficacy, we must also consider some effectiveness concepts. For instance, although outcome efficacy, for heuristic purposes, is considered as the highest level in the economic efficacy model, it does not ensure good performance over time in a broader effectiveness model. For instance, in order for the person to learn which decks are rewarding (or to unlearn previous impressions), one must have outcome efficacy and experience the differences in their outcomes.[425] Yet that experience alone does not insure that learning will occur. Thus, to understand performance on the IGT, one must also consider various learning abilities, as outlined in chapter 4. These learning capacities, in turn, depend on previously discussed factors, such as the reward variance. The rate at which knowledge of a deck's outcome is used to update expectations depends partly on one's prior estimate of the inherent uncertainty in the outcomes.

More Specific Tests

In addition, we may learn about more specific study differences. For example, the type of diagnostic uncertainty appears to affect anticipatory evaluations at the management level. The IGT does not initially specify the probabilities of winning or losing gambles, whereas the Rogers Gambling tasks discussed in chapter 3 do. In the latter case, people may behave somewhat more like rational economists and make numerical calculations, thus relying on abstract thought. They are then less likely to generate anticipatory SCRs. But in the former case, when subjects in the IGT have only ambiguous information about probabilities, they do generate SCRs. They may then need to rely more on feeling states, which involve bodily as well as brain responses.[426]

Likewise, one must consider whether the tasks merely engage passive evaluation mechanisms or actions as well. For instance, actions may influence not only the occurrence of outcomes but also their subjective experience. Neural activities appear to differ in response to rewards, depending on whether or not the subject acted to obtain them. In passive learning studies, in which no action is required, one sees activations of the ventral striatum.[427] When action is permitted, one sees activations of the dorsal striatum, including the caudate.[428]

In addition, a similar interaction may occur between two components of management efficacy, involving actions and anticipations. While the medial

PFC (mPFC) is not involved directly in the learning of associations, it does signal the capacity for controlling outcomes, which can reduce anticipatory stress.[429] In fact, it exerts this inhibition indirectly through GABA (gamma-aminobutyric acid) systems in the brain—the same systems that are affected by many tranquilizers. Thus, taking control of one's environment may be somewhat like taking a valium or having a drink. The effect is oddly reminiscent of peoples' perceptions of environmental risks, which are greatly reduced when the risks seem controllable.[430]

Other Experimental Differences

Beyond the task differences suggested by concepts of efficacy and effectiveness, the field of epidemiology identifies many other variations in study design—so many, in fact, that one is likely to need a more substantial science of "neuroepidemiology" to begin to characterize their differences. Although such a description is far beyond the scope of this book, let us briefly note a few important sources of differences between studies, as well as factors affecting the meaning of results.

Methods for the Selection and Comparison of Subjects

Studies commonly differ depending on how subjects are selected as well as compared—for example, cross-sectionally at a single time or longitudinally over time, as well as prospectively or retrospectively. In addition, there are case reports, similar to those sometimes seen in neuroeconomic articles— even the latter studies with extremely small samples come close to being case reports.[431] The field of epidemiology considers advantages and disadvantages of all these competing methods. For instance, the case reports may enable much more detailed analyses of particular cases, but only at the expense of increased biases.

The Populations

The field of epidemiology has identified many possible variations in the type, extent, and stage of different diseases, which may be studied. The neuroeconomic studies of patients in a clinic, for example, may have different mixtures of cases, with different types and rates of comorbid illnesses, in addition to the illness that is the focus of the study. Another common type of variation is the type of neural lesion being studied. Some lesions are so general that they affect adjoining regions; for instance, a lesion to the ACC might affect the dorsomedial prefrontal cortex (DMPFC); so when considering the results of a study of the decisions of lesioned patients, one could misattribute a function of the DMPFC incorrectly to the ACC. Likewise, different neuroeconomic measures may have more or less value, depending on the type and severity of the disorder. For instance, some measures may differ from controls in severely but not mildly impaired patients.

The Measures

The field of epidemiology in medicine has also emphasized the importance of carefully considering how variations in the measures may influence their apparent associations with different populations. The sources of variation may include differences between populations, random biological changes in the individual, and errors of measurement. Neuroeconomic measures often entail additional considerations specific to the method. For example, in fMRI studies, the definition of an activation depends on complex determinations of statistical power and on the intensity of noise, as well as many assumptions and interpretations, which often vary between studies (for a review of issues in fMRI interpretation, see Brett et al.).[432] In particular, the studies presuppose common maps of brain anatomy, which in reality may vary across different people. Likewise, many studies use average activations across a given time period and discard potentially useful information about dynamic changes within an individual. The QALMs model discussed earlier shows why such dynamic patterns of change—visible with other, more time-sensitive technologies—can provide very useful information that may also ultimately tell more about how different brain regions interact.

Beyond the epidemiologic and technology-specific considerations, however, identifying the level of measurement itself is often a critical but subtle problem in neuroeconomic studies. For instance, contrary to the authors' intent, one might misinterpret a study of Coke versus Pepsi preferences as indicating that neurobiologic measures predict future preferences better than people themselves can predict future likes.[433] Yet, the neural measures were made when the subjects *experienced* a taste of the drink and were compatible with the criterion to be predicted—the stated preference after the *experienced* taste. However, the prior preference measures were *anticipatory* ones and thus incompatible with the *experienced* taste. To conclude that neural measures predict better than peoples' own preferences, one would need to compare the reported taste preferences with anticipatory, rather than experienced, neural activities (e.g., prior to being told that they were to receive a bolus of Coke or Pepsi).

Likewise, if one elicits choices in time tradeoff discounting tasks, measures of discounting choices are evaluations related to management efficacy (E_H in Figure 5–1); whereas, anticipatory neural recordings after a choice but before the outcome (E_A) can be viewed are related to outcome effectiveness. The former may reflect decisional effort, while the latter may reflect anticipatory anxiety from not knowing the result. Some anticipatory SCR measures confound these two temporally separable stages of management efficacy and outcome effectiveness. Yet other studies report subjective ratings of anticipation after an outcome occurs. These are remembered utilities, which may differ in yet other ways.

If we distinguish still more complex forms of evaluation, we may identify important dissociations between capacities in some individuals. For instance, although some expectancy-related anticipations might be viewed as a type of prediction, some studies try to predict the anticipations themselves. Accordingly, cigarette smokers may make smoking decisions based on one form of anticipatory evaluation (E_H)—their expected craving—but their anticipations of craving when they make the choice often do not agree with their actual experience of craving while they await a cigarette (E_A).[434] In fact, their dispassionate predictions of future craving after smoking may elicit expectancy-related utilities, whereas their predictions during a period of withdrawal may elicit more goal-related utilities that engage very different neural circuits.

In addition, if we distinguish different forms of evaluations, we may also better understand how different studies produce apparently contradictory results. As noted in the section on Changes in reference points in chapter 4, some imaging studies have suggested that the active areas of the brain differ during gain or loss. However, other studies have not found such differences. Many inter-study differences may account for the different conclusions. Some studies involve gambles that are all losses or all gains and others involve gambles with mixed outcomes. Others also add certain outcomes and have people choose between a gamble and a certain outcome. Some evaluate risky choices, and find no differences in the regions of brain activation for gains and losses.[435] Other studies measure experienced or riskless multiattribute evaluations and do find such differences.[436] If the risky/riskless distinction proves to be one significant factor underlying the disagreements, it is possible that risky and riskless choices are processed differently. Such a finding would be consistent with multiattribute utility methods, which first assess the value of an outcome ($v(x)$) in riskless choices, then estimate the utility of this value ($u(v(x))$) in risky decisions.[437]

The Models

The models assumed to underlie neuroeconomic measures may also lead to differences in study results. For example, in a manner analogous to some prior studies of loss aversion, suppose that we search for brain regions in which the activities correspond linearly to the monetary change, x (i.e., $v(x) = x\beta_{gain}$ and $v(-x) = x\beta_{loss}$) then $(v(-x) - v(x)) = (\beta_{loss} - \beta_{gain})x$. If we take the value $(\beta_{loss} - \beta_{gain}) = \lambda$, to be the loss aversion coefficient, that coefficient will be the slope of a regression of the change in $v(x)$ on x, (with zero intercept). However, suppose that one searched for brain regions whose activities did not correlate linearly with behaviorally derived values $v(x)$ but rather with the log of these values (X). Then $(\beta_{loss} - \beta_{gain})$ could have no such relation to loss aversion and instead reflect the relative curvatures of the value functions.[438] Thus, it would be possible for studies using these two methods to make very different conclusions about the value of the loss aversion coefficient.

Spurious Correlations and Confounded Variables

The field of epidemiology also describes numerous possible sources of bias that can lead to spurious associations between the measures and populations being studied. In neuroeconomics, factors that affect neural activations include idiosyncratic stimulus features, such as the direction an arrow is pointing to indicate a reward or penalty. Such variables can produce epiphenomena, or spurious correlations, between irrelevant stimuli and neural activities.[439]

Furthermore, some studies confound multiple neuroeconomic variables. For instance, the original versions of the IGT confounded the expected value and the riskiness of the decks as well as ambiguities about the probabilities and outcomes. The decks with positive expected value were also less risky, and those with negative expected value were more risky. So one could not determine whether neurologically impaired subjects performed more poorly because they did not calculate the expected values of gambles or because they preferred more risks than did normal individuals. More recent evidence, in fact, indicates that risk preference may have been a factor. One study found that impaired subjects outperformed the normals when the positive expected value decks were the riskier ones.[440]

Finally, when actions are involved, one must recognize that anticipatory measures of neural activity may confound the disappointment over a below-expectation or unobtained outcome, given one's choice, and the regret over an unobtained outcome, which would have resulted if one chose differently. However, methods such as Mellers' decision affect theory discussed in chapter 4, enable one to separate the two components and test whether the disappointment and regret have different neural correlates.

Toward a Broader Set of Neuroepidemiologic Tests

In the future, we will need to do more than clarify the structure of existing studies and the meaning of the evidence they provide. In order to make neuroeconomic measures even more generally useful in describing decisional capacities, future studies will need to consider a broader range of outcomes. These should include nonmonetary outcomes in more realistic environments and not simply monetary ones in laboratory settings.

The more extensive use of nonmonetary risks and rewards will be important for several reasons. First, since different nonmonetary outcomes can engage different emotions and neural systems, their use in gambling experiments may affect descriptive neuroeconomic variables in different ways. For example, when the outcomes are monetary rewards and engage the approach systems in the brain, a better-than-expected outcome normally would produce elation and a worse-than-expected outcome would produce disappointment, reflected in the different coefficients of the disappointment model in chapter 4. However, social gains or losses may endow the coefficients with new meaning. For instance, if one imagines giving a public speech and sees it as a social opportunity, a better-than-expected outcome may result in pride and a worse-than-expected outcome may trigger embarrassment. However, if it is seen as a social threat, the better-than-expected outcome will provide relief and the bad outcome shame or guilt.[441]

Likewise, very different emotions are likely to occur when a more substantive physical threat—such as the warning of a possible electric shock—occurs and engages the avoidance systems. In this case, a better-than-expected outcome normally provides relief and a worse-than-expected one produces distress. In these cases, one could compute the "elation" and "disappointment" coefficients, but their meanings would now differ, and they would be more aptly named "relief" and "distress" coefficients. One could use such coefficients to estimate the function of distinct neural systems, which mediate safety and fear learning.

In addition, the use of nonmonetary outcomes, which generate strong emotional responses, may affect the values of the parameters themselves. For example, people anticipating a kiss or an electric shock have different attitudes toward risk. Such strong emotional outcomes also can alter loss aversion and the sensitivity to changes in probability.[442]

Furthermore, some inconsistencies in choice may emerge only when the decisions involve "colder" attributes, such as small monetary gains, or "hot" attributes, which stimulate strong feelings. Clearly, strong feelings may involve primitive neural systems that mediate goal-related emergency responses, which differ from those that mediate deliberative, expectancy-related processing.[443] For instance, strong feelings from drug-related rewards may stimulate the inconsistent choices of some addicts who want to use drugs even when they will get little pleasure. Intense fear from social or environmental threats may engage the inappropriate responses of anxious patients, who avoid situations that they know will not produce harm. At the same time, patients with obsessive-compulsive personality disorder may focus too much on objective attributes like monetary gains and too little on the likely impact of their decisions on future feelings (recall the miserly Mr. Scrooge). An excessive focus on objective, seemingly "rational" factors in a choice can cause people to make choices that they later will not like.[444]

Eliciting strong feelings also can suggest the need for new models. For example, the presence of such feelings can make discount rates more reflective of anticipatory emotion than the value of end outcomes. One study elicited monetary evaluations of outcomes such as "kiss from the movie star of your choice" or "a nonlethal 110 V electric shock" occurring at different points in time. Subjects were willing to pay the most to delay the kiss and wanted to get the shock done as soon as possible. Since ordinary positive discount rates imply a desire to delay bad outcomes and hasten good ones, the results suggested negative discount rates.[445] However, the altered meaning of the discount rates here suggested the need for more complex models—such as the anxiety or QALMs models—that consider the quality and duration of anticipatory emotions. Such models provide parameters that might better explain the desire to prolong the pleasurable anticipation of a kiss and to diminish the unpleasurable anticipation of a shock.

Beyond this, we may need more realistic environments to adequately explore the factors affecting choice. For instance, economists do not distinguish such costs that involve the effort versus the delay required to obtain a reward, yet different neural systems seem to be involved in the two cases.[446]

By developing alternative models for variables such as effort and delay, we also may begin to better understand the importance of effort and motivation, and this may lead to better models of decision making. Consider the decision weights in current behavioral decision theory models. They may reflect action tendencies in low-effort problems such as selecting gambles but not in more effortful, real-world situations. For instance, a depressed patient might do well in playing lotteries on the computer. But in order to play the gambles of life—for example, to interview for a job and risk not getting it—the depressive must first get up in the morning and find the energy to go to the interview.

SUMMARY

This book has put forth many cautions about neuroeconomic models. Beyond the neuroepidemiologic factors previously noted, other limitations concern the biological processes being modeled. Currently, it is difficult to match specific neural circuits to particular neuroeconomic parameters. Our understanding of any correspondences is likely to change, and some circuits may serve general cognitive functions that do not correspond well to any existing economic models. In addition, the complex modular operations of the brain also limit what we can say about the importance of any particular brain structure's role in decision making.

Likewise, the present book's survey of the components of decision-making capacities is far from complete, and the whole is likely to be greater than the sum of its parts. As discussed in the section on future models, many brain systems perform complementary and compensatory functions. In the future, therefore, we will see need for more measures not merely of brain activity but also interactivity, as illustrated by QALMs models discussed in chapter 4.

Even then, however, many critical components of human performance may be found to derive from the brain's software more than in its hardware. And unfortunately, we cannot yet identify the neurobiological processes underlying the complex software problems that arise from unique individual histories of learning, memory, and habit.

Indeed, even at the level of analysis that is currently feasible, the generalizability of the findings often remains uncertain. For example, many neuroeconomic studies involve research with animals, whose brains differ from ours. In monkeys, perceptual decisions may be coordinated: Seeing a stimulus and deciding what to do is sufficient for determining a motor response. However, in humans, decisions do not determine actions so simply.[447]

Yet, humans are still part of the animal kingdom; Wall Street is still a jungle; and animals not working in this human jungle show many of the same violations of economic axioms that have been demonstrated empirically in humans.[448] When foraging for flower nectar, bumblebees violate the independence axiom of the economic theory and demonstrate the Allais paradox, much as humans do.

Capuchin monkeys demonstrate changes in risk preference depending on whether gambles are presented as gains or losses.[449] Likewise, the increased risk seeking for losses relative to gains that prospect theory predicts is not merely seen in role-seeking starlets but also in food-pecking starlings (blackbirds).[450] In addition, nonhuman primates, like humans, demonstrate an aversion to inequity. For example, many monkeys refuse to continue an experiment when they receive cucumber rewards but see another group receiving better-tasting grapes. In fact, some not only refuse to eat their cucumbers, they angrily hurl them back at the researcher.[451]

Thus, even animals exhibit some uncanny similarities to humans. And so neuroeconomics may not be for the birds, or the bumblebees, or the monkeys alone. In fact, humans who wish to hurl the limited neuroeconomic rewards, like cucumbers, back at the researchers who offered them would do well to consider the alternatives.

In fact, some would argue that, despite its limitations, the neuroeconomic approach has already extended beyond its precursors: neurobiology and economics. It reaches beyond some purely descriptive neuroscientific approaches, which examine increasingly detailed cellular and subcellular processes, then reason inductively about what is being seen. While highly useful, such reasoning alone can be difficult to reconcile with alternative theories, increasingly distanced from actual behavior and often hard to test. The neuroeconomic theory also reaches beyond the economic theory, which has limitations opposite to those of the descriptive neurobiologic approaches. While the economic method is explicit in its assumptions and can be clearly tested, it is also a highly abstract view that ignores many important but untidy details needed to explain behavior.

The neuroeconomic theory attempts to take advantage of the strengths of both neurobiology and economics. It may use economic models to describe neural events and thereby give us new ideas about rational capacities. At the same time, neuroeconomics may incorporate detailed findings from neurobiology into economic models. The resulting concepts reach beyond economic principles based on monetary gain or consciously stated preferences. They reach toward possible biologic correlates of the capacities to act in a way that improves our well-being.

Also, the neuroeconomic concepts clarify the need to consider aspects of well-being that the economic theories do not address. For example, in economics, action is merely a means to obtain good outcomes. In reality, however, the mere sense of control—the belief that our actions control outcomes—directly affects our well-being. Beyond this, in economics, the anticipation of future outcomes simply predicts the likely value of future experiences. Yet, clearly, regardless of future outcomes, our well-being depends directly on many anticipatory emotions, from financial or health worries to the desires that drive long-term career goals. At times, such emotions can be harmful. When a person continually worries about improbable events, such anticipation may produce fear that is unnecessary. But when a person is losing his sight or dying of a terminal illness, his anticipation may provide hope that is essential. In fact, the pursuit of such hope may itself be essential to rational choice.

Reminiscence is important as well. According to economic analysis, we must look forward toward the possible future consequences of different actions to make rational choices and achieve well-being. However, we can sometimes merely look back at the past to experience a similar sense of well-being.[452] Happiness derives in part from one's ability to recall a rich history, and this capacity becomes even more important as life progresses. As such, even when patients with terminal cancer lack a forward-looking hope for the future, they can still receive pleasure by looking back upon a life well led. In many of life's most painful situations—even when awaiting gas chambers in concentration camps—people use the past to create meaning for their lives.

The changes in expectations and adaptations discussed in chapter 4 are also important to well-being. For example, people quickly adapt to continual rewards, such as financial gain; and animals run faster toward goals that provide intermittent rather than continuous reward. Also, people who move to California in search of the continual rewards of an ideal climate do not become happier in the long run.[453] After being in California for a while, they learn to expect good weather and then become uncomfortable with only slightly colder temperatures that would have felt wonderful had they still been living in the northeastern United States.[454]

Finally, although the prototypic, economically rational individual achieves well-being by acquiring desired commodities and reaching goals, some economists have recognized that, in reality, such achievement is not sufficient. As one economist noted, "I imagined that all my goals were satisfied. Would that make me happy? No." People need to strive for goals. They enjoy the struggle itself. In fact, their efforts to achieve goals may contribute more to a sense of well-being than the achievement of the goals themselves. To understand the importance such struggles and other noneconomic pleasures, consider the following story of Iceland.

Emotional Warmth in Iceland

If the happiest people in the world do not all live in California, where else could they possibly come from? The answer may surprise you. At odds with economic theory, a Gallup poll more than a decade ago found that they did not even come from the wealthiest countries, including the entire United States, in which 72% reported satisfaction, or Japan, in which only 42% reported satisfaction during a period of economic prosperity. Paradoxically, they came from a windswept island encircled by glaciers and volcanoes, where life seemed the most difficult. Despite having less than 4 hr of daylight and a fishing industry that is endangered daily by unpredictable weather, 82% of the inhabitants of Iceland said they are satisfied with their lives.[455]

Some scientists believe that the Icelander's happiness derives partly from the land's discomforts. Because they do not expect good weather or a comfortable existence, life seldom disappoints them. At the same time, they do enjoy other social benefits, which come from a culture of greater compassion and cooperation. Many Icelandic families embrace people, such as the alcoholic or the illegitimate child, who have become outcasts in our society. Their culture also helps its members to learn to make social commitments, involving the ability to see their neighbors' views. As a result, Iceland has an excellent system of universal education and medical care, with the world's lowest infant mortality rate and nearly the highest longevity.

Thus, the Icelanders' apparent happiness may derive in part from some previously discussed neuroeconomic factors: the pleasure of variety and surprise related to expectations and uncertainty, as well as the capacity for adaptively framing problems in different perspectives and learning to make social commitments. Their capacities may also involve what philosophers and religious visionaries have called "eudaimonic"—the well-being that arises from engagement in actions, which also has some previously discussed neuroeconomic correlates.

To be sure, the ideas of the visionaries may go a step beyond neuroeconomic factors, which may produce mere happiness. They maintain that, beyond the mere pleasure of action or attaining goals, one's engagement in the community gives people a deeper sense of involvement and even meaning in life.[456] Indeed, some have argued that a loss of such meaning—the extinction of value altogether—can be a much more serious threat than loss of pleasure or even of life in some circumstances.[457] They point out that some people may use such a sense of meaning to adapt to illness, whereas people with good physical health may become depressed when they lose the sense of meaning in their lives. Thus, the meaning of life may not lie simply in the satisfaction of existing needs and values, as present economic theories may suggest.

Clearly the present text does not reveal the meaning of life or address many other important religious and philosophical issues. It does not even address some aspects of long-term well-being. However, it does suggest neurobiologic correlates of some capacities to achieve short-term well-being—in a sense, a form of "happiness." These include a degree of consistency of present, past, and future evaluations, the calibration of beliefs and values, and the ability to adapt.

Thus, neuroeconomics may still help us understand many capacities that promote well-being, even if it cannot yet explain human capacities to attain a sense of identity, find a sense of meaning, and appreciate particular pleasures of the mind.[458] In addition, before one extols the miracle of such complexities in human mental life, one must note that the power of any theory of decision making derives in part from its simplicity and economy. So, although there may be many values and virtues and more profound meanings in life, it may not be entirely dissolute to start with one simple goal of choice: the attainment of happiness. While other factors also may contribute to well-being, there can be little controversy about the importance of happiness itself.

As once noted in a poem by Ogden Nash:

> Lot's of truisms don't have to be repeated but there is one that has got to be,
> Which is that is much nicer to be happy than it is not to be,
> And I shall even add to it by stating unequivocally and without restraint
> That you are much happier when you are happy than when you ain't.[459]

Glossary

Affect The subjective experience of a transient emotional state.

Allais paradox A pattern of inconsistent choices that violate the independence axiom. According to the paradox, people value certain gains more than the theory of expected utility would predict, based on the values derived from choices between gambles.

Ambiguity Uncertainty about the true value of the probability of an event. For example, flipping a fair coin offers a .5 chance winning or losing for sure and there is no ambiguity. More ambiguity exists if we are randomly given either an advantageous deck of cards to pick from, in which case the chances of winning are 70%, or a disadvantageous deck to pick from, in which case the chances of winning are 30%. The overall chance of winning or losing in the latter case is still .5, but we do not know whether we will get the deck in which the chances of winning are really .7 or .3.

Amygdala An almond-shaped structure in the medial temporal lobe that coordinates the actions of the autonomic and endocrine systems in emotion. It appears to be part of a defense response system, and bilateral damage to the amygdala often results in an inability to protect oneself. Conditions such as anxiety, autism, depression, narcolepsy, posttraumatic stress disorder and phobias also may be linked to abnormal functioning of the amygdala.

Anterior cingulate cortex (ACC) A structure involved in error detection, attention, pain, social attachment, and many other functions. It lies on the medial surface of the frontal lobes. The cingulate cortex is part of the limbic system and is the cortical part of the cingulate gyrus.

Antisocial personality disorder (ASPD) Individuals with this disorder often believe their desires justify their actions and that other peoples' needs and safety are not important. Such people often lie and engage in reckless behavior that poses risks to themselves as well as others. They often have a history of multiple arrests. They must have a history of conduct problems during childhood to receive the diagnosis of ASPD.

Awareness calibration The calibration of measures of one's confidence in his own probability estimates.

Basal ganglia The basal ganglia are structures involved in many automatic motor functions and motivational processes. They lie beneath the cerebral cortex. The basal ganglia consist of several interconnected forebrain nuclei: the substantia nigra (SN), subthalamic nucleus (SN), the globus pallidus (GP), and the striatum (the caudate nucleus, putamen, and nucleus accumbens).

Basolateral amygdale The basolateral nucleus is the largest of three groups of nuclei in the amygdala. It connects with the thalamus as well as the temporal, insular, and prefrontal cortices. Its neurons project to excitatory portions of the striatum.

Behavioral decision making/behavioral economics A study of how people do make decisions and why they do not make decisions as they should, according to normative economic models. Behavioral economics concerns mainly studies of individual decision making in financial matters, as well as social cooperation and competition.

Bipolar disorder A recurrent mood disorder consisting of manic/hypomanic episodes with or without depressive episodes. Manic behavior is characterized by hyperactivity, rapid speech, impulsivity and a diminished need for sleep. Hypomanic symptoms are similar but milder.

Borderline personality disorder (BPD) People with borderline personality disorder, have a marked instability of mood, relationships, and self-image. Those with BPD often exhibit suicidal or self-injurious behavior, unprovoked anger, rapid mood shifts, lack of identity, a sense of emptiness, and a fear of abandonment.

Brainstem The brainstem controls many autonomic functions, such as heartbeat and respiration. It is a stalk beneath the cerebrum that connects the forebrain, spinal cord, and peripheral nerves. It is also a term for the midbrain and hindbrain.

Calibration A measure of the quality of subjective probability estimates, which is determined according to whether the subjective estimate of the likelihood of an event matches the actual frequency of its occurrence.

Caudate nucleus As part of the striatum, the head of the caudate head connects with the putamen, and its tail ends in the amygdala of the temporal lobe. It is part of the basal ganglia, which lies beneath the cortex.

Cerebellum A large part of the brainstem that helps integrate sensory information and motor commands to enable coordinated actions.

Cerebral cortex The outer surface of the brain, containing most of the neurons in the cerebrum.

Cerebrum A major subdivision of the forebrain.

Certainty effect This reflects peoples' tendencies to value certain gains or reject certain losses more than the expected utility theory would predict (see Allais paradox).

Certainty equivalent The "certainty equivalent" of a gamble is the minimum payment that the subject will take to play a gamble (or the maximum he will take to give it up). The difference between the certainty equivalent and the expected value of the gamble is called the risk premium and is a measure of risk aversion (or seeking).

Cingulate cortex This outfolding of the cerebral cortex runs front to back, and is hidden from view within the gap separating the two cerebral hemispheres. It is part of the limbic system.

Comparators Neural circuits that enable computation of the match between real or imagined outcomes and the person's goals.

Confidence A pattern of bias in the calibration of subjective probabilities. In one usage of the term, underconfidence occurs when the person's probability estimates are not extreme enough (e.g., when the person underestimates the chance of winning a gamble with a high frequency of wins and underestimates the chances of losing a gamble with a high frequency of losses). Overconfidence occurs when the estimates are not extreme enough. When applied to the awareness of one's estimates, however, overconfidence may also mean that a person is too sure that his estimate is correct (i.e., an overly narrow 95% confidence interval for the estimate).

Corticotrophin-releasing factor (CRF) CRF is a biologically active neurochemical that helps integrate the endocrine, autonomic, immune, and behavioral responses of the stress response. It does so in part via feedback loops, which involve the hypothalamus and the pituitary and adrenal glands. However, CRF genes in the cortex also play an important role in the stress response.

d-amphetamine (dextroamphetamine) Dextroamphetamine (dexedrine) is a stimulant that enhances alertness and increases motor activity. Like ritalin, it stimulates dopamine systems in the brain and is used to treat individuals with attention deficit hyperactivity disorder (ADHD).

Decision utility Decision utility is the value assigned to a possible future stimulus or outcome, as inferred from the person's choices. This use of the term "utility" corresponds roughly to the modern 20th-century conceptions of utility as an unobservable value, which is inferred from people's choices. The present book distinguishes two aspects of decision utility that are not entirely unrelated but which appear to have some distinct neurobiologic features: expectancy-related and goal-related utility.

Delay aversion coefficient The ratio of the marginal rate of change of benefits to that of the costs of waiting for an outcome.

Dendrite A long, thin extension from the nerve cell. Through connections with the axons of other nerve cells, it receives messages.

Depression Depression can refer either to the symptom of low mood or to a more enduring episode of a mood disorder (such as major depression, defined in the following text).

Discounting When a person assigns lesser importance to delayed than to immediate outcomes of the same monetary amount, she is said to "discount" the deferred outcomes. In most economic models, the discount rate is assumed to be constant. That assumption is relaxed in hyperbolic and hybrid models.

Discrimination In the context of probability judgment, discrimination reflects the capacity to sort events into different groups (e.g., in meteorologic predictions, cases in which daily rainfall will or will not occur). The discriminatory capacity is independent of the calibration, which measures the quality of the actual numerical probabilities assigned to the events (e.g., the subjective probability of rainfall).

Discriminatory bias In signal detection theory, the discriminatory bias is the tendency to respond "yes" on a task independently of whether or not the response is correct.

Discriminatory sensitivity In signal detection theory, the discriminatory sensitivity depends on the ability to make distinguishing judgments, for example, to say "yes" more often when that response is correct than to say "yes" when that response is incorrect.

Dominance In the usual usage of the term, one option dominates another if it offers at least as much as compared with the second, no matter what happens and at least one of its outcomes is strictly better (see probabilistic dominance for another usage of the term).

Dopamine Dopamine is a neurotransmitter released from the terminal of one neuron to stimulate another. It modulates some motor actions as well as approach and avoidance responses. It also plays an important role in motivating the use of some drugs of abuse.

Dorsal striatum (DS) The dorsal striatum is the sensorimotor part of the striatum. Antipsychotic drugs that simulate motor symptoms of Parkinson's disease affect the DS.

Dorsolateral prefrontal cortex (DLPFC) The DLPFC is a region on the lateral surface of the brain in front of the premotor region. It plays an important role in language, attention, working memory and calculative functions, which may affect impulsivity and decision making, as well as attention and language. Patients with DLPFC lesions often have deficiencies in these functions, as well as apathy, indifference, and psychomotor retardation.

Economic optimality A neoclassical view holds that decisions are optimal if they maximize the forward-looking expected utility of choices. Optimality, as such, requires only an internal consistency of stated preferences with each other and with the axioms. A less commonly held concept of optimality would consider the maximization of utility of the experienced outcomes.

Effectiveness Elements of the capacity to make rational choices not considered by a neoclassical economic model.

Efficacy The capacity to make rational choices according to a neoclassical economic model.

Error-related negativity (ERN) ERN is a part of the event-related brain potential (ERP), which is linked to error detection and action monitoring. As an abrupt negative deflection occurring 50–150 ms following a response, it has been associated with activity involving the anterior cingulate cortex (ACC).

Evaluations The degree of subjective well-being experienced in response to a real or imagined outcome, such as the occurrence of an event or the acquisition of an object. It is an affective state that may occur in response to memory, experience, or anticipation.

Event-related potential or evoked potential Extremely low voltage activity in the brain, which is ordinarily concealed, but occurs at specific times after a stimulus.

Expectancy-related utility A form of anticipatory or future evaluation that represents the predicted value assigned to a future outcome based on past experience. It is the value that steers choice in a particular direction based on past learning; whereas, goal-related utility is the value that motivates action based on current wants or needs. The two types of values may coincide but do not always do so.

Expected utility The sum of the utility of the outcomes, each multiplied by the chance that they will occur.

Expected value The sum of the amount of the outcomes, each multiplied by the chance that they will occur.

Experienced or present evaluation Experienced utility is the person's instantaneous subjective well-being in the present moment. It may be a response to a specific stimulus or outcome. It corresponds to Kahneman's use of the term utility as an observable and potentially measurable value. For didactic purposes, the book refers to experienced utility as a "present evaluation."

Forebrain The most complex and frontal part of the developing brain. Its two divisions include the lower diencephalon, which contains the thalamus and the hypothalmus, and the upper telencephalon, which contains the cerebrum.

Frontal cortex (FC) The cortical part of the frontal lobe, which is located anterior to the central sulcus. It includes the primary motor, premotor, and prefrontal regions.

Fronto-median cortex (FMC) The FMC is the median wall of the posterior frontal lobe. It plays a role in associations that develop over a long period of time.

Future or anticipatory evaluation Evaluations of the future involve our anticipation of events that might affect our future well-being. It encompasses expectancy and goal-related utilities. Predictive and decision utilities discussed elsewhere would also fall into this category.

GABA (gamma aminobutyric acid) An inhibitory neurotransmitter that is augmented by alcohol and benzodiazepines, such as Valium.

Generalized anxiety disorder (GAD) GAD is characterized by pervasive anxiety symptoms that are not restricted to specific situations. Typical symptoms are tension and excessive worry, sometimes with irritability, fatigue, insomnia, and edginess.

Globus pallidus One of the basal ganglia of the forebrain. With the putamen, it forms a cone-like structure, whose tip extends medially toward the thalamus.

Glutamate An amino acid (glutamic acid) used as a neurotransmitter at many excitatory synapses in the central nervous system.

Goal-related utility The value assigned to a future outcome that motivates action based on current wants or needs. It is distinguished from expectancy-related utility, which is the value that steers choice in a particular direction based on past learning.

Goals The states that one is motivated to seek or avoid.

Hindbrain The most posterior of the three brain regions that arise at the anterior end of the neural tube during embryonic development of the brain. It is the most posterior part of the adult brain and includes the pons, medulla, and cerebellum.

Hippocampus The hippocampus is part of the limbic system. Like the amygdala, it is located deep in the medial temporal lobe. It is thought to be involved in certain types of memory.

Hypothalamus The hypothalamus is a small structure in the limbic system. In part through its control of the pituitary gland, it is involved in autonomic, endocrine, and homeostatic functions, which mediate many emotions and drives.

Importance weight The importance of one feature of an outcome relative to the other features. In a sense, this weight is an "exchange rate" which determines how much of one feature one is willing to give up in order to get more of another.

Independence axiom An axiom of expected utility theory that states that one's preferences should not be changed by an independent and irrelevant event. For example, suppose one prefers $3,000 for sure to a gamble that offers a .8 chance to win $4,000 but does not prefer a .25 chance to win $3,000 over a .2 chance to win $4,000. If one had these preferences, it would be equivalent to changing them capriciously, based upon a completely independent event. To illustrate why, suppose one is offered a two-stage gamble and that the chance of rain is .75. If it does rain, he gets nothing. If it does not rain ($p = .25$), then he gets to choose between $3,000 or a .8 chance to win $4,000. Now one may prefer the former option. Yet considering the chance of rain, that two-stage gamble is the same as the choice between a .25 chance of $3,000 and a .2 chance of $4,000. And in this case, he previously preferred the latter. Thus, he is changing his preference based upon an independent and irrelevant event (the rain).

Insula/insular cortex The insular cortex plays a role in visceral functions and in the integration of autonomic information. It is located beneath the flaps of the frontal, parietal, and temporal lobes.

Iowa Gambling Task (IGT) In this task, a person repeatedly chooses between decks of cards that offer differing amounts of gain (x) or loss (y) with varying probabilities. Thus, the individual gradually learns to distinguish between a "good" deck providing positive expectations of reward and a "bad" deck providing negative expectations of loss.

Limbic system A brain system involved in the regulation of emotion, motivation, and homeostasis.

Locus coeruleus The locus coeruleus lies in the floor of one of the fluid-containing sacs in the brain—the fourth ventricle. Holding the main noradrenergic neurons of the brain, it activates the sympathetic nervous system and thereby helps regulate arousal, attention, and autonomic tone.

Loss aversion coefficient The ratio of the absolute value of the value of a loss divided by the value of an equivalent gain. Conventionally, the ratio is taken as the value at $x = 1$ unit; however, that often yields different values for different measurement units, for example, euros or dollars. So alternative, scale-independent measures have been developed as discussed in chapter 4.

Major depressive episode Major depression is a depressive episode lasting more than 2 weeks, commonly accompanied fatigue, guilt, poor motivation, lack of pleasure, sleep disturbance, and sometimes by anhedonia and, hopelessness.

Mania An episode of a mood disorder characterized by elevated mood and often accompanied by diminished sleep need, hyperactivity, racing thoughts, agitation, and impulsivity such as excessive spending.

Marginal utility The marginal utility is the amount of additional utility obtained from an additional increment of an outcome. If someone has decreasing marginal utility, he obtains less benefit from additional increases.

Medial prefrontal cortex (mPFC) The mPFCis the portion of the PFC toward the midline. It contains the anterior cingulate cortex and is important in attention and motivation.

Mental health A concept of health based on the person's functioning (e.g., work or social relations), risk-taking behavior, and reported types and levels of distress.

Mesolimbic The mesolimbic dopamine system (or the mesocorticolimbic system) originates in the midbrain ventral tegmental area, which lies medial to the substantia nigra, a region affected by Parkinson's disease. Dopaminergic neurons in this area send projections upward to limbic structures, such as the nucleus accumbens and amygdala, as well as to associated cortical structures, particularly the prefrontal cortex. The mesoaccumbens projection is believed to regulate the rewarding properties of a wide variety of stimuli, including drugs of abuse. The mesocortical projection is believed to be a major target for the antipsychotic properties of dopamine receptor antagonist drugs.

Methamphetamine Methamphetamine is a stimulant that has even stronger CNS effects than amphetamine. It is often a drug of abuse; it increases mood, wakefulness, and physical activity, and decreases appetite.

Methylphenidate (Ritalin) Methylphenidate is a mild CNS stimulant that is often used to treat attention deficit/hyperactivity disorder. It may exert its stimulant effect by activating the brain stem arousal system and cortex.

Midbrain The middle of the three brain regions that arise from the neural tube during embryonic development. In adults, it consists of the superior colliculus, the inferior colliculus, and parts of the reticular formation.

Mood A pervasive and sustained emotion. A sustained disturbance in mood can meet the criteria for an affective disorder or syndrome such as mania or depression.

Morphine Morphine is a narcotic pain reliever and is a common drug of abuse. When injected intravenously, it produces intense euphoria. In addicts, its discontinuation leads to profound withdrawal symptoms.

Multi-attribute utility A common currency for combining different features of an outcome into an overall evaluation.

Neuroeconomics Neuroeconomics is the study of what happens in the brain when we make decisions, assess risks and rewards, and interact socially.

Neuron A nerve cell.

Nigrostriatal tract The nigrostriatal dopamine system lies in part of the substantia nigra and sends upward projections to the dorsal striatum, particularly the caudate and putamen. This projection modulates motor functions, which are disturbed in Parkinson's disease. The extrapyramidal adverse effects of antipsychotic drugs are believed to result from the blockade of striatal dopamine receptors.

Norepinephrine (NE, also called noradrenaline) A neurotransmitter released by sympathetic motor neurons and by some neurons in the central nervous system.

Nucleus accumbens The nucleus accumbens is the region that fuses the putamen and caudate. It is part of the ventral continuation of the dorsal striatum (caudate, putamen). It helps mediate reward, pleasure, and addiction.

Orbitofrontal cortex (OFC) Lying above the eye sockets, the orbitofrontal cortex overlaps with the ventromedial prefrontal cortex (VMPFC). Its lateral portion is part of the VMPFC. The OFC receives information about what is happening in the environment and what plans are being made by other parts of the frontal lobes. Its output affects many behaviors and physiological responses, including emotional responses organized by the amygdala. Damage to the orbitofrontal cortex results in many emotional disturbances: disinhibition, impulsivity, poor empathy, and a failure to plan ahead. Yet such damage often produces few cognitive deficits.

Outcomes Ongoing as well as imagined events that carry affective significance. They include rewards, such as the receipt of a paycheck, and penalties, such as the loss of money or a family member. Outcomes also can be purely internal and biological, such as bodily signals of excess or deficiency. More broadly conceived, outcomes can also represent bodily events or values, such as the blood concentration of a chemical like sodium.

Panic disorder In panic disorder, recurrent attacks of panic often occur unpredictably and without obvious precipitants. The attacks consist of severe cognitive anxiety with physical and psychological symptoms. Physical symptoms include rapid heart beat tachycardia, palpitation, sweating, tremor, shortness of breath, dizziness, and numbness. Cognitive symptoms may include a fear of dying or going crazy.

Parietal cortex The parietal cortex is one of the four major hemispheres of the brain (the others being the frontal, temporal, and occipital cortices). Its anterior portion is the primary somatosensory cortex. Its posterior portion mediates many complex visual and somatosensory functions.

Past evaluation or remembered utility A past evaluation is the subjective value assigned to an outcome that is remembered from the past. For didactic purposes, this term is used in place of Kahneman's term remembered utility but is, for practical purposes, equivalent.

Personality disorder People with personality disorders have symptoms characterized by deviance and distress. Regarding deviance, the person's behavior differs from the "norm" in one of several possible ways: for example, a tendency toward overreliance on others in dependent personality disorders or an inability to form lasting attachments in schizoid personality disorders. Borderline, antisocial, avoidant, compulsive, or narcissistic traits can meet criteria for the diagnosis of personality disorders.

Phobia A phobia is a fear that is disproportionate to the specific situation that prompts it and typically leads to avoidance of the feared stimulus. Specific phobias typically involve fears of situations for which people are evolutionarily "prepared," for example, snakes, heights, open spaces. Social phobia typically involves a profound fear of social interaction—of talking to others, eating, drinking, and speaking in public as well as a fear of humiliation or embarrassment.

Pituitary gland A major endocrine gland at the base of the brain, which is controlled in turn by the hypothalamus.

Postsynaptic cell The target cell at the synapse—the connection between two neurons.

Posttraumatic stress disorder (PTSD) Posttraumatic stress disorder is a prolonged reaction to a life-threatening or catastrophic stressor. It often lasts for years and is accompanied by flashbacks, nightmares, avoidance of memories of the stress, excessive vigilance, anger, and a loss of interest in life.

Predictive utility Predictive utility is the forecast of well-being due to an outcome that may occur in the future.

Premotor cortex Part of the frontal lobe, the premotor cortex contains primary motor and prefrontal regions. Like those of the motor cortex, premotor neurons terminate in the spinal cord to engage motor behavior. It receives information from higher-order somatosensory and visual areas of the posterior parietal cortex.

Present evaluation or experienced utility A present evaluation is the person's instantaneous subjective well-being in the present moment. It may be a response to a specific stimulus or outcome. It corresponds to Kahneman's use of the term experienced utility as an observable and potentially measurable value.

Probabilistic dominance Roughly, one option probabilistically dominates another if the chances it offers of preferred outcomes are greater or the same and at least one such chance is strictly greater than that of the alternative option.

Prospect theory A behavioral economic theory motivated by violations of expected utility theory. It has two phases, one involving the editing of gambles and the other related to the evaluation of probabilities and outcomes.

Putamen Part of the basal ganglia, lying beneath the cortex. Together with the caudate, the putamen is part of the striatum. It lies in the brain medial to the insula and is continuous with the head of the caudate nucleus.

Quality calibration Quality calibration is the match of the subjective probabilities to the objective ones.

Rationality The ability to make choices that foster well-being. Note that the definition of rationality in neoclassical economics would involve only the ability to make choices consistent with one another and with a set of axioms.

Reference point A reference point is a standard to which outcomes are compared. For example, having a million dollars in the bank might be evaluated positively by those who previously had nothing, but may be valued negatively by those who had 2 million dollars a year ago. Here differences in the reference point—the prior assets—would determine the hedonic importance of the million dollars.

Relative performance The relative performance (RP) considers how much better the subjects' choices are than random selection, given the subject's own values, as determined in a gambling task.

Remembered utility or past evaluation Remembered utility is the subjective value assigned to an outcome that is remembered from the past. For didactic purposes, this is referred to as a past evaluation in this book.

Risk adjustment Risk adjustment is the sensitivity of decisions to changes in risk— for example, the tendencies of subjects to wager more in a gambling task as the probability of winning increases.

Risk attitude A person's attitude toward risk reflects roughly the tendency to prefer to play or avoid gambles, which is not explained by the expected value of the gambles. A person is risk-averse if she would rather have a payment equal to the expected value of the gamble instead of playing the gamble itself. A person is risk- seeking if she would rather play the gamble than have a certain payment equal to the gamble's expected value.

Risk premium The difference between the expected value of the gamble and its certainty equivalent. It is a measure of risk aversion (or seeking).

Rogers' decision quality task In this type of experiment, subjects are offered gambles with a specified chance, p, of either winning or losing a fixed number of points. Subjects must first choose the type of bet they want—one with a high or low probability of winning—then they decide how many points to wager on the gamble.

Rogers' risk attitude task Subjects make choices between multiple gambles, with differing probabilities and amounts to win or lose.

Schizophrenia Schizophrenia is a major mental illness characterized by "positive" and "negative" symptoms. The "positive" symptoms include false perceptions, called hallucinations, and false beliefs, called delusions. The "negative" symptoms include diminished affect, ambivalence, and illogical patterns of thought and speech as well as impaired cognitive function. These symptoms typically are followed by a progressive decline in social and work performance.

Serotonin (5-hydroxytryptamine, or 5-HT) Serotonin is a neurotransmitter that mediates many behaviors and physiological functions, including mood, emotion, sleep, and appetite. It plays a role in the biochemistry of depression, bipolar disorder, anxiety, and sexual function.

Social phobia Social phobia typically involves a profound fear of social interaction—of talking to others; of eating, drinking, and speaking in public—as well as a fear of humiliation or embarrassment.

Somatic loop/somatic marker hypothesis Damasio's somatic marker hypothesis seeks to explain how "gut feelings" arise. To enable gut feelings to occur, structures including the prefrontal cortex—particularly the VMPFC—facilitate the learning of associations between environmental situations and the emotional states that usually occur in such situations. The physical component of emotional states is often relayed from the body to the somatosensory and insular cortices. Then, at a later time, when a similar environmental situation occurs, there is a reactivation of the same somatosensory pattern that encoded the prior somatic state. The reactivation can occur either through a "body loop" or "somatic loop" that entails actual bodily changes stimulated by the prefrontal cortex and then registered again in the somatosensory cortex. Alternatively, the reactivation of the somatosensory pattern can bypass the body when prefrontal signals are directly transmitted to the somatosensory cortex. The somatosensory pattern enables one to label the environmental situation as good or bad, creating what we commonly call *gut feelings*.

Somatosensory (SS) cortex and somatosensory/insular (SSI) cortex The primary somatosensory cortex is located in the anterior parietal lobe. It is part of a sensory system that processes sensory information from the body, including the skin, muscles, and joints. The somatosensory/insular (SSI) cortex also includes the insula and plays a role in the conscious recognition of emotional states.

Stria terminalis A ribbon of fibers emerging from the posterior part of the amygdala and from the expansion of the tail of the caudate, the stria terminalis is involved in unlearned fear responses. The bed nucleus of the stria terminalis also is heavily innervated by mesolimbic dopamine neurons from the ventral tegmental area and, like the nucleus accumbens, is sensitive to the dopamine stimulant actions of many drugs of abuse.

Striatum A collective term for the caudate nucleus and putamen, which are two of the basal ganglia of the forebrain. The ventral striatum (VS) plays an important role in reward learning and the dorsal striatum (DS) is also involved in action motivated by learning signals.

Subjective probability The person's subjective interpretations of the probability of an outcome, which may differ from the frequency based on objective statistics or the known properties of a gamble.

Subjectively expected utility (SEU) The sum of the amount of each outcome of a gamble, multiplied by the subjective probability that it will occur.

Substantia nigra (SN) A midbrain region involved in the control of motor behavior. Loss of dopamine neurons of the substantia nigra occurs in the movement disorder called Parkinson's disease.

Subthalamic nucleus (STN) The subthalamic nucleus is in the back of the substantia nigra. Damage to the subthalamic nucleus in humans leads to hemiballismus, a syndrome of violent or dance-like movements. Lesions of this nucleus in cocaine-addicted animals may turn them into overeaters.

Sympathetic nervous system A part of the autonomic nervous system, containing neurons that release norepinephrine. Actions of the sympathetic nervous system typically oppose the actions of the other division of the autonomic nervous system, the parasympathetic division.

Synapse The contact point where a neuron transfers information to a target cell.

Temporal lobe The superior portion of the temporal lobe contains the primary auditory cortex and other auditory regions; the inferior portion contains regions devoted to complex visual functions. In addition, some regions of the superior temporal sulcus receive a convergence of input from the visual, somatosensory, and auditory sensory areas.

Thalamus The two thalami lie each beneath one side of the cerebral hemispheres. They act as a relay between sensory information and regions of the cerebral cortex and play an important role in motor control. In addition, recurrent cortico-thalamo-cortical volleys of impulses are thought to underlie conscious experience.

Tradeoff The importance of one feature of an outcome relative to that of another feature. For instance, one might give up salary to have more free time in a job if the latter is more important.

Tryptophan Tryptophan is an amino acid that is essential in human nutrition.: It is also a precursor for serotonin, and its depletion causes decision-making deficits. Tryptophan is plentiful in chocolate, oats, bananas, dried dates, milk, cottage cheese, meat, fish, turkey, and peanuts.

Utility The subjective worth of an outcome.

Utility function A utility function indicates the subjective worth of particular levels of an outcome inferred from choices between risky gambles.

Value function In standard forms of decision theory, a value function indicates the subjective worth of different levels of an outcome inferred from choices in the absence of risk. However, in many behavioral decision models, such as prospect theory, the term also is used to denote the subjective worth of outcomes inferred from risky choices. The book uses the term in the latter sense to distinguish it from utilities, inferred from neoclassical economic models, such as expected utility.

Ventral striatum (VS) The ventral striatum includes the olfactory tubercle and the nucleus accumbens, which is the region where the putamen and the head of the caudate nucleus fuse. It plays an important role in the generation of signals, which enable learning.

Ventral tegmental area (VTA) The ventral tegmental area is a part of the tegmentum, and midbrain, medial to the substantia nigra. Its dopaminergic neurons project to limbic structures, such as the nucleus accumbens (NA) and amygdala, as well as associated cortical structures, such as the prefrontal cortex (PFC). The projection to the NA is believed to regulate the rewarding properties of a wide variety of stimuli, including drugs of abuse. The projection to the PFC may gate goal changes, which produce motivated actions.

Ventromedial prefrontal cortex (VMPFC) The ventromedial prefrontal cortex is the part of frontal cortex that lies toward the midline. It overlaps with the orbitofrontal cortex (OFC). It plays a role in processing information about past punishments and rewards. Signals from this area of the brain may be associated with the unconscious emotional responses that are registered as "gut feelings" or intuition.

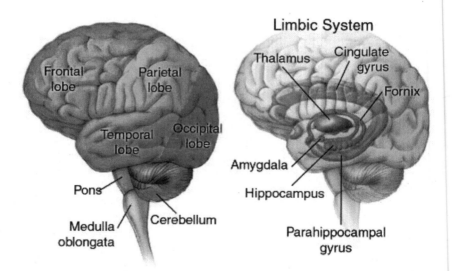

Figure A–1 The cortex and limbic system (www.ahaf.org/alzdis/about, reprinted with permission from the Alzheimer's Association of America).

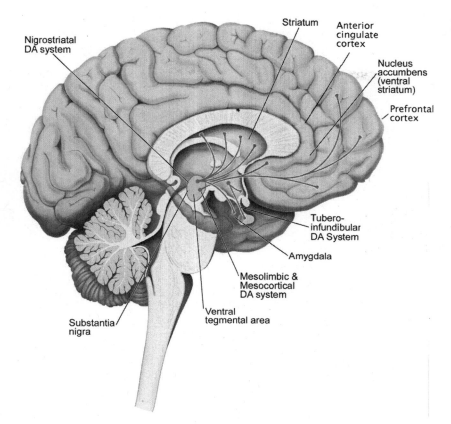

Figure A–2 Some key circuits and structures involved in decision and action. (Zabo, S. T., Gould, T. D., & Manji, H. K. (2004). Neurotransmitters, receptors, signal transduction, and second messengers in psychiatric disorders. In A. F. Schatzberg & C. B. Nemeroff (Eds.), *American Psychiatric Publishing Textbook of Psychopharmacology* (3rd ed., pp. 3–52). Washington, DC: American Psychiatric Press. Retrieved from http://www.wellesley.edu/Chemistry/Chem101/brain)

Notes

1. http://www.math.tamu.edu/~dallen/masters/egypt_babylon/babylon.pdf.
2. Damasio (1995)
3. Ibid.
4. Glimcher (2003).
5. Cacioppo, Berntson, Lorig, Norris, and Rickett (2003).
6. Montague, Dayan, and Sejnowski (1996); Schultz and Dickinson (2000).
7. Gehring and Willoughby (2002); Knutson, Fong, Bennet, Adams, and Hommer (2003); Platt and Glimcher (1999).
8. Camerer, Loewenstein, and Prelec (2004); Dickhaut et al. (2003); Johnson (2005); Weber (2006).
9. Camerer (2003); Delgado, Frank, and Phelps (2005); McCabe, Houser, Ryan, Smith, and Trouard (2001); Sanfey, Rilling, Aaronson, Nystron, and Cohen (2003).
10. Kahneman, Diener, and Schwartz (1999).
11. Berridge (1999), p. 525; Shizgal (1999).
12. Bechara and Damasio (2002).
13. Ernst et al. (2003); Robbins (2003); Rogers et al. (1999); Bernheim, and Rangel (2004).
14. Nestler and Self (2002); Paulus (2005).
15. Sometimes, efficacy research uses controlled, randomized clinical trials to assess the value of a technology. Other times, it uses economic decision theory to assess the value of technologies under ideal circumstances (Fryback, 1983).
16. Mandelblatt, Fryback, Weinstein, Russell, and Gold (1997).
17. The efficacy model applies to human performance as well as to diagnostic tests because the quality of a test derives not merely from the test results but also from the skill of at least one human being who interprets the results (e.g., the physician). In the analysis of diagnostic tests, their quality often is determined by averaging the performance measures of a test across the different humans who use it. For instance, multiple radiologists may judge whether a tumor is present in a mammogram; one averages across all their interpretations to estimate the accuracy of the test. However, in the evaluation of human capacities, one averages test performance measures across many applications of a test by the same person (e.g., seeing how accurately a particular radiologist interprets the mammograms). The neuroeconomic approach similarly seeks to determine the performance of a human by averaging her performance across multiple tests. In theory, the

155

approach would resemble averaging several questionnaire items that measure a particular judgment skill, to determine the person's ability in a particular area.

18. Although some of these concepts are not typically addressed in economic models, they are consistent with the economic concepts of rationality.

19. Suppose that S is a measure of the stimulus. D is an event, such as danger. Deniro's diagnostic efficacy depends on the extent to which he appropriately revises his estimates of danger after seeing a stimulus (see Figure 2–1a). The degree of revision is determined by the likelihood ratio: LR = P(S|D)/P(S|not D) when the person is exposed to the stimulus. The LR represents the extent to which a person experiences a change in beliefs about the likelihood of danger (D) after exposure to an informative stimulus. More specifically,

(1) the LR = (the posterior odds of D given S)/(the prior odds of D)
= {P [D|S]/(1 − P (D|S))]/[p/(1 − p)] where p = Pr(D)}.

20. Usher, Cohen, Servan-Schreiber, Rajkowski, and Aston-Jones (2000).

21. McClure, Gilzenrat, and Cohen (2006).

22. Ledoux (1996).

23. That is, he may feel unduly certain that there is an increased risk of danger when he believes some increased risk exists. Or he may feel unduly certain that there is no danger when he believes a decreased risk of danger exists. Conversely, he may be underconfident a not revise his estimates of the likelihood of danger enough.

24. Wiedmann, Paulie, and Dengler (2001).

25. More broadly, management efficacy also involves the ability to convert unconscious biases into automatic actions.

26. Such evaluations are likely to involve not merely outcomes but outcomes weighted by their probability of occurrence.

27. Bechara and Damasio (2002); Bechara, Dolan, and Hindes (2002).

28. Bernstein, Newman, Wallace, and Luh (2000); Hollander, Posner, and Cherkasky 2002).

29. vonWinterfeldt and Edwards (1986).

30. Mayer, Salovey, and Caruso (2000a, 2000b).

31. In a cost-effectiveness analysis, one divides the cost of information by the expected value of sample information (EVSI). An incremental cost-effectiveness model considers the added benefit of a departure from one's default strategy, such as habitual action compared with the added "cost" in terms of time or effort. Their ratios would guide priorities for attending to the stimuli with the most value in enabling appropriate actions.

32. Cost-effectiveness applies not merely to perception but also to other functions, such as action. For example, people must decide whether a particular action should be taken in lieu of actions one might take to solve other problems. For example, Deniro clearly could save his life by attending to the possible danger from the mobster. So he would likely do this before attending to something less important, like his income taxes.

33. Kroeze and vanden Hout (2000).

34. Gorman, Kent, Sullivan, and Coplan (2000).

35. In particular, the lack of inhibition of the ventromedial caudate may account for the failure of patients with OCD to inhibit persistent attention to stimuli that would ordinarily be ignored (Berthier, Kulesevski, Gironelli, & Lopez, 2001).

36. Manoach (2002).

37. Walton, Ruderbeck, Bannerman, et al. (2006).

38. De Quervain, Fishbacher, Treyer, et al. (2004).
39. Ibid.
40. King-cassas, Tomlin, Anen, et al. (2005).
41. McCabe et al. (2001).
42. Hill and Sally (2002).
43. Lilenfeld and Penna (2000).
44. This aspect of outcome efficacy involves the extent to which one can experience simulated pleasures ordinarily experienced with certain simulated outcomes. Although management efficacy also involves simulation, it is determined by whether or not simulations can change actions and not the extent of their hedonic effects.
45. Jevons (1871).
46. Pirsig (1991).
47. Berns, Chappelow, and Cekic (2006).
48. Event-related potentials (ERPs) are electrical potentials measured at the scalp that are small relative to EEG activity. They are so small that they usually cannot be discriminated from noise on any single trial in which a stimulus is presented for evaluation. But they can be seen using techniques known as digital filtering and ensemble averaging across repeated trials.
49. Shizgal (1999).
50. Knutson, Taylor, Kaufman, Peterson, and Glover (2005).
51. Lucas, Clark, Georgellia, and Diener (2003).
52. Woody Allen, *Love and Death* (1975).
53. vonWinterfeldt and Edwards (1986).
54. Pliskin, Shepard, and Weinstein (1980).
55. Volkow, Chang, Wang, et al. (2001).
56. Delgado, Locke, Stenger, and Flez (2003).
57. To my knowledge, no experiments have attempted to correlate multiattribute utility tradeoffs with patterns of neural activity. However, one might test whether the structures, which respond not merely to the valence of reward but also to its magnitude, better reflect the quantitative tradeoffs (e.g., dorsal striatum).
58. Baunez, Dias, Cador, and Amarlik (2005).
59. Denk, Walton, Jennings, et al. (2005).
60. The economic model asserts that the probabilities and outcomes are combined by a multiplication rule, but further research is needed to clarify how such combination occurs at a neural level. Several neural network models have addressed the issue in other contexts (Bugmann, 1991, 1992).
61. This is called the "law of large numbers."
62. Bechara, Damasio, and Damasio (2003).
63. Whether or not this hunch enables decisions without conscious recognition has been the subject of some recent debate (Maia & McClelland, 2004).
64. Wagar and Thagard (2004).
65. However, the Iowa group contended the preceding experiment did not adequately explain data on the skin conductance responses (SCRs; Bechara, Damasio, Tranel, & Damasio, 2005; Maia & McClelland, 2004).
66. North and O'Carroll (2001).
67. One study suggested that the SCR magnitude appeared to be related to the magnitude of experienced outcomes but not to the riskiness of gambles. Yet, the study implicitly assumed that the SCRs could only bias people away from the selection of bad decks and not toward good decks (Tomb, Hauser, Dedlin, & Caramazza, 2002).
68. Batson and Engel (1999).

69. Knutson and Peterson (2005).
70. Knutson et al. (2005).
71. People will also pay surprising little for a gamble with an infinite expected value
    that is extended indefinitely in time. Daniel Bernoulli once asked people how
    much they would be willing to pay to play a game in which a coin is repeatedly
    tossed until a head appears. The game would give the player $2 if head appears
    on the first toss, $2^2 = 4 on the second, $2^3 = 8 on the third and so on, ad
    infinitum. Rarely would people pay more than $4 to play such a game. But the
    game actually offers a .5 chance of winning $2, a $.5^2 = .25$ chance of winning 2^2
    $= 4, a $.5^3 = .125$ chance of winning $2^3 = 8 and so on. Hence, if the game is
    continued ad infinitum, its expected value is

    $$.5\ (\$2) + .25(\$4) + .125(\$8) +\ldots = \$1 + \$1 + \$1 +\ldots = \text{infinity}.$$

    The fact that people usually prefer a small certain amount of money over this
    gamble, which has infinite expected value, has been termed the "St. Petersburgh
    paradox." The paradox has been used to argue that people do not follow an
    expected value strategy. Alternative explanations also have been offered to explain
    the St. Petersburgh paradox—for example, the fact that a game cannot be contin-
    ued ad infinitum or that a lottery commission would be unable to actually pay
    the maximum possible prize. For a summary, see Neuman and Politser (1992).
72. A person who wishes to play larger stakes gambles, with equal expected value, is
    also more risk-seeking. For instance, if a person is offered a choice whether or not
    to play a gamble involving a 50:50 chance to win or lose $10, depending on the flip
    of a coin, both options will have an expected value of zero. Yet the risk-seeking
    individual will want to play the gamble and the risk-averse individual will not.
       Likewise, a person who prefers to gamble for larger, rather than smaller,
    stakes with the same expected values is more risk-seeking than risk-averse. Such
    a person, for example, would prefer a risky chance to win a large amount of
    money—say, a 10% chance of winning $100 (otherwise to win nothing)—over a
    50% chance to win $20 (otherwise to win nothing). In both cases, the expected
    value—the amount one would win in the long run with repeated plays of the
    gamble—is the same $10, but the amount of risk is greater in the first gamble
    (i.e., one stands to win more, but the chances of winning nothing are 90%).
73. Platt and Glimcher (1999).
74. McCoy and Platt (2005).
75. Fishbein, Eldreth, Hyde, et al. (2005).
76. Bayer, Delgado, Grinband, Hirsch, and Weber (2006).
77. Rogers (2003).
78. Preuschoff, Bossaerts, and Quartz (2006a, 2006b).
79. Mohr, Biele, Krugel, Li, and Heekerin (2007)
80. Rogers, Tunbridge, Bhaqwagar, et al. (2003).
81. Rogers et al. (1999). The more common type of dominance that has been studied
    involves the outcomes. For instance, if you are offered a choice between a 60%
    chance to win $10 (otherwise zero) and a 60% chance to win $5 (otherwise $0),
    you are better off with the first option if you win and no worse off than the sec-
    ond option if you lose. By this definition, the first option dominates the second.
    If you fail to choose it, you are not seeking greater risk; rather, you are violating
    a basic principle of rational choice.
82. Rogers et al. (1999).

83. As the probability of winning increases beyond .5, the expected value of the gamble increases and the variance of the gamble $[(x - y)^2 p(1 - p)]$ actually decreases, since $p(1 - p)$ is maximal at $p = .5$. One might expect that normal subjects would increase their bets both to gain more money on average and to reach a higher, more preferred level of risk.

84. The same unawareness could also prevent them from increasing their gambles when the probability of winning rises.

85. Mavaddat, Kirkpatrick, Rogers, and Sahakian (2000).

86. Preuschoff et al. (2006a, 2006b).

87. Ledoux (1996).

88. Lerner and Keltner (2000); Nielen, Veltman, de Jong, Mulder, and den Boer (2002).

89. Preuschoff et al. (2006a, 2006b).

90. Politser (1991a); vonWinterfeldt and Edwards (1986).

91. Although this section illustrates its use in determining subjects' performance according to an expected utility model, it could also be based on alternative, nonexpected utility models, as discussed in chapter 5.

92. Each deck had 40 cards: 20 with a black face and 20 with a red face. When subjects play every 10 cards from deck A over the course of trials, they gain $1,000, but they also encounter five unpredictable punishments ranging from $150 to $350, bringing the total loss to $1250. When subjects play every 10 cards from deck B, they gain $1,000, but they also find one big punishment for $1250. The net loss from these "disadvantageous" decks is $250. By contrast, when subjects play every 10 cards from deck C or D, they obtain a gain of only $500, but the losses also are also smaller, that is, $250 (ranging from $25 to $75 in deck C and one $250 loss in deck D). These "advantageous decks" yield a net gain of $250.

93. Tranel, Bechara, and Denburg (2002).

94. When the gambles described above were presented, the SCRs in response to the actual outcomes were measured as the 5-s interval immediately after a choice was made and the outcome of the gamble was displayed on the computer screen. The anticipatory SCRs were taken during the subsequent period, which varied in duration but averaged 5 s, before the next choice was made.

    One possible issue in using the experienced and anticipatory SCRs as measures of discrete psychological processes is that, in theory, the experiential SCRs may not have completely decayed by the time that the anticipatory SCRs for the next choice have begun. The hypothesis that one may have affected the other was tested and disconfirmed for the methods used by Tranel et al. However, an alternative would be to actually estimate jointly the two partly overlapping experiential and anticipatory response functions, based upon a model of each. Future experimental studies may be able to provide such estimates. Tranel, Bechara, and Denburg (2002).

    In any case, note that the SCR measurements in the Tranel et al. study were derived from a computerized procedure that removed the effects of some background "noise," such as the downward drift typically observed over time in the SCRs. However, it is likely that other background influences reflected in the skin conductance levels (SCLs) will also need to be removed in order to adequately predict the anticipatory SCRs from the experienced ones. While further empirical work in this area will be needed, Nagai et al. have suggested taking the derivative of the SCLs to more adequately measure SCR (Nagai, Critchley, Featherstone, Trimble, & Dolan, 2004).

95. Given adequate data, one can compute the value of the ideal strategy from each play of the gamble. However, to illustrate the application of the measure from published aggregate data in the Tranel et al. study, I used the advantageous deck's outcome as the "ideal." With this assumption, I calculated the RP = $(EU_{avg} - EU_r)/(EU_I - EU_r)$ = $(.82 - .56)/(2.26 - .56)$ = .15 for subjects without right-sided damage and RP = $(EU_{avg} - EU_r)/(EU_I - EU_r)$ = $(.79 - .92)/(1.82 - .92)$ = $-.14$ for those with right-sided VMPFC damage.

96. Yates (1990).

97. Ibid.

98. For instance, if the objective frequency of an event is .4, the variability index, VI = $.4(.6)$ = .024. VI is maximized when the average frequency = .5, indicating maximal uncertainty; it is minimized when the average frequency = 0 or = 1.

99. Yates (1990).

100. Huettel, Mack, and McCarthy (2002).

101. Gomez-Beldarrain, Harries, Garcia-Monco, Ballus, and Grafman (2004).

102. Ibid.

103. Such children who think about the future have the ability to defer gratification by distracting themselves (Damasio, 1999; Metcalfe and Mischel, 1999).

104. In fact, Bechara found in a study comparing the decision-making skills of addicts and "normal people" that a significant number of the latter had decision-making impairments similar to those of the addicts but without the signs of neurologic impairment in the latter group (Bechara, 2001).

105. Ainslie (1992).

106. The function used is reported in Laibson (1997). A similar, alternative method is reported by Odonogue and Rabin (1999).

107. McClure, Laibson, Lowenstein, and Cohen (2004).

108. The study gave subjects a variety of choices between one immediate and one delayed reward or between two delayed rewards. The areas on fMRI which reflected the parameter β or the relative value of immediate rewards were taken to be those activated when a choice has an immediate reward as one option. These areas included midbrain dopamine systems in the limbic system and surrounding cortex: the ventral striatum, medial OFC, and medial PFC. These limbic structures and associated paralimbic cortical projections receive dense innervation from midbrain dopamine systems and are responsive to reward expectation. The areas that reflected the value of K or delayed rewards were taken to be those activated nonspecifically, since all decisions involved at least one outcome with a delayed reward. These areas, including the lateral prefrontal and parietal areas, were uniformly activated regardless of delay, but more so when subjects choose longer-term options. Moreover, the relative activities of these two sets of areas, once they are normalized by their degree of variation, actually predict whether the immediate or delayed option will be chosen.

109. Fellows and Farah (2005).

110. As has been done previously in studies of risk assessment (Fischoff, 1995).

111. Grisso et al. (2003).

112. Politser (1991a).

113. Ibid.

114. Berlin, Rolls, and Kishka (2004).

115. Sayette, Loewenstein, Kirchner, and Travis (2005).

116. Giordano, Bickel, Loewenstein, et al. (2002).

117. Bickel and Vuchinich (2002).

118. Giordano et al. (2002).

119. Ainslie (1992).

120. Monterosso, Erhman, Napier, O'Brien, and Childress (2001).

121. Kheramin, Body, and Ho (2003). The previously cited animal experiments found that under conditions of large delays, the OFC-damaged rats were actually more tolerant of delay, a fact which ordinarily would be obscured by the opposing effects of changes in risk, unless the effects of uncertainty and delay discounting are separately estimated. Also, other experiments have shown that delay and odds discounting are not equally affected by lesions to the serotonergic nervous system (Mobini, Body, Ho, et al., 2002). Further, delay and odds discounting are negatively correlated in humans. In addition, some differences in delay discounting in humans (smokers vs. nonsmokers) are not mirrored by similar changes in odds discounting (Richards, Zhang, Mitchell, & de Wit, 1999).

122. For example, using a discrete-time example, if the risk of an outcome occurring during each successive hour is p, if it has not already occurred, then the outcome is expected to occur, on average, during hour $1/p$. So, for example, if there is a $p = .5$ or 50% chance of the outcome occurring in each hour, it can be expected to occur, on average, during hour $1/(.5) = 2$—that is, during the second hour. Similarly, if there is a $p = .1$ or 10% chance, one would expect it to occur during hour $1/(.1) = 10$—that is, during the 10th hour. Since the expected delay is related to the risk of the outcome, it is likely that a person's attitude toward the risk of an outcome will be related to his attitude toward the delay in its occurrence.

123. Rogers et al. (1999).

124. Winstanley et al. found that serotonergic lesions did not cause delay discounting: however, individuals who have low serotonin-related chemicals in the urine—including many antisocial, impulsive, and aggressive individuals—have been found to discount delayed outcomes (Winstanley, Theobald, Dalley, & Robbins, (2005); and SSRI treatment normalizes delay discounting (Bickel & Vuchinich, 2002).

125. Acheson, Farrar, Patak, et al. (2006).

126. Cardinal and Cheung (2005).

127. Robbins (2003).

128. Cardinal, Pennicott, Sugathapala, Robbins, and Everitt (2001).

129. Normally, the dopamine neurons that mediate such pleasurable emotions remain active for prolonged periods when reward is delayed. But such sustained activation could not occur in rats with NA damage (Fiorillo, Tobler, & Schultz, 2003).

130. Camerer and Loewenstein (2003).

131. Van Osch, Wakker, van den Hout, and Stiggelbout (2004).

132. Bentham (1948).

133. Damasio (1999).

134. Kahneman et al. (1999).

135. Similar ratings of quality over longer periods of chronic illnesses are often used in economic analyses to determine measures of "quality adjusted life years" (Oliver, 2003).

136. Damasio (2002).

137. Redelmeier and Kahneman (1996).

138. Ibid.

139. Hsee, Zhang, and Chen (2006).

140. Gabrielli (2003).
141. Rilling, Glenn, Jairam, et al. (2005).
142. SCLs can reflect slow shifts in electrodermal activity; while SCRs reflect more rapid, transient events.
143. Sharpe (2004).
144. Although the study unfortunately did not control the amounts of the imagined gains or losses across different individuals, controlled studies of experienced evaluations in patients with VMPFC damage produce similar results. In any case, the study's methods themselves do offer an additional portal through which we may view people's evaluations of past experience.
145. Drevets (2003); Phelps (2003).
146. Also, perhaps due to dysfunction of the hippocampus and medial prefrontal cortex, they have trouble recalling other past occurrences, even when they are asked to do so (Saigh & Bremner, 1999).
147. More specifically, it reduces the bias people have to recall emotionally charged words more than neutral words, particularly the immediately preceding ones (Strange, Hurleman, & Dolan, 2003).
148. Vaiva, Ducrocq, Jezequel, et al. (2003).
149. Anxiety level and benzodiazepine use were marginally significant ($p = .05$) (Wooley and Goethe, 2005).
150. Sir Francis Bacon (1624) Apophthegms no. 36. Printed by John Haviland for H. Barret and R. Whittaker. London, England.
151. Ellsberg (1961).
152. Let us suppose that we are offered choices between two urns containing red and white balls. Urn 1 contains 50 red and 50 white balls. Urn 2 contains 100 balls but the number of red and white is unknown. You are told that you will win $1,000 if a red ball is randomly picked, otherwise you will win nothing. When asked to choose, most people prefer to draw a ball from Urn 1, since its composition is known. Given that the payoffs are the same in either choice, we can infer that your subjective probability (sp) of winning with a red ball from Urn 1 (R1) is sp(R1) > sp(R2), the subjective probability of picking a red ball from Urn 2.

   Given the same payoff amounts, suppose we now are asked to make a similar choice between either red or white from Urn 1 and will win if our chosen ball is picked. You choose red. Then, since you must either win or lose, the subjective probability of winning [sp(R1)] and losing [sp(W1)] must add to one. Thus, sp(R1) = 1 − sp(W1). Similarly, if we instead made a choice between red and white in Urn 2, and chose red, we must recognize that sp(R2) = 1 − sp(W2). Substituting these values for sp(R1) and sp(R2) into the prior equation, sp(R1) > sp(R2), we obtain:

$$sp(W2) > sp(W1).$$

   That is, we should believe that selecting a white ball from Urn 2 is more likely to win than selecting one from Urn 1. So if we are given a choice between the two urns and told that we will win if we select white, we should clearly choose Urn 2. Yet this is the urn with an ambiguous composition, and most people actually prefer selecting from the urn with the more clearly specified chance of winning, Urn 1.
153. Basili, Chateauneuf, and Fontini (2004).
154. Shafer (1976); Dempster (1964).
155. Slovic (2001).

156. Slovic, Finucane, Peters, and MacGregor (2004).
157. Berns et al. (2006).
158. Although the cited experiment did not introduce elements of uncertainty, one might expect similar activations when uncertainty is ignored and only the magnitude of the outcome considered.
159. Hsu, Bhatt, Adolphs, Tranel, and Camerer (2006).
160. Hsu and Camerer (2004).
161. Bechara (2004).
162. Bechara, Levin, Weller, and Shiv (2006).
163. For instance, state lotteries offer well-defined but very low probabilities of winning large amounts of money. Also, in the Ellsberg paradox, most people would estimate that the chance of winning when drawing from an urn with unknown composition is substantial—close to 50%. Similar uncertainties may exist when subjects estimate the chances of winning early in the IGT.
164. Hsu et al. (2006).
165. Paulus, Rogalsky, Simmons, Feinstein, and Stein (2003).
166. Nesse and Klaas (1994).
167. Yu and Dayan (2005).
168. Huettel (2005).
169. Kahneman et al. (1999).
170. Ibid.
171. Lowenstein and Schkade (1999).
172. Ibid.
173. Christensen-Szalanski (1984).
174. Loewenstein (1999).
175. Slovic (2000).
176. Slevin, Plant, Lynch, Drinkwater, and Gregory (1988).
177. Baron, Asch, Fagerlin, et al. (2003).
178. Schkade and Kahneman (1998).
179. Baron et al. (2003).
180. McClure et al. (2004).
181. Kahneman and Snell (1992).
182. Hsee et al. (2006).
183. Nisbett and Wilson (1977).
184. Although the study of sales forecasts did assess the implicit use of advice, it did so only indirectly, by inferring this from consciously stated estimates.
185. Slovic (2001).
186. Whether they follow their gut feelings in advance of conscious choice is currently unresolved (Damasio, 1995; Maia and McClelland, 2004).
187. When patients with damage to the amygdala are conditioned to expect an unconditioned stimulus, such as a shock, they do show an experienced SCR even though they do not do so for conditioned stimuli, such as monetary win (Phelps, 2003).
188. To the extent that the underanticipation of patients with right-sided VMPFC damage reflects underconfidence in actual behavior, it is consistent with observations that VMPFC-damaged subjects take longer to make a decision and with speculations that they do so due to a lack of confidence (Rogers et al., 1999).
189. Since subjects in the Iowa Gambling Task did not initially know the chances of winning or losing, they could have been slower to learn and underconfident.

That is, if the VMPFC patients had uninformative estimates of the probability of gain or loss—for example, assigning the same subjective probability to highly probable events as to highly improbable ones—then they would underestimate the chance of winning when the chances of winning were high and underestimate the chance of losing when the chance of losing was very high. When these biased estimates of probability were multiplied by the values of the outcomes and summed the result would appear to be underanticipation. However, in the previously discussed calibration studies, another group of patients with right-sided VMPFC damage actually demonstrated overconfidence rather than underconfidence in conscious probability estimates.

190. That is, if the calibration results pertained to first- rather than second-order confidence estimates (quality rather than awareness calibration).

191. Knutson et al. (2003).

192. The publications relating to valuations in different groups of substance abusers did not report all the SCR data needed for the present analysis; therefore, the experiment on VMPFC damage is used to illustrate the analysis. Tranel, Bechara, and Denburg (2002).

193. Although aggregated results across different individuals showed no significant intergroup differences, a significance might be achieved through within-subject analysis of SCR changes, which can greatly increase the discriminatory power of an analysis (Politser, 1985).

194. To verify this hypothesis, one would need not merely to test whether group differences exist in the SCR responses to each possible outcome. Rather, one could test whether differences exist across groups in the parameters of "utility functions" for each individual, which describe the pattern of reactions across all the outcomes. For instance, if the "utility function" is an exponential, such as $u(x) = A \exp(-Bx)$, then one could estimate the value of the parameter A as well as B, which is the ratio of u''/u'', proposed by Arrow and Pratt to be an index of "risk aversion," as discussed in chapter 3.

195. Rogers et al. (1999).

196. Nevertheless, Figure 4–1 displays values for experienced outcomes rather than risky prospects. And when subjects are offered the choice of a certain outcome that will be experienced immediately, as opposed to risky prospects whose possible effects can only be expectancy-related, the values for certain outcomes elicit simpler neural processing mechanisms tied to direct action. More complex mechanisms, therefore, may be needed to fully explain the apparent risk aversion of patients with VMPFC damage. In the choice of certain outcomes, activity occurs throughout neural systems involved in coordinated motor action including premotor areas, cerebellum, and various frontal and motor regions (Dickhaut et al., 2003; Cacioppo and Nusbaum, 2003).

By contrast, the evaluation of risky outcomes involve more information and elicit activity in a different set of neural structures that mediate more complex processing mechanisms and calculations. These structures include the precuneus, central sulcus, paracentral sulcus, and parietal cortices. However, even in prospective choices that involve uncertainty, differences appear to exist between responses to gains and losses. For instance, there is more orbitofrontal and left frontal pole activity when people choose between gains as opposed to losses (O'Doherty, Kringelbach, Rolls, Hornak, & Andrews, 2001).

197. Dickhaut et al. (2003).

198. The term utility function is in parentheses because, by definition, a true utility function is not directly measured but rather inferred from stated preferences.
199. Coombs (1976); Davidson, Suppes, and Siegel (1957); Miyamoto and Politser (1981).
200. Searjeant (2002).
201. Not to mention lawyers' fees or the risks to her future income if she were to be put in jail for shoplifting.
202. Kahneman and Tversky (1979).
203. This pattern of preferences represents a violation of the independence axiom. If you had these preferences, it would be equivalent to changing them capriciously, based upon completely independent events. For instance, suppose you are offered a two-stage gamble and that the chance of rain is .25. If it does not rain, you get nothing. If it does rain ($p = .25$), then you get to choose between $3,000 or a .8 chance to win $4,000. Considering the chance of rain, that two-stage gamble is the same as the choice between a .25 chance of $3,000 and a .2 chance of $4,000. So if you prefer the latter, you are changing your preference based upon an independent and irrelevant event (the rain).
204. If one prefers $3,000 for sure to a gamble that offers a .8 chance to win $4,000, otherwise nothing, then one should also prefer a two-stage gamble that offers a .25 chance to win either the $3,000 or a chance to play the gamble. But when the latter option is summarized to subjects as a choice between ($3,000, .25, 0) and ($4,000, .2), many prefer the latter gamble. This is a violation of the independence axiom.
205. Rogers et al. (1999).
206. The investigators found increased activity in the OFC for gains (vs. losses) when risky choices were compared. They found no such activity when a risky option was compared with a certain outcome (Dickhaut et al., 2003).
207. Paulus (2005).
208. Rogers et al. (1999).
209. Rottenstreich and Hsee (2001).
210. Paulus (2005).
211. Misra and Ganzini (2005).
212. Van Osch et al. (2004).
213. The loss aversion is typically evaluated at $x = 1$. Note, however, that when the exponent determining the value of the gains and losses is not the same, then changes in the scale of the outcomes—for example, using Euros instead of Dollars—could change the value of the loss-aversion coefficient. To deal with this problem, consider a model that derives the value functions from two separate sets of transformation (Kobberling & Wakker, 2005). The first transforms the monetary outcomes into "basic" magnitudes with no sign, the second into values specific to the different gain and loss functions. In the "basic" transformation:

$$u(x) = (1 - e^{-\beta x})/\beta.$$

The next major step includes a series of evaluative transformations. The authors transform the "basic" function into two functions more specific to gains and losses, such as:

$u^+(x) = (1 - e^{-\mu x})/\mu$ to describe the basic utility for gains and $u^-(x) = \lambda(e^{-\upsilon x} - 1)/\upsilon$ to describe the basic utility for losses (this could be accomplished through separate transformations to reflect the decreasing marginal value of gains (μ) and losses (*v*) and to reflect loss aversion (λ). Here the value of the loss aversion does not depend on the scale of the outcomes.

214. Rogers (2003).
215. Rogers et al. (1999).
216. Rogers (2003).
217. Camerer et al. (2004); Dickhaut et al. (2003).
218. Dickhaut et al. (2003).
219. Ursu and Carter (2004).
220. Elliott (2002).
221. Seo and Lee (2006).
222. Tom, Fox, Trepel, and Poldrack (2007).
223. For instance, if subjects evaluate each gamble individually, through the editing mechanisms of prospect theory, the initial payment to subjects of a $30 fee could, in theory, transform a 50:50 chance to gain $12 or lose $14 into a 50:50 chance to gain $42 or $16 total.
224. Tom et al. (2007).
225. Annoni, Ptak, Caldara-Schnetzer, Khateb and Pollermann (2003).
226. Linked with decreased flow in frontal and thalamic regions during the recall of a narrative (Andreasson, O'Leary, Cizadloe, et al., 1996).
227. Bechara et al. (2002).
228. Turhan, Sivers, Thomason, et al. (2004).
229. Increased self-referential interpretations also occur in borderlines and appears related to activity in the medial PFC (Kelley, Macrae, Wylan, et al., 2002).
230. Thaler (1980).
231. Ibid.
232. McNeil, Weichselbaum, and Pauker (1978).
233. Bechara and Damasio (2005).
234. Gonzalez, Dana, Koshino, and Lust (2005).
235. Ibid.
236. Ursu and Carter (2004).
237. Elliott (2002).
238. Chua, Golzalez, and Liberzon (2005).
239. Camile, Coricelli, Sallet, et al. (2004).
240. For a review, see Loewenstein and Lerner (2003).
241. Josephs et al. (1992).
242. He has a similar but separate model for regret (Bell, 1985).
243. However, they assign different importance to high or low probabilities in general (not differing for gains and losses).
244. Note that, while prospect theory uses separate decision weights for gains and losses, the weights are assumed to sum to one in the complex disappointment model. As noted earlier, that is problematic in some cases, as when the probabilities are ambiguous. However, neurobiologists will need to determine if the simpler model provides an adequate fit for practical purposes, as when the data only permit estimation of one attention weight parameter.
245. These areas include the midbrain ventral tegmental area, which lies medial to the substantia nigra and contains dopaminergic neurons that give rise to the mesocorticolimbic dopamine system. These neurons send ascending projections that innervate limbic structures, such as the NAc and amygdala,

as well as associated cortical structures, particularly the prefrontal cortex. The mesoaccumbens projection is believed to regulate the rewarding properties of a wide variety of stimuli, including drugs of abuse (Daniel, Egan, and Wolf, 2000). Note also that neurons responding to rewards also are found in other structures, including the striatum, subthalamic nucleus, dorsolateral and orbitofrontal cortex, anterior cingulate cortex, amygdala, and lateral hypothalamus (Schultz, 2002).

246. Schultz and Dickinson (2000).

247. Likewise, when a predictable lack of reward occurs, the prediction error is nil and little or no decline of dopamine neuron activity occurs when the reward does not materialize (Montague et al., 1996).

248. Ernst, Kimes, London, et al. (2003).

249. Such neurobiologic evidence of dual reward signals seems consistent not merely with disappointment theory but also with very simple economic models that explain peoples' preferences in terms of two distinct properties of gambles: the expectation of the gamble and its variance. Here the variance is similar to the psychological value of a gamble and its value as a teaching signal. The variance, then $= (x - y)^2p(1 - p)$ and is also maximal at $p = .5$.

250. Berridge (1999); Fiorillo et al. (2003).

251. At the same time, however, a stimulus that is merely uncertain—according to the definition of Fiorillo and Schultz—does not necessarily provide important information for learning. Specifically, to provide good diagnostic information, the stimulus must enable a change in decisions and improved outcomes. Also, the significance of any stimulus information depends on the structure of the task.

252. Coombs (1975).

253. Krebs, Ericksson, Webber, and Charnor (1977).

254. Glimcher (2003).

255. Bazanis, Rogers, Dowson, et al. (2002).

256. Ibid.

257. Ernst, Kimes, et al. (2003).

258. Ernst, Grant, et al. (2003).

259. Dahl (2003).

260. Chambers and Potenza (2003).

261. Ibid.

262. Spitzer (1999).

263. Rubinsztein et al. (2001); Murphy et al. (2001).

264. The constellation of structures included the left insula, inferior frontal gyrus, middle frontal gyrus, precuneus, and inferior parietal lobule. Methamphetamine-dependent subjects did have an activation in other neural structures that varied with expected value but the activations was significantly less than that seen in normal controls (Paulus et al., 2002a, 2002b).

265. Volkow (2004).

266. Volkow et al. (2004).

267. Rogers et al. (1999).

268. In the IGT, the magnitude of the outcomes also is unknown to the subjects initially.

269. Busemeyer and Stout (2002).

270. Ibid.

271. To understand the basis of this model, let us suppose that a sequence of rewards or penalties may occur during successive time intervals. The expectation at a given time t, E_t can then be written as an infinite series of the expectations for all future time intervals, discounted successively by a factor, γ. In other words:

$$E_t = \bar{E}_t + \gamma\bar{E}_{t+1} + \gamma^2\bar{E}_{t+2} + \gamma^3\bar{E}_{t+3} + \dots$$

where $\bar{E}_t$ is the reward or penalty occurring between time t and $t + 1$. Multiplying the infinite series for E_{t-1} by γ and subtracting it from the infinite series for E_t one obtains $E_{t-1} - \gamma E_t = \bar{E}_{t-1}$.

So if the change in expectation during interval $t - 1$ to t, after outcome x is:

$$\Delta E_t = E_t - E_{t-1} = a[v(x) - \bar{E}_{t-1}]$$

This can be re-expressed as:

$\Delta E_t = a[v(x) - (E_{t-1} - \gamma E_t)] = a[v(x) + \gamma E_t - E_{t-1}] = a\delta$, where δ is a learning signal.

It is interesting to compare the learning signal in the TD model with the experienced reward in the disappointment model. In the TD model, the learning signal, $\delta = v(S) - \bar{E}_{t-1}$. In the disappointment model,

$E_r = e[v(S) - EV]$, where $S = x$, the monetary reward and $E_p = -d[v(S) - EV]$ where $v(S) = y$ if S denotes a loss. Here v denotes the monetary value of the outcome and EV is the expected monetary value of a gamble with known outcomes and probabilities.

272. The parameters a, w, and θ are all estimated from these choices using maximum likelihood methods.

273. In Busemeyer and Stout's model, the parameter, a, is the rate at which changes in expectations occur. For an outcome, S, the new expectation is:

$$\Delta E_t = E_t - E_{t-1} = a[v(S) - E_{t-1}],$$

$$\text{where } v(S) = (1 - w)R(S) + wP(S),$$

where $R(S)$ is the value of the reward component of the stimulus and $P(S)$ is the penalty component; $(1 - w)$ is the weight placed on rewards and w is the weight placed on penalties. There is also another parameter θ which represents how dependent the choice is on the expectations. According to the model, when one is presented with a choice between multiple gambles, the strength of motivation for choice i is $Q_i = \exp(\theta E_i)$.

where E_i is the anticipated value of the ith choice. In a two-alternative probabilistic choice model, therefore, the probability of choosing the advantageous deck (a) is $\text{Pr(advantageous deck)} = Q_a/(Q_a + Q_d)$. So when the consistency of choice, θ, is zero, choice is random and one is as likely to choose one alternative as the next. As θ becomes very large, the most advantageous deck is chosen with near certainty. θ is therefore termed a consistency parameter. The parameters a, w, and θ are all estimated from these choices using maximum likelihood methods. Busemeyer and Stout also illustrate a possible extension of their model through a temporal discounting model. In this model, $E_t - E_{t-1} = a[v(x) + \gamma E_t - E_{t-1}]$ where γE_t reflects the future expectation subsequent to the outcome, weighted by a discount parameter γ.

274. The TD-EV model corrects an error made by some other TD models, which have been applied to preferential choice. Some of these models have assumed that the probability of making a particular choice is a simple function of the

learning signal. In other words, you will make a choice if you learned enough about its advantage on the previous trial. That is not a reasonable assumption. For example, once one learns which decks in the IGT yield the largest reward, one will continue selecting those decks for their monetary rewards, even when the learning signal is nil.

275. Hou, Adams, and Barto (1995).

276. The amount of inhibition is not the total expectation of future reward, E_{t-1}, but rather the expectation of reward between time $t-1$ and t, which is $\bar{E}_{t-1} = E_{t-1} - \gamma E_t$, where γ is a discount factor (see Figures 4-3 and 4-4).

277. Montague et al. (1996).

278. Busemeyer and Stout (2002).

279. Busemeyer, Stout, and Finn (in press).

280. The consistency parameter was significantly lower only in the cocaine abusers.

281. This asymmetric coding of positive and negative prediction errors is thought by some to be an inevitable result of the low baseline dopamine activity levels (Niv, Duff, & Dayan, 2005).

282. Accordingly, when serotonin is low, even in normal volunteers, learning is often impaired. Medications that enhance serotonin activity can improve reward learning in depressed patients, and the administration of a serotonin precursor, tryptophan, can enhance such learning among depressed patients even before their mood improves (Cohen, Weingartner, Smallberg, Pickar, & Murphy, 1982; Park et al., 2002).

283. Serotonin may alter the representation of reward in the orbital frontal cortex through associated dopamine systems that link the reward to a stimulus (Rogers et al., 2003). At the same time, while the depletion of serotonin in normal controls does appear to impair discrimination of different degrees of reward, however, such depletion does not appear to impair the discrimination of different degrees of penalty.

284. The TD models presented ascribe all such asymmetries of learning to the altered values of rewards and penalties and do not explicitly consider the different efficiencies of learning signals arising only from disappointment or elation. In the TD-EV model, once one computes the value of a stimulus, deviations from expectations are weighted equally, whether the deviations are positive or negative. If the expectation is $25 and one receives $5 more ($30), there will be the same change in expectation that there will be if one receives $5 less ($20). Yet much evidence suggests that the loss of $5 from the expectation will loom larger than the gain of $5, and that these discrepancies are the central component of the learning signal.

285. Daw and Touretzky (2002).

286. An average reward TD model explains adaptations to experienced rewards, and corresponding changes in the learning signals they convey in terms of the average past reward. In one such model, the error signal is $\delta = r(t) - (E_{t-1} - \gamma E_t) - r = r(t) - \bar{E}_{t-1} - r$, where $r(t) - \bar{E}_{t-1}$ is a phasic signal from the reward at time t and r is the average past reward rate.

The average reward model has an advantage over the previously described TD model, which uses arbitrary discounting assumptions to try to model the diminishing effects of the learning signal over time. In the latter model, no explicit link is made to the past mean levels of reward, which may not be fully reflected in the expectations. Also, the average reward adjustment has proven useful in building a more coherent theory tied to the underlying neurobiology, as described in the article by Daw and Touretzky (2002).

287. Ursu and Carter (2004).

288. Fellows (2004).

289. However, a mere deficit in reversal learning does not appear to explain the apparent deficits of male drug abusers, who often have VMPFC impairments. A study that presented explicit probabilities and minimized learning effects still found decision-making deficits in such patients (Stout, Rock, Campbell, Busemeyer, & Finn, 2005).

290. Huettel, Song, and McCarthy (2005).

291. Solomon (1980).

292. Siegel, Krank, and Hinson (1988).

293. Siegel, Hinson, Krank, and McCully (1982).

294. The Liabson model represents a more general case (2001), of which the Becker-Murphy model of advertising is a special case (Becker & Murphy, 1993).

295. The economic model of environmental cues assumes that there is a variable x that summarizes a compensatory physiological process activated by the cue. The model proposes a utility function that depends on the physiological state (x), which changes with consumption induced by the presence or absence of the cue. In the model, there are two physiologic processes that evolve over time, denoted by the superscript i: one that occurs when a red cue appears, signaling the person to consume, and one when it does not, signaling abstinence These processes grow with experience over time (Laibson, 2001).

   For an opponent process in which consumption decreases appetite, Laibson proposes a utility function: $u(a^i - \lambda x^i) + (1 - a^i)\xi$, where x^i_t is the value of the physiologic process at time t, and α^i is an indicator variable valued at 1 when cue-induced consumption occurs and 0 otherwise; λ is a scaling constant (when multiplied by λ, the physiologic process takes on values between zero and one). Also, ξ is the utility of the act that is the alternative to consumption—for example, the utility of nondrug use. Laibson, in addition, assumes an exponential discounting of future hedonic experiences.

   For a stimulatory process in which consumption increases appetite, he suggests an alternative utility function:

   $$u(a^i x^i - \lambda x^i) + (1 - a^i)\xi.$$

   He shows that the same conclusions, described next for the inhibitory process, also apply for such stimulatory processes (see Figure 4–5 in the body of the text).

296. For simplicity of explanation, the value of alternative activities is assumed to be zero here. But the same arguments will apply when it is not zero (see Figure 4–5).

297. Some evidence suggests that, while opponent processes mediating tolerance and withdrawal operate during the process of addiction itself, different processes may operate when people have been abstinent for prolonged periods. In such cases, imagining drug use often has proponent, drug-like effects (Nestler & Self, 2002).

298. Implicitly, this model assumes that the incremental utility between use and nonuse is related to wanting; whereas, the incremental utility between use and the original status quo [$u(0)$] determines satisfaction. This assumption is potentially testable.

299. Tecott (2000).

300. Although Berridge has suggested that other neural receptors—such as opiate and GABA receptors—may have more to do with such experienced evaluations (Berridge, 2003).

301. For example, overexpression of CREB may lead to increased dynorphin in the nucleus accumbens, which creates dysphoria and diminishes pleasure in response to cocaine (Carlezon, 2004).

302. Piazza (2005).

303. Daw, Kakade, and Dayan (2004).

304. At the same time, Berridge questions the interpretation of cues as giving rise to negative, opponent processes, but rather sees them as a positive influence, intensifying states of wanting and sometimes even pleasure. For instance, the sight of a food may trigger salivation and other physiological changes that increase the pleasure of consuming the food. Likewise, in some cases, drug consumption may lead to sensitization which increases its effects. Such changes may be partially captured in the "excitement" which can drive risky thrill-seeking, as previously addressed by the "anxiety" model. However, they are not incompatible with the environmental cues model. In fact, Laibson examined a stimulatory process and found the same conclusions about increased "wanting" with increased drug use.

Laibson's work extends Gary Becker's theory of "rational addiction," which explains how an addict could rationally be impelled to use drugs in order to be consistent with his values. In fact, the addict may even use drugs when there is no fundamental change in values. The utility function is the same before and after the addiction. In this model, the physiologic process—the new status quo—explains why the addict's wanting increases his drug consumption.

305. Bentham (1948).

306. Ibid.

307. In the case of drug addiction, one could hypothesize that the need to prevent withdrawal symptoms is a reason for the continuance of drug-seeking behavior. But addicts still crave the drugs long after the disappearance of the withdrawal symptoms (Berridge, 1999).

308. Cabanac and Leblanc (1983).

309. Not having been told what they chose, many addicts even insisted that they had taken the salt solution rather than the cocaine (Fischman & Foltin, 1992).

310. One possible explanation for observed dissociations of action and other types of utility is that the value experienced at a particular instant does not attain consciousness. It is possible that the action tendency will more closely reflect the experienced value reported when the experienced value gains access to consciousness. Nevertheless, as discussed later, economic theory often assumes that values can be consciously stated.

311. Dayan and Balleine (2002).

312. Berridge (2003).

313. McClure, Daw, and Montague (2003).

314. Ibid.

315. The responses of the "critic" appear to be reflected sometimes also in the anterior cingulate cortex.

316. Berridge (2003).

317. Berridge (1999)

318. Montague, Hyman, and Cohen (2004).

319. Dreher, Kohn, and Berman (2006).
320. Robinson, Smith, Mizumori, and Palmiter (2005).
321. Berridge (2005).
322. Daw, Div, and Dayan (2005).
323. This reference value can be viewed as an individual-specific mean within range of values representing normal variability for serum sodium. Normal serum sodium levels range from about 136 to 145 milliequivalents per liter. If a person's values fall outside this interval, they are considered abnormal.
324. It may also reflect a special type of "experienced utility"—the immediate anticipatory value, such as the savoring, of a coming meal. The prediction can be modeled as an expectation from any of the models previously discussed—such as expected utility, disappointment theory, or even temporal discounting. Such models predict whether or not consumption of the food is likely to provide pleasure if the organism decides to select it.
325. In addition, there is a type of encoding for the normal range of variation, which developed through the course of evolution to ensure our survival. Deficient sodium levels can result in lethargy, weakness, nausea, vomiting, confusion, and even seizures. Excessive sodium levels can result in muscle irritability, respiratory paralysis, confusion, and even death. However, it is not merely the absolute levels of sodium that determine whether the person experiences these symptoms but also the rate of change of the sodium levels, as if neurons compute changes in blood sodium levels and do not merely monitor their absolute levels. The trend in sodium level would be a kind of expectation of future blood sodium levels and the person's distress when the values are too large or too small represent a kind of "disappointment"—a signal of possible error in the maintenance of physiological stability.
326. The degree of wanting even can affect the experience of a food's "saltiness." When a salty food is consumed, sensory neurons, called "salt best" neurons, fire not according to the actual concentration of sodium but according to the degree of the discrepancy between the salty food stimuli and the body's "wanting" of salt (Parrot & Schulkin, 1993).
327. Daw et al. (2005).
328. Niv, Daw, and Dayan (2006, in press); Dayan and Balleine (2002).
329. Niv et al. (2006, in press).
330. Satoh, Nakai, Sato, and Kimura (2003).
331. Dayan and Balleine (2002).
332. Goudriaan, Ooserlaan, de Beurs, and ran den Brink (2005).
333. Swanda, Haaland, and Larue (2000).
334. Fishbein et al. (2005).
335. Ibid.
336. Lopes and Oden (1999).
337. Many other alternatives to the SPA model also have been proposed. However, no consensus yet exists on the best one.
338. The decision weights apply to a range of these outcome values rather than a single outcome. The model multiplies each decision weight by the "relative value" of the outcomes—the difference in value between the reference outcome and the next smallest one. Originally, the motivation for such RDU models was that, since the decision weights in prospect theory can distort the apparent value of a gamble, their use can sometimes lead to cases in which

the model will "select" an alternative which is dominated (the "poor quality" choices, in Rogers's terminology). That fact led to considerable consternation among economists, who wished to maintain some semblance of rationality in the model's selections and who did not think that reasonable people would make such choices. Thus, the simple form of prospect theory was modified and has led to a broad variety of competing models. Unlike the simpler prospect theory model such models avoid the selection of dominated options; and they reformulate the decision weights in a broader context.

339. From a technical standpoint, the RDU models assess the decision weights only after one identifies and ranks the possible outcomes. Also, one assigns weights not to the probabilities of each outcome but to their "decumulative" probabilities. Decumulative probabilities can best be understood by analogy to the "p-values" in statistics. In t-tests, for example, one computes the p-value, or significance level, of an outcome, X, by determining the probability that X will exceed a critical value, t. Thus, one does not merely consider the chance of observing a particular value of X, but rather the probability of observing a range of potential outcomes. Similarly, in RDU theories, one finds the chance that a given outcome will be less than a particular outcome (an example is cumulative prospect theory). In decumulative probabilities, one finds the chance that an outcome will be greater than or equal to a particular value. For instance, suppose a gambling task gave us the choice between a "safe" gamble with a $p = .9$ chance of $37.50 and a .1 chance of −$87.50. One would rank the outcomes from lowest to highest. Then, in a decumulative model, one would first find the chance that the actual outcome of a gamble would be greater than or equal to the lowest value (−$87.50), which is $D_1 = 1$, and the chance that the value would be greater than or equal to the highest outcome ($37.50), which is $D_2 = .9$. The chance of exceeding the highest outcome, D_3 is 0, so we now have a 0–1 scale of decumulative probabilities. One then assigns weights $h(D_i)$ to each of these decumulative probabilities, somewhat as one did before in prospect theory, by transforming the probabilities.

340. Davies (2003).

341. Cromwell, Hassani, and Schultz (2004).

342. Data were not sufficient to determine the exact nature of the function but it was to be presumed to be similar to the range or variance.

343. Tobler, Fiorillo, and Schultz (2005).

344. Padoa-Schioppa and Asaad (2006).

345. The search for cheaper gas could make sense if we are learning to find a gas station that we would repeatedly use, if we could find a more efficient way to reach it (Thaler, 1999).

346. Ernst et al. (2003).

347. Wu (1999).

348. A more general form of Wu's model asserts that: $U =$ expected value $+ e^* p^* (1 − p)[v(x) − v(y)] − d^*(1 − p^*) p[v(x) − v(y)]$. The introduction of the value function $v(\cdot)$ allows one to assign a nonconstant marginal value for money.

349. This model resembles a quality adjusted life years model, which multiplies the length of survival by an estimate of the quality of life, although the gain and loss parameters in the anxiety model themselves may depend on the length of the time period, whereas time and quality are separate arguments in the quality adjusted life years model (Pliskin et al., 1980).

350. Wu's anxiety model might describe both expectancy and goal-related feelings but does not distinguish anticipatory and experienced feelings which may differ.

351. Note that the anxiety model provides normative rather than descriptive information. According to such model, anxious people act impulsively to diminish their anxiety; and it is economically "rational" to sacrifice future payoffs in order to decrease such distress. Such behavior is compatible with some biological responses. Through short-term mechanisms of neural change, the set point of the stress response system can be temporarily altered to maintain the higher levels of stress response. Such changes enable the organism to respond more effectively to temporary problems. After the stress is removed, and the uncertainties resolved, the system usually returns to its normal set points and emotional responses. Thus, anxiety due to a stress response can be terminated. However, when stress is inescapable and prolonged, anxiety sometimes cannot be "turned off." The stress can alter the expression of genes and alter neural structures. For instance, it may produce toxic neurotransmitters, such as glutamate, leading to shrinkage of the hippocampus. It may thereby impair the memory of contextual cues that normally modify fear responses. Chronic stresses also decrease the number of dendrites in the prefrontal cortex, which plays a role in fear extinction. Likewise, they increase the number of dendrites in the basolateral amygdala, and increase the size of the amygdala, which may increase anxiety and fear-related memories. Enlargement of the amygdala may also be related to heightened aggression and increased fear conditioning (Mcewen, 2003).

    The latter also occurs in many nondrug-related forms of associative learning (Hyman, 2002).

    Similar disturbances and long-term alterations of set point are also likely to occur in systems that mediate approach rather than avoidance. For instance, some investigators believe that the dopamine receptors that mediate craving may become sensitized in some cases of drug abuse. Such changes may result from the adaptations of nerve cells, alterations in the proteins, and even changes in the synapses that connect nerve cells. If we wish to model such changes in set point, we may therefore need alternative models, which do not assume that anxiety or craving can be effectively "turned off" once a gamble is resolved.

352. Galaverna et al. (1999).

353. Berridge (1999).

354. Bazanis et al. (2002).

355. Loewenstein and Thaler (1989).

356. For the simplest hyperbolic model, $V = v(x)/t$, the value is the average reward value per unit time.

357. Kalenscher et al. (2005).

358. In order to allow for the apparent discount rate to vary with the size of the reward, some papers have proposed a modified hyperbolic model, in which $V(x,t) = v(x)/(1 + Kt)^s$ where s is a constant and $v(x)$ is the value of the reward obtained immediately.

359. Also, although one could assign "negative discount rates" to account for such phenomena, the methods used to estimate the discount rates may give little attention to such anticipatory emotions, in part, because they typically ask people to state their preferences between immediate small rewards or larger delayed ones. Thus, they may focus peoples' attention on the receipt of the reward rather than the feelings they will have while they are waiting.

360. The benefits and costs correspond to the previously mentioned $G(t)$ and $L(t)$ functions, weighted by the amount of time spent thinking about gains versus losses [denoted $h(p)$ and $1 - h(p)$].
361. Kalenscher, Ohmann, and Gunturkun (2006).
362. McClure et al. (2004).
363. Durstewitz, Seamans, and Sejnowski (2000); Usher and McClelland (2001).
364. Feng and Li (2001).
365. Isles, Humby, and Wilkinson (2003).
366. Evenden and Ryan (1999); Winstanley, Theobald, Dalley, et al. (2005).
367. Winstanley et al. (2005).
368. Evenden and Ryan (1999).
369. Winstanley et al. (2005); Mateo, Budygin, John, and Jones (2004).
370. Likewise, when animals receive a lesion to dopamine neurons in the NAc, their time preferences do not conform well to a single-rate hyperbolic model. While these animals do have more trouble learning the value of delayed rewards, the hyperbolic model predicts that this impairment would affect the discount rates, not the form of the model. Contrary to this prediction, the dopamine lesion may instead alter the model itself by interfering with a complex system of interactions (Acheson, 2005).
371. Formulae analogous to the QALMs model derive from one compartment's activity, which is the equilibrium solution to a linear system of differential equations. The solution can be found using the command in Mathematica: DSolve $[\{x'_1[t] = \rho_1 - k_{10} x_1[t] - \beta_{21}x_2[t], x'_2[t] = \rho_2 - k_{20} x_2[t] - \beta_{12} x_1[t]\}, \{x_1[t], x_2[t]\}, t]$ a, b, c, d in the QALMs model are complex functions of the ρi, kij, and βij.

   Usher and McClelland (2001) discuss methods for preventing the solutions from taking on negative values. One may also assume that the rates vary with time and involve additional compartments. However, when one must add these and other complexities to create an adequate model, an even simpler, single rate model becomes much less likely to suffice—thus reinforcing the main point of the text.
372. Loewenstein (1987).
373. In such models, for example

$$U(b, t) = A\, H(b)[1 - \exp(-kt)] \text{ for } k > 0$$
$$U(b, t) = -A\, H(b)[1 - \exp(-kt)] \text{ for } k < 0$$

(as k approaches zero, the exponential functions approach the linear function $U(b, t) = A\, H(b)t$, which is the simplest and most widely applied form of quality adjusted life years, which assumes risk neutrality; Miyamoto, 1999).
These functions have a known axiomatic basis: Maas and Wakker (1992) showed that if survival duration is utility independent of health quality, then the function must be linear or exponential; and since linearity is implausible, it must be exponential.
374. Laibson (2006). Citation of an unpublished paper by McClure, S., Ericson D., Laibson D., Loewenstein, G., and Cohen, J. (2006).
375. Berns et al. (2006).
376. The constant term is analogous to the reaction time, such as the differences in distances traveled before the first and second drivers hit the brakes.
377. The conditions determining the form of the QALMs function derive from the following analysis. Suppose $V = V(x_1, t) = a + (b/c)(1 - \exp[-ct]) - (d/e)(1 - \exp[-et]$

Then $V' = b \exp(-ct) - d \exp(-et) = 0$ at a critical point, in which case, $t_c = (\log (b/d))/(c - e)$. The critical point is a maximum if $V'' = -bc \exp(-ct_c) + de \exp(-et_c) < 0$, which reduces to $e < c$. That is, the relation of marginal rates of change for costs and benefits (e and c) determines whether the critical point is a maximum or minimum.

In the former case, when delay aversion also is lower ($d < b$), a single peaked function (case 1 in Figure 4–10) will occur—providing that the critical point is greater than zero or $t_c = (\log (b/d))/(c - e)$ or $(\log (d/b))/(e - c) > 0$. Since $e < c$, this occurs when $d < b$.

In this case, the benefits are more important than the costs ($b > d$), and they also rise more rapidly ($c > e$), but after they approach an asymptote, the slowly rising costs cut into their advantage, gradually reducing the initial advantage of delay. The result is a single peaked function (SPF, Case 1). Note also that, while the marginal disutility (e vs. c) determines whether the critical point is a maximum, the general importance of costs versus benefits or delay aversion (d vs. b) determines whether this critical point occurs in a realistic range ($t_c > 0$). Thus, when the costs of waiting loom larger than the benefits ($d > b$), and they also rise slowly ($e < c$), leading to further, delayed reductions in utility after the benefits have neared a plateau, the costs increasingly dominate the benefits, leading to a monotone decreasing function for the realistic range of $t_c > 0$ (Case 2).

Two other conditions can arise when the critical point, t_c is a minimum rather than a maximum: that is, when $e > c$. First, the critical point $t_c < 0$ when $d < b$, and we find a monotone increasing function (Case 3). Here the costs are less important than the benefits (the delay aversion $d/b < 1$) and the benefits continue to increase once the costs have approached a plateau (since $c < e$, reflecting a low marginal change for benefits). Second, the critical point— here, a minimum—occurs at a positive t_c, when the delay aversion is initially large ($d/b > 1$). In this case, the delay aversion and increased marginal rate of change of the costs lead to an initial fall in value, followed by a more prolonged increase in benefits (due to $c < e$). This produces a single dipped function (SDF, Case 4). Coombs and Avrunin have described less-specific conditions to clarify the form that more general functions of this form will take.

378. The original study also found a better fit by adding the voltage by it to a single exponential model, rather than multiplying by it.
379. Ochsner and Gross (2004); Rogan, Leon, Perez, and Kandel (2005).
380. Mitchell (2004).
381. Ibid.
382. Malone et al. (2003).
383. Bickel and Vuchinich (2002).
384. Giordano et al. (2002).
385. Such variations can also be interpreted as a weakening of utility independence assumptions underlying some exponential QALY models. Such time-varying parameter values can sometimes be accommodated using models similar to RDU. These models also resemble the more general form of the anxiety model, and bear some similarities to nonlinear compartmental models in which the parameters themselves are time dependent.

Note also that a violation of utility independence would imply that the exponential function cannot apply. The more general form of the model, which may be related to nonlinear kinetics, for $G(t) < 0$ is

$U(b, t) = A\,H(b)\,[1 - \exp(G(t)]$. Miyamoto (1992) discusses the axiomatization of this model in a RDU framework.

Such models, in which the discount rate is not constant but a function of time is reminiscent of biophysical models, based on Michaelis-Menten kinetics, which have been used to describe many chemical interactions, such as receptor binding, which may play an important role in the generation of value. The QALMs model still can be adapted to such problems. Coombs and Avrunin (1977) have developed more general guidelines for defining whether cost and benefit functions of various forms may yield a net single peaked function or some other form.

386. The form of the preference functions illustrated still can be predicted from the shapes of the component curves using weaker mathematical assumptions, outlined by Coombs and Avrunin (1977).

387. These factors include different receptor affinities and efficacies of tissue responses, They are compatible with various models, which consider, at a far more detailed level, second messenger systems, the effects of different dopamine receptors on cyclic AMP levels, the role of NMDA as a second messenger through protein kinases which play a role in long-term potentiation and depression, as well as complex interactions between DA and glutamate systems mediated by G proteins and protein kinases. Similar models could also consider phasic and tonic activations of DA cells (Ashby & Casale, 2003).

388. Paraphrase of a quote attributed to Albert Einstein, American-born physicist, 1879–1955.

389. Note that elements of outcome efficacy, such as experienced utilities do not exist in the neoclassical economic model but can be accommodated in the more general model of Bentham.

390. Recall that according to the independence axiom, if a choice A is preferred to a gamble $G = (x,p,y)$, then (A,P,C) is preferred to (G,P,C), where p and P are probabilities. But people often switch preferences when uncertainty is added.

391. Although the result would have been stronger if changes in the individual subject's choices varied with DLPFC activity, the result still suggests that the violation of the independence axiom may not always be irrational.

392. Sanfey, Hastie, Colvin, and Grafman (2003).

393. Fishbein et al. (2005). One more sign of an independence from expectancies is the fact that the error signal emanating from the ACC after a loss (called the error related negativity, ERN) is present for small losses even when large losses might have occurred but did not (Gehring & Willoughby, 2002).

394. Berridge (2003).

395. In other experiments, however, the ACC does not simply deactivate when one satisfies goals but also activates somewhat in response to rewards . Such findings could be consistent with the view that goal-aspiration is not a simple all-or-none phenomenon. Rather, people may treat some aspiration levels in a manner similar to the reference point in prospect theory. Thus, below-aspiration outcomes are treated as losses, and loom much larger than gains, but gains may still have some value. Such a theory would be supported by findings that losses loom larger than gains in recordings of error in the ACC (Heath, Larrick, & Wu, 1999; Rushworth, Walton, Kennerley, & Bannerman, 2004).

396. Neurobiologic research is already uncovering neural mechanisms underlying addition, subtraction, multiplication, and division (Grossberg, 2000a, 2000b, 2000c; Romo and Salinas, 2003).

397. Machens, Romo, and Brody (2005).
398. Although the application involved dopamine modulation of attention rather than anticipated reward, the basic principles for studying the latter should be similar (Ashby & Casale, 2003).
399. Ashby and Casale (2003).
400. Payne, Bettman, and Johnson (1993).
401. Although the evidence concerning left and right brain functions is not entirely consistent (Wohlford, Miller, and Gazzaniga, 2000).
402. Rushworth et al. (2004).
403. In fact, the latter structures appear also associated not only with differences in the way we evaluate risky or ambiguous gambles but also in the way we assess familiar or unfamiliar foods. For instance, monkeys with bilateral amygdala or OFC lesions have less consistent preferences over time for unfamiliar foods (Baylis and Gaffin, 1991). However, the same is not true for familiar foods, suggesting that additional neural structures also may "back-up" and preserve well-established preferences (Fellows, 2004).
404. Yu and Dayan (2005).
405. One may question, then whether the loss of the ability to distinguish ambiguity versus risk in OFC-damaged patients is related to their inability to change learned contingencies, which appears to account for much of their poor performance on the IGT, a task involving ambiguous probabilities. If so, then the quality of learning may not be adequately measured by TD models, which do not distinguish ambiguity and risk.
406. Loewenstein and O'Donoghue (2005).
407. Hollander (2002).
408. Rogan et al. (2005).
409. Furthermore, the latter component may have dual effects. First, it could moderate the extent of loss aversion through an effect on fear-learning systems. Second, due to an effect on pleasure systems. it could independently affect other model components, including decision weights or marginal utilities.
410. Daw et al. (2005).
411. Bernheim and Rangel (2004).
412. Politser (1991c).
413. Walton, Rudebeck, Bannerman, and Rushworth (2007).
414. Kant (1959).
415. The latter brain areas are older regions that are thought to mediate evolutionary or culturally learned biases that favor or oppose particular types of actions. Thus, some scientists have questioned whether deontological judgments really reflect the "rationalist" consideration of principles advocated by philosophers such as Kant, or whether they really reflect a basic emotional response that is subsequently rationalized. When difficult moral judgments are made, ACC activation could reflect not only an effort to resolve the conflict between principle and calculation but also to rationalize emotional judgments (Greene, Nystrom, Engell, Darley, and Cohen 2004; Greene, Sommerville, & Nystrom, 2001). Such interesting and provocative suggestions have already contributed to a lively debate among philosophers in the growing field of "neuroethics."
416. Greene et al. (2001, 2004).
417. Bleichrodt, Diecidue, and Quiggin (2004).

418. For instance, people can reduce regret by comparing their own bad experiences with those of others who obtained even worse outcomes (Harreveld and van der Pligt, 2003).
419. Fellows (2004).
420. For example, suppose that an experiment shows the person a gamble, and then asks him or her if he or she wishes to place a bet on it (analogous to the Rogers Gambling tasks). Hypothetically, suppose that one then measured the percent of "correct" choices of positive expected value gambles. Then, if such gambles are much more frequent than negative expected value gambles, one person could be more accurate than another merely choosing to gamble more often, then the second person is a more conservative bettor but can better discriminate the positive from the negative expected value bets.
421. Nesse and Klaas (1994).
422. Drevets et al. (1997).
423. Rogers et al. (2003).
424. Rogers, Lancaster, Wakeley, and Bhagwagar (2004).
425. We have discussed learning in the section on effectiveness, since most learning models are non-economic.
426. Hsee, Zhang, Yu, and Xi (2003); Wilson, Hodges, and LaFleur (1995).
427. McClure, Berne, and Montague (2003).
428. When action occurs and is linked to an unpredictable outcome, the caudate is activated. Since the caudate is also activated when there is no such linkage but time pressure exists in making a response, Delgado suggests that it is the perception of whether a linkage to action exists which determines caudate response and that the caudate reflects reinforcement of action, not rewards per se. Tricomi, Delgado, and Fiez (2004).
429. Structures in the rat which are analogous to the human VMPFC send projections to serotonin neurons in the dorsal raphe. Parts of it indirectly inhibit serotonin neurons in the dorsal raphe, which are involved in the stress response (Robbins, 2005).
430. Slovic (2001).
431. Stone, Cosmides, Tooby, Kroll, and Knight (2002).
432. Brett, Johnsrude, and Owen (2002).
433. McClure et al. (2004).
434. Sayette et al. (2005).
435. Seo and Lee (2006); Tom et al. (2007).
436. Knutson et. al. (2007).
437. vonWinterfeldt and Edwards (1986).
438. For example, suppose that we use the exponential form of the value function suggested by Kahneman and Tversky. Then the neural activity measure as a function of x would be $V = \log v(x)$ and $V(-x) - V(x) = \log |v(-x))| -\log v(x) = \log (\lambda(x\beta loss/x\beta gain)) = L + (\beta loss - \beta gain)X$, where $L = \log \lambda$ and $X = \log x$. In this case, the value $(\beta loss - \beta gain)$ would reflect the relative curvatures of the behavioral value functions, and only the intercept of the regression would be related to loss aversion (i.e., its logarithmically transformed value (L)).
439. For example, the sensory correlates of the direction an arrow is pointing appeared to be reflected in the lingual gyrus in one study and unrelated to subject evaluations or choices (Robbins & Everitt, 1992).

440. Shiv, Loewenstein, Bechara, Damasio, and Damasio (2005).
441. Nesse (2004).
442. Rottenstreich and Hsee (2001); Johnson, Bayer, Brodscholl, and Weber (2005).
443. Ledoux (1996).
444. Hsee et al. (2003); Wilson et al. (1995).
445. Loewenstein (1987).
446. Denk et al. (2005).
447. Rorie and Newsome (2005).
448. Camerer et al. (2004).
449. Lakshminarayanan, Chen, and Santos (2006).
450. Marsh and Kacelnik (2002); Real (1996).
451. Brosnan and de Waal (2003).
452. An economic decision analysis could consider one option as "doing nothing but sitting and reminiscing." However, any customary analysis would have difficulty explaining how a good choice provides benefit not merely in its substantive future outcomes but also in the pleasurable recollection that a good choice was made. Such pleasure can be the mirror-image of postdecisional regret, which is usually excluded from economic analysis and its consideration in decisions is generally taken to be "irrational." The ability to recall past outcomes unrelated to one's actions adds yet another layer of complexity to the value of reminiscence, which is not considered in economic analysis.
453. Schkade and Kahneman (1998).
454. The question then arises: If people adapt to good outcomes and have happiness set points that often do not depend on outcomes, does this mean that efforts to improve welfare are futile? One answer suggested to this question is that such efforts are not futile if we can improve objective happiness—the average instantaneous happiness, a factor that may be ignored if satisfaction only is measured.
455. This description is adapted from Morais (1995).
456. Ryan and Deci (2001).
457. Rescher (1993).
458. Kubovy (1999).
459. Nash (1938).

References

Acheson, A. (2005). *The role of the nucleus accumbens in reinforcer discounting*. Unpublished dissertation submitted to the graduate school of the State University of New York at Buffalo. Department of Psychology, State University of New York at Buffalo, Buffalo, NY.

Acheson, A., Farrar, A., Patak, M., Hausknecht, K., Kieres, A. K., Choi, S., et al. (2006). Nucleus accumbens lesions decrease sensitivity to rapid changes in the delay to reinforcement. *Behavioural Brain Research, Brain Res. 173*, 217–228.

Ainslie, G. (1992). *Picoeconomics: The strategic interaction of successive motivational states within the person (Studies in rationality and social change)*. Cambridge, MA: Cambridge University Press.

Allen, W. (Director) (1975). *Love and Death*. Jack Rollins, J. and Charles H. Joffe Productions, USA.

Andreasson, N., O'Leary, D., Cizadloe, T., Arndt, S., Rezai, K., Ponto, L. L., et al. (1996). Schizophrenia and cognitive dysmetria: A positron emission tomography study of dysfunctional prefrontal-thalamic-cerebellar circuitry. *Proceedings of the National Academy of Sciences of the United States of America, 93*, 9985–9990.

Annoni, J., Ptak, R., Caldara-Schnetzer, A., Khateb, A., & Pollermann, B. Z. (2003). Decoupling of autonomic and cognitive emotional reactions after cerebellar stroke. *Annals of neurology, 53*, 654–658.

Ashby, F. G., & Casale, M. (2003). A model of dopamine-modulated cortical activation. *Neural Networks, 16*, 973–984.

Baron, J., Asch, A., Fagerlin, A., Jepson, C., Loewenstein, G., Riis, J., et al. (2003). Effect of assessment methods on the discrepancy between judgments of health disorders people have and do not have. *Medical Decision Making, 23*, 422–434.

Basili, M., Chateauneuf, A., & Fontini, F. (2004). *Choices under ambiguity with familiar and unfamiliar outcomes*. Working paper, Department of Economics, University of Siena, Siena, Italy.

Batson, C., & Engel, C. (1999). Value Judgments: Testing the somatic-marker hypothesis using false physiological feedback. *Personality and Social Psychology Bulletin, 25*, 1021–1032.

Baunez, C., Dias, C., Cador, M., & Amarlik, M. (2005). The subthalamic nucleus exerts opposite control on cocaine and "natural" rewards. *Nature Neuroscience, 8*, 484–489.

Bayer, H., Delgado, M., Grinband, J., Hirsch, J., & Weber, E. (2006). *Neural substrates of risky decision making.* Paper presented at the 2006 Annual Meeting of the Society for Neuroeconomics, Park City, UT.

Baylis, L., & Gaffin, D. (1991). Amygdalectomy and ventromedial prefrontal ablation produce similar deficits in food choice and in simple object discrimination in experimental learning for an unseen reward. *Experimental Brain Research, 86,* 617–622.

Bazanis, E., Rogers, R., Dowson, J., Taylor P., Meux, C., & Staley, C., et al. (2002). Neurocognitive deficits in decision-making and planning of patients with DSM-III-R borderline personality disorder. *Psychological Medicine, 32,* 1395–1405.

Bechara, A. (2001). Neurobiology of decision-making: Risk and reward. *Seminars in Clinical Neuropsychiatry, 6,* 205–216.

Bechara, A. (2004). The role of emotion in decision-making: Evidence from neurological patients with orbitofrontal damage. *Brain and Cognition, 55,* 30–40.

Bechara, A., & Damasio, A. (2005). The somatic marker hypothesis: A neural theory of economic decision. *Games and Economic Behavior, 52,* 336–372.

Bechara, A., & Damasio, H. (2002). Decision-making and addiction (part I): Impaired activation of somatic states in substance-dependent individuals when pondering decisions with negative future consequences. *Neuropyschologica, 40,* 1675–1689.

Bechara, A., Damasio, H., & Damasio, A. (2003). The role of the amygdala in decision-making. *Annals of the New York Academy of Sciences, 985,* 356–369.

Bechara, A., Damasio, H., Tranel, D., & Damasio, A. R. (2005). The Iowa Gambling Task and the somatic marker hypothesis: Some questions and answers. *Trends in Cognitive Sciences, 9,* 159–162.

Bechara, A., Dolan, S., & Hindes, A. (2002). Decision-making and addiction (part II): Myopia for the future or hypersensitivity to reward? *Neuropsychologica, 40,* 1690–1705.

Bechara, A., Levin, I., Weller, J., & Shiv, B. (2006). *The neural basis of decisions under uncertainty: Separate systems for choice under ambiguity and uncertainty (2005).* Paper presented at the Annual Meeting of the Society for judgment and decision making, Toronto, Canada.

Becker, G., & Murphy, K. (1993). A simple theory of advertising as a good or bad. *Quarterly Journal of Economics, 108,* 941–964.

Bell, D. (1985). Disappointment in decision-making under uncertainty. *Operations Research, 33,* 1–27.

Bentham, J. (1948). *An introduction to the principles of morals and legislation.* Oxford, UK: Blackwell (originally published in 1789).

Berlin, H., Rolls, E., & Kishka, U. (2004). Impulsivity, time perception, emotion and reinforcement sensitivity in patients with orbitofrontal cortex lesions. *Brain, 127,* 1108–1126.

Bernheim, D., & Rangel, A. (2004). Addiction and cue triggered decision processes. *American Economic Review, 94,* 1558–1590.

Berns, G., Chappelow, J., & Cekic, M. (2006). Neurobiologic substrates of dread. *Science, 312,* 754–758.

Bernstein, A., Newman, J. P., Wallace, J. F., & Luh, K. E. (2000). Left hemisphere activation and deficient response modulation in psychopaths, *Psychological Science, 11,* 414–418.

Berridge, K. (1999). Pleasure, pain, desire and dread: Hidden core processes of emotion. In Kahneman, D., Diener, E., & Schwartz, N. (Eds.), *Well-being: The foundations of hedonic psychology* (p. 525). New York: Russell Sage Foundation.

Berridge, K. (2003). Irrational Pursuits: Hyper-incentives from a visceral brain. In Brocas, I. & Carrillo, J. (Eds.), *The psychology of economic decisions: Volume 1 Rationality and well-being* (pp. 17–40). Oxford: Oxford University Press.

Berridge, K. (2005). Hold the dopamine Espresso reward learning, hold the dopamine theoretical comment on Robinson et al. *Behavioral Neuroscience, 119*, 336–341.

Berthier, M. L., Kulesevski, J. J., Gironelli, A., & Lopez, A. L. (2001). Obsessive-compulsive disorder and traumatic brain injury: Behavioral, cognitive and neuroimaging findings. *Neuropsychiatry, Neuropsychology, and Behavioral Neurology, 14*, 23–31.

Bickel, W. K., & Vuchinich, R. E. (2002). *Reframing health behavior change with behavioral economics*. Mahwah, NJ: Lawrence Erlbaum Associates.

Bleichrodt, H., Diecidue, E., & Quiggin, J. (2004). Equity weights in the allocation of health care: The rank-dependent QALY model. *Journal of Health Economics, 23*, 157–171.

Brett, M., Johnsrude, I., & Owen, A. (2002). The problem of functional localization in the human brain. *Nature Reviews. Neuroscience, 3*, 243–249.

Brosnan, S., & de Waal, F. (2003). Monkeys reject unequal pay. *Nature, 425*, 297–299.

Bugmann, G. (1991). Summation and multiplication: Two distinct operation domains of leaky integrate-and-fire neurons. *Network, 2*, 489–509.

Bugmann, G. (1992). Multiplying with neurons: Compensation for irregular input spike trains by using time dependent synaptic efficiencies. *Biological Cybernetics, 68*, 87–92.

Busemeyer, J. R., & Stout, J. C. (2002). A contribution of cognitive decision models to clinical assessment: Decomposing performance on the Bechara gambling task. *Psychological Assessment, 14*, 253–262.

Busemeyer, J., Stout, J., & Finn, P. (in press). Using computational models to help explain decision-making processes of substance abusers. In Barch, D. (Ed.), *Cognitive and affective neuroscience of psychopathology*. Oxford, UK: Oxford University Press.

Cabanac, M., & Leblanc, J. (1983). Physiological conflict in humans: Fatigue versus cold discomfort. *American Journal of Physiology, 244*, R621–R628.

Cacioppo, J., Berntson, G., Lorig, T., Norris, C., & Rickett, T. (2003). Just because you're imaging the brain doesn't mean you can stop using your head: A primer and set of first principles. *Journal of Personality and Social Psychology, 83*, 630–661.

Cacioppo, J., & Nusbaum, H. S. (2003). Component processes underlying choice. *Proceedings of the National Academy of Sciences of the United States of America, 100*, 3016–3017.

Camerer, C. (2003). *Behavioral game theory: Experiments in strategic interaction*. Princeton, NJ: Princeton University Press.

Camerer, C., & Loewenstein, G. (2003). Behavioral economics: Past, present, future. In C. Camerer, G. Loewenstein, & M. Rabin (Eds.), *Advances in behavioral economics* (pp. 3–52). Princeton, NJ: Princeton University Press.

Camerer, C., Loewenstein, G., & Prelec, D. (2004). Neuroeconomics: Why economics needs brains. *Scandanavian Journal of Economics, 106*(3), 555–579.

Camile, N., Coricelli, G., Sallet, J., Pradat-Diehl, P., Duhamel, J., & Sirigu, A. (2004). The involvement of the orbitofrontal cortex in the experience of regret. *Science, 304*, 1167–1170.

Cardinal, R., & Cheung, T. (2005). Nucleus accumbens core lesions retard instrumental learning and performance with delayed reinforcement in the rat. *BMC Neuroscience, 6*, 36.

Cardinal, R. N., Pennicott, D. R., Sugathapala, C. L., Robbins, T., & Everitt, B. (2001). Impulsive choice induced in rats by lesions of the nucleus accumbens core. *Science, 292*, 2499–2501.

Carlezon, W. A. (2004). *Roles for CREB and dynorphin in depressive-like behaviors associated with drugs of abuse.* Paper presented at the Annual Meeting of the Society of Biological Psychiatry, New York.

Chambers, R., & Potenza, M. (2003). Neurodevelopment, impulsivity and adolescent gambling. *Journal of Gambling Studies, 19*, 53–84.

Christensen-Szalanski, J. J. (1984). Discount functions and the measurement of patients' values: Women's decisions during childbirth. *Medical Decision Making: An International Journal of the Society for Medical Decision Making, 4*, 47–58.

Chua, H., Gonzalez, R., & Liberzon, I. (2005). *Regret, disappointment, and risky choices.* Poster presented at the Annual Meeting of the Society for Biological Psychology, Atlanta, GA.

Cohen, R. M., Weingartner, H., Smallberg, S. A., Pickar, D., & Murphy, D. L. (1982, May). Effort and cognition in depression. *Archives of General Psychiatry, 39*(5), 593–597.

Coombs, C. (1975). *Portfolio theory and the measurement of risk*, Michigan Mathematical Psychology Program Technical Report, University of Michigan, Ann Arbor, MI.

Coombs, C. (1976). *A theory of data.* Ann Arbor, MI: Matheis Press.

Coombs, C., & Avrunin, G. (1977). Single peaked functions and the theory of preference. *Psychological Review, 84*, 216–230.

Cromwell, H., Hassani, O., & Schultz, W. (2004). Relative reward processing in the primate striatum. *Experimental Brain Research, 162*, 520–525.

Dahl, R. (2003). *Risk taking and thrill seeking: The psychobiological roots of behavioral misadventures.* Paper presented at the Lipsitt-Duchin lecture series: What's killing our Kids? Brown University, Providence RI.

Damasio, A. (1995). *Descartes' error: Emotion, reason, and the human brain.* New York: Avon Books.

Damasio, A. (1999). *The feeling of what happens.* New York: Harcourt, Brace and Co.

Damasio, A. (2002). Remembering when. *Scientific American, 287*, 66–73.

Daniel, D., Egan, L., & Wolf, S. (2000). Neuropsychiatric aspects of movement disorders. In B. Sadock & V. Sadock (Eds.), *Kaplan and Sadock's comprehensive textbook of psychiatry* (pp. 285–229). Philadelphia, PA: Lippincott, Williams and Wilkins.

Davidson, D., Suppes, P., & Siegel, S. (1957). *Decision-making: An experimental approach.* Palo Alto, CL: Stanford University Press.

Davies, G. (2003). *Risky aspirations: The role of risk in choice between continuous distributions.* Paper presented at the Centre for Decision Research Seminars (G Villejoubert, Chair). Leeds University Business School, Leeds, UK.

Daw, N., Div, Y., & Dayan, P. (2005). Actions, policies, values and the basal ganglia. Paper in preparation for Recent Breakthroughs in Basal Ganglia Research. Nova Science Publishers.

Daw, N., Kakade, S., & Dayan, P. (2004). Opponent interactions between serotonin and dopamine. *Neural Networks, 15*, 603–616.

Daw, N., & Touretzky, D. S. (2002). Long-term reward prediction in TD models of the dopamine system. *Neural Computation, 14*, 2567–2583.

Dayan, P., & Balleine, B. (2002). Reward, motivation and reinforcement learning. *Neuron, 36*, 285–298.

Delgado, M., Frank, R., & Phelps, E. (2005). Perceptions of moral character modulate the neural systems of reward during the trust game. *Nature Neuroscience, 8*, 1611–1618.

Delgado, M., Locke, H., Stenger, V., & Flez, J. A. (2003). Dorsal striatum responses to reward and punishment: Effects of valence and magnitude manipulations. *Cognitive, Affective and Behavioral Neuroscience, 3*, 27–38.

Dempster, A. (1964). On the difficulties inherent in Fisher's fiducial argument. *Journal of the American Statistical Association, 59*, 56–66.

Denk, F., Walton, M., Jennings, K., Sharp, T., Rushworth, M. F., & Bannerman, D. M. (2005). Differential involvement of serotonin and dopamine systems in cost-benefit decisions about delay or effort. *Psychopharmacology, 179*, 587–596.

De Quervain, D., Fishbacher, U., Treyer, V., Schellhammer, M., Schnyder, U., Buck, A., et al. (2004). The neural basis of altruistic punishment. *Science, 305*, 1254–1258.

Dickhaut, J., McCabe, K., Nagode, J. C., Rustichini, A., Smith, K., & Pardo, J. V. (2003). The impact of the certainty context on the process of choice. *Proceedings of the National Academy of Sciences of the United States of America, 100*, 3536–3541.

Dreher, J., Kohn, P., & Berman, K. (2006). Neural coding of distinct statistical properties of reward information in humans. *Cerebral Cortex, 16*, 561–573.

Drevets, W. C. (2003). *Abnormalities in the Neural Circuits subserving decision reward processing in mood disorders*. Paper presented at the annual meeting of the Society for Biological Psychiatry, San Francisco.

Drevets, W., Price, J., Simpson, J., Todd, R. T., Reich, T., Vannier, M. et al. (1997). Subgenual prefrontal cortex abnormalities in mood disorders. *Nature, 386*, 824–827.

Durstewitz, D., Seamans, J., & Sejnowski, T. (2000). Dopamine-mediated stabilization of delay-period activity in a network model of prefrontal cortex. *Journal of Neurophysiology, 83*, 1733–1750.

Elliott, R. (2002). Dissociable roles for ventral, frontal and striatal regions in human reinforcement processing. *Biological Psychiatry, 49*, 10S.

Ellsberg, D. (1961). Risk, ambiguity and the Savage axioms. *Quarterly Journal of Economics, 75*, 643–669.

Ernst, M., Grant, S. J., London, E. D., Contoreggi, C. S., Kimes, A. S., & Spurgeon, L. (2003). Decision making in adolescents with behavior disorders and adults with substance abuse. *American Journal of Psychiatry, 160*, 33–40.

Ernst, M., Kimes, A., London, E., Matochik, J. A., Eldreth, D., Tata, S., et al. (2003). Neural substrates of decision-making in adults with attention deficit hyperactivity disorder. *American Journal of Psychiatry, 160*, 1061–1070.

Evenden, J., & Ryan, C. (1999). The pharmacology of impulsive behavior in rats VI. The effects of ethanol and selective serotonergic drugs on response choice with varying delays of reinforcement. *Psychopharmacology (Berlin), 128*, 161–170.

Fellows, L. (2004). The cognitive neuroscience of human decision making. *Behavioral and Cognitive Neuroscience Reviews, 3*, 159–172.

Fellows, L., & Farah, M. (2005). Dissociable elements of human foresight: A role for the ventromedial prefrontal lobes in framing the future but not in discounting future rewards. *Neuropsychologica, 43*, 1214–1241.

Feng, J. & Li, G. (2001). Behavior of two-compartment models. *Neurocomputing, 38–40*, 205–211.

Fiorillo, C. D., Tobler, P. N., & Schultz, W. (2003). Discrete coding of reward probability and uncertainty by dopamine neurons. *Science, 299*, 1898–1902.

Fischman, N. W., & Foltin, R. W. (1992). Self-administration of cocaine by humans: A laboratory perspective. In G. R. Bock & J. Whelan (Eds.), *Cocaine: Scientific and social dimensions* (pp. 165–180). Chichester, England: Wiley.

Fischoff, B. (1995). Risk perception and communication unplugged: Twenty years of process. *Risk Analysis, 15*, 137–145.

Fishbein, D., Eldreth, B., Hyde, C., Matochik, J. A., London, E. D., Contoreggi, C., et al. (2005). Risky decision making and the anterior cingulate cortex in abstinent drug users and non-users. *Cognitive Brain Research, 23*, 119–136.

Fryback, D. G. (1983). A conceptual model for output measures in cost-effectiveness evaluation of diagnostic imaging. *Journal of Neuroradiology, 10*(2), 94–96.

Gabrielli, J. D. (2003). *Neural systems mediating cognitive and emotional learning.* Paper presented at the annual meeting of the Society for Biological Psychiatry, San Francisco.

Galaverna, O., Seeley, R., Berridge, K., Grill, H. J., Epstein, A. N., & Schulkin, A. (1999). Lesions of the central nucleus of the amygdala, I. Effects on taste reactivity, taste aversion learning and sodium appetite. *Behavioural Brain Research, 59*, 11–17.

Gehring, W. J., & Willoughby, A. R. (2002). The medial prefrontal cortex and the rapid processing of monetary gains and losses. *Science, 295*(5563), 2279–2282.

Giordano, L., Bickel, W., Loewenstein, G., Jacobs, E. A., Marsch, L., & Badger, G. J. (2002). Mild opioid deprivation increases the degree that opioid-dependent outpatients discount delayed heroin and money. *Psychopharmacology, 163*, 174–182.

Glimcher, P. (2003). *Decisions, uncertainty and the brain: The science of neuroeconomics.* Cambridge, MA: MIT Press.

Gomez-Beldarrain, M., Harries, C., Garcia-Monco, J. C., Ballus, E., & Grafman, J. (2004). Patients with right frontal lesions are unable to assess and use advice to make predictive judgments. *Journal of Cognitive Neuroscience, 16*, 74–89.

Gonzalez, C., Dana, J., Koshino, H., & Just, M. (2005). The framing effect and risky decisions: Examining cognitive functions with fMRI. *Journal of Economic Psychology, 26*, 1–20.

Gorman, J. M., Kent, J. M., Sullivan, G. M., & Coplan, J. D. (2000). Neuroanatomical hypothesis of panic disorder. *American Journal of Psychology, 157*, 493–505.

Goudriaan, A., Oooserlaan, E., De Beurs, E., & van den Brink, W. (2005). Decision making in pathological gambling: A comparison between pathological gamblers, alcohol dependents, patients with Tourette's syndrome, and normal controls. *Cognitive Brain Research, 23*, 137–151.

Greene, J., Nystrom, L., Engell, A., Darley, J. M., & Cohen, J. D. (2004). The neural bases of cognitive conflict and control in moral judgment. *Neuron, 44*, 389–400.

Greene, J., Sommerville, R., & Nystrom, L. (2001). An fMRI investigation of emotional engagement in moral judgment. *Science, 293*, 2105–2108.

Grisso, T., Steinberg, L., Woolard, J., Cauffman, E., Graham, E., Scott, S., et al. (2003). Juveniles' competence to stand trial: A comparison of adolescents' and adults' capacities as trial defendants. *Law and Human Behavior, 27*, 333–363.

Grossberg, S. (2000a). How hallucinations may arise from brain mechanisms of learning, attention, and volition. *Journal of the International Neuropsychological Society, 6*, 583.

Grossberg, S. (2000b). The complementary brain: Unifying dynamics and modularity. *Trends in Cognitive Sciences, 4*, 233–246.

Grossberg, S. (2000c). The imbalanced brain: From normal behavior to schizophrenia. *Biological Psychiatry, 48*, 81–98.

Harreveld, F., & van der Pligt, J. (2003). *Social comparison as a way to reduce regret University of Amsterdam Social Psychology.* Paper presented at the 19th Biannual conference on subjective probability, utility and decision making (SPUDM 19), Zurich, Switzerland.

Heath, C., Larrick, R., & Wu, G. (1999). Goals as reference points. *Cognitive Psychology, 38,* 79–109.

Hill, E., & Sally, D. (2002). *Dilemmas and bargains: Theory-of-mind cooperation and fairness.* Working paper. University College, London.

Hinson, J., Jameson, T., & Whitney, P. (2002). Somatic markers, working memory, and decision making. *Cognitive, Affective, and Behavioral Neuroscience, 2,* 341–353.

Hollander, E. (2002). *The impulsive-aggression symptom domain in borderline personality disorder.* Paper presented at the annual meeting of the American Psychiatric Association, Philadelphia, PA.

Hollander, E., Posner, N., & Cherkasky, S. (2002). Neuropsychiatric aspects of aggression and impulse control disorders. In S. C. Yudofsky & R. E. Hales (Eds.), *Neuropsychiatry and clinical neurosciences* (pp. 579–596). Washington, DC: American Psychiatric Publishing.

Hou, J., Adams, J., & Barto, A. (1995). A model of how the basal ganglia generate and use neural signals that predict reinforcement. In J. Hou, J. Davis, & D. Beiser (Eds.), *Models of information processing in the basal ganglia* (pp. 249–274). Cambridge, MA: MIT press.

Hsee, C., Zhang, J., & Chen, J. (2006). Internal and substantive inconsistencies in decision making. In D. Koehler & N. Harvey (Eds.), *Blackwell handbook of judgment and decision making* (pp. 360–378). Oxford, England: Blackwell.

Hsee, C., Zhang, J., Yu, F., & Xi, Y. (2003). Lay rationalism and inconsistency between predicted experience and decision. *Journal of Behavioral Decision Making, 16,* 257–272.

Hsu, M., Bhatt, M., Adolphs, R., Tranel, D., & Camerer, C. (2006). Neural systems responding to degrees of uncertainty in decision making. *Science, 310,* 680–683.

Hsu, M., & Camerer, C. (2004). *Ambiguity aversion in the brain.* Caltech. Working paper.

Huettel, S. (2005). Neural substrates for the resolution of uncertainty. Poster presentation at the annual meeting of the Society for Neuroeconomics. Kiawah Island, SC.

Huettel, S., Mack, P., & McCarthy, G. (2002). Perceiving patterns in random series: Dynamic processing of sequence in prefrontal cortex. *Nature Neuroscience, 5,* 485–490.

Huettel, S., Song, A., & McCarthy, G. (2005). Decisions under uncertainty: Probabilistic context influences activation of prefrontal and parietal cortices. *Journal of Neuroscience, 25,* 3304–3311.

Hyman, S. (2002). Dopamine, gene expression, and the molecular mechanisms of synaptic plasticity. *Biological Psychology, 49,* S1.

Isles, A., Humby, T., & Wilkinson, S. (2003). Measuring impulsivity in mice using a novel delayed operant reinforcement task: Effects of behavioral manipulation and d-amphetamine. *Psychopharmacology, 170,* 376–382.

Jevons, W. S. (1871). *The theory of political economy.* London and New York: Macmillan and Co.

Johnson, E. (2005). *Behavioral economics and decision making.* Paper presented at the annual meeting of the Society for Neuroeconomics, Kiawah Island, SC.

Johnson, E., Bayer, H., Brodscholl, J., & Weber, E. (2005). *Query theory, inhibition, and individual differences in value construction.* Paper presented at the Annual Meeting of the Society for Neuroeconomics. Kiawah Island, SC.

Josephs, R., Larrisck, R., Steele, C., Larrick, R. P., Steele, C. M., & Nisbet, R. E. (1992). Protecting the self from the negative consequences of risky decisions. *Journal of Personality and Social Psychology, 62,* 26–37.

Kahneman, D., Diener, E., & Schwartz, N. (Eds.). (1999). *Well-being: The foundations of hedonic psychology.* New York: Russell Sage Foundation.

Kahneman, D., & Snell, J. (1992). Predicting a changing taste: Do people know what they will like. *Journal of Behavioral Decision Making, 5,* 187–200.

Kahneman, D., & Tversky, A. (1979). Prospect theory: An analysis of decision under risk. *Econometrica, 47,* 263–291.

Kalenscher, T., Ohmann, T., & Gunturkun, O. (2006). The neuroscience of impulsive and self-controlled decisions. *International Journal of Psychophysiology, 62,* 203–211.

Kalenscher, T., Windmann, S., Diekamp, B., Rose, J., Güntürkün, O., & Colombo, M. (2005). Single units in the pigeon brain integrate reward amount and time to reward in an impulsive choice task. *Current Biology, 15,* 594–602.

Kant, I. (1959). *Foundation of the metaphysics of morals.* Indianapolis, IN: Bobbs Merril.

Kelley, W. M., Macrae, C. N., Wylan, C., Caglar, S., Inati, S., & Heatherton, T. F. (2002). Finding the self: An event-related fMRI study. *Journal of Cognitive Neuroscience, 14,* 785–794.

Kheramin, S., Body, S., & Ho, M. (2003). Role of the orbital prefrontal cortex in choice between delayed and uncertain reinforcers: A quantitative analysis. *Behavioural Processes, 64,* 239–250.

King-Cassas, D., Tomlin, B., Anen, C., Camerer, C., Quartz, S. R., & Montague, R. (2005). Getting to know you: Reputation and trust in a two-person economic exchange. *Science, 308,* 78–83.

Knutson, B., Fong, G., Bennet, S., Adams, C. S., & Hommer, D. (2003). A region of mesial prefrontal cortex tracks monetarily rewarding outcomes: Characterization with rapid event-related fMRI. *NeuroImage, 18,* 263–272.

Knutson, B., & Peterson, R. (2005). Neurally reconstructing expected utility. *Games and Economic Behavior, 52,* 305–315.

Knutson, B., Taylor, J., Kaufman, M., Peterson, R., & Glover, G. (2005). Distributed neural representation of expected value. *Journal of Neuroscience, 25,* 4806–4812.

Kobberling, V., & Wakker, P. (2005). An index of loss aversion. *Journal of Economic Theory, 122,* 119–113.

Krebs, J. R., Ericksson, J. T., Webber, M., & Charnov, E. L. (1977). Optimal prey selection in the grey tit. *Animal Behavior, 25,* 30–38.

Kroeze, S., & vanden Hout, M. A. (2000). Selective attention for cardiac information in panic patients. *Behavior Research and Therapy, 38,* 63–72.

Kubovy, M. (1999). On the pleasures of the mind. In D. Kahneman, E. Diener, & N. Schwartz (Eds.), *Well-being: The foundations of hedonic psychology* (pp. 134–154). New York: Russell Sage Foundation.

Laibson, D. (1997). Golden eggs and hyperbolic discounting. *Quarterly Journal of Economics, 112,* 443–477.

Laibson, D. (2001). A cue theory of consumption. *Quarterly Journal of Economics, 116,* 81–119.

Laibson, D. (2006). *Intertemporal choice*. Stanford Economics/Neuroeconomics Summer School, Stanford University, Palo Alto, CA. Citation of an unpublished paper by McClure, S., Ericson, D., Laibson, D., Loewenstein, G., & Cohen, J. (2006).

Lakshminarayanan, V., Chen, M., & Santos, L. (2006). *The evolution of decision-making under uncertainty: Framing effects in non-human primates*. Paper presented at the Annual Meeting of the Society for Neuroeconomics, Park City, UT.

Ledoux, J. (1996). *The emotional brain: The mysterious underpinnings of emotional life*. New York: Simon and Schuster.

Lerner, J. S., & Keltner, D. (2000). Beyond valence: Toward a model of emotion-specific influences on judgment and choice. *Cognition and Emotion, 14*, 473–494.

Lilenfeld, S. O., & Penna, S. (2000). Anxiety sensitivity: Relations to psychopathy, DSM-IV personality disorder features, and personality traits. *Anxiety Disorders, 113*, 367–393.

Loewenstein, G. (1987). Anticipation and the valuation of delayed consumption. *The Economic Journal, 97*, 666–684.

Loewenstein, G. (1999). A visceral account of addiction. In J. Elster & O.-J. Skog (Eds.), *Getting hooked: Rationality and addiction* (pp. 236–264). Cambridge, UK: Cambridge University Press.

Loewenstein, G., & Lerner, J., (2003). The role of affect in decision-making. In R. Davidson, K. Scherer, & H. Goldsmith (Eds.), *Handbook of affective sciences* (pp. 619–642). Oxford, UK: Oxford University Press.

Loewenstein, G., & O'Donoghue, T. (2005). *Animal spirits: Affective and deliberative processes in economic behavior*. Working paper. Department of Social and Decision Sciences, Carnegie Mellon University.

Lowenstein, G., & Schkade, D. (1999). Wouldn't it be nice? In D. Kahneman, E. Diener, & N. Schwartz (Eds.), *Well-being: The foundations of hedonic psychology* (pp. 85–105). New York: Russell Sage Foundation..

Loewenstein, G., & Thaler, R. (1989). Anomalies: Intertemporal choice, *Journal of Economic Perspectives, 3*, 181–193.

Lopes, L., & Oden, G. (1999). The role of aspiration level in risky choice: A comparison of cumulative prospect theory and SP/A theory. *Journal of Mathematical Psychology, 43*, 286–313.

Lucas, R., Clark, A., Georgellia, Y., & Diener, E. (2003). Reexamining adaptation and the set point of happiness reactions to changes in marital status. *Journal of Personality and Social Psychology, 84*, 527–539.

Maas, A., & Wakker, P. (1992). Additive conjoint measurement of multiattribute utility. *Journal of Mathematical Psychology, 38*, 86–101.

Machens, C., Romo, R., & Brody, C. (2005). Flexible control of mutual discrimination: A neural model of two-interval discrimination. *Science, 307*, 1121–4.

Maia, T., & McClelland, J. (2004). A reexamination of the evidence for the somatic marker hypothesis: What participants really know in the Iowa gambling task. *Proceedings of the National Academy of Sciences, USA, 101*, 16,075–16,080.

Malone, K., Waternaux, C., Haas, G., Cooper, T., Li, S., & Mann, J. (2003). Cigarette smoking, suicidal behavior, and serotonin function in major psychiatric disorders. *American Journal of Psychiatry, 160*, 772–779.

Mandelblatt, J., Fryback, D., Weinstein, M., Russell, L., & Gold, M. (1997). Assessing the effectiveness of health interventions for cost-effectiveness analysis. Panel on cost-effectiveness in health and medicine. *Journal of General Internal Medicine, 12*(9), 551–558.

Manoach, D. S. (2002). *Prefrontal cortex dysfunction during working memory performance in schizophrenia: Reconciling discrepant findings.* Paper presented at the annual meeting of the Society for Biological Psychiatry, Philadelphia, PA.

Marsh, B., & Kacelnik, A. (2002). Framing effects and risky decisions in starlings. *Proceedings of the National Academy of Sciences of the United States of America, 99,* 3352–3355.

Mateo, Y., Budygin, E., John, C., & Jones, S. R. (2004). Role of serotonin in cocaine effects in mice with reduced dopamine transporter function. *Proceedings of the National Academy of Sciences, USA, 101,* 372–377.

Mavaddat, N., Kirkpatrick, P., Rogers, R., & Sahakian, B. (2000). Deficits in decision-making in patients with aneurisms of the anterior communicating artery. *Brain, 123,* 2109–2117.

Mayer, J., Salovey, P., & Caruso, D. (2000a). Emotional intelligence as Zeitgeist. In R. Bar-On & J. Parker (Eds.), *Handbook of emotional intelligence* (pp. 99–117). San Francisco, CA: Jossey-Bass.

Mayer, J., Salovey, P., & Caruso, D. (2000b). Selecting a measure of emotional intelligence. In R. Bar-On & J. Parker (Eds.), *Handbook of emotional intelligence* (pp. 320–342). San Francisco, CA: Jossey-Bass.

McCabe, K., Houser, D., Ryan, L., Smith, V., & Trouard, T. (2001). Functional imaging study of cooperation in two-person reciprocal exchange. *Proceedings of the National Academy of Sciences, USA, 98*(20), 11832–11835.

McClure, S., Berne, G., & Montague, P. (2003). Temporal prediction errors in a passive learning task activate ventral striatum. *Neuron, 38,* 339–346.

McClure, S., Daw, N., & Montague, R. (2003). A computational substrate for incentive salience. *Trends in Neurosciences, 26,* 423–428.

McClure, S., Gilzenrat, M., & Cohen, J. (2006). An exploration–exploitation model based on norepinephrine and dopamine system activity. *Journal of Neural Information Processing Systems, 18,* 867–874

McClure, S., Laibson, D., Lowenstein, G., & Cohen, J. D. (2004). Separate neural systems value immediate and delayed rewards. *Science, 306,* 503–507.

McClure, S., Lee, J., Tomlin, D., Cypert, K., Montague, L., & Montague P. R. (2004). Neural correlates of behavioral preferences for culturally familiar drinks. *Neuron, 44,* 379–387.

McCoy, A., & Platt, M. (2005). Risk-sensitive neurons in macaque posterior cingulate cortex. *Nature Neuroscience, 8,* 1220–1227.

Mcewen, B. (2003). Mood disorders and allostatic load. *Biological Psychiatry, 54,* 200.

McNeil, B. J., Weichselbaum, R., & Pauker, S. G. (1978). The fallacy of the five-year survival in lung cancer. *The New England Journal of Medicine, 299,* 397–401.

Metcalfe, J., & Mischel, W. (1999). A hot/cool-system analysis of delay of gratification: Dynamics of willpower. *Psychological Review, 106,* 3–19.

Misra, S., & Ganzini, L. (2005). *The influence of mood state on the capacity to consent to research in bipolar patients.* Paper presented at the Annual Meeting of the American Psychiatric Association, Atlanta, GA.

Mitchell, S. (2004). Effects of short-term nicotine deprivation on decision making: Delay, uncertainty, and effort discounting. *Nicotine and Tobacco Research, 6,* 819–828.

Miyamoto, J. (1999). Quality adjusted life years (QALY) utility models under expected utility and rank-dependent utility assumptions. *Journal of Mathematical Psychology, 43,* 201–237.

Miyamoto, J., & Politser, P. (1981). *Risky utilities and riskless values: A comparison of assessment procedures.* Paper presented at the Annual Meeting of the Society for Medical Decision-making, University of Pennsylvania.

Mobini, S., Body, S., Ho, M., Bradshaw, C. M., Szabadi, E., Deakin, J. F., et al. (2002). Effects of lesions of the orbitofrontal cortex on sensitivity to delayed and probabilistic reinforcement. *Psychopharmacology, 160*(3), 290–298.

Mohr, P., Biele, G., Krugel, L., Li, S.-C., & Heekerin, H. (2007). *Risk-value tradeoff in investment decisions.* Paper presented at the Annual Meeting of the Society for Neuroeconomics, Hull, MA.

Montague, P. R., Dayan, P., & Sejnowski, T. J. (1996). A framework for mesencephalic dopamine systems based on predictive Hebbian learning. *Journal of Neuroscience, 16*, 1936–1947.

Montague, P. R., Hyman, S. E., & Cohen, J. D. (2004). Computational roles for dopamine in behavioural control. *Nature, 431*, 760–767.

Monterosso, J., Ehrman, R., Napier, K., O'Brien, C. P., & Childress, A. R. (2001). Three decision-making tasks in cocaine-dependent patients: Do they measure the same construct? *Addiction, 96*, 1825–1837.

Morais, R. (1995). Saga of fire and ice. *Forbes, 156*, 160–164.

Murphy, F. C., Rubensztein, J. S., Michael, A., Rogers, R. D., Robbins, T. W., Paykel, E. S., et al. (2001). Decision-making cognition in mania and depression. *Psychological Medicine, 1*, 671–693.

Nagai, Y., Critchley, H., Featherstone, E., Trimble, M., & Dolan, R. (2004). Activity in ventromedial PFC co-varies with sympathetic skin conductance level: A physiological account of a "default mode" of brain function. *NeuroImage, 22*, 243–251.

Nash, O. (1938). *I'm a stranger here myself.* Boston: Little, Brown, and Company.

Nesse, R. (2004). *What social phobia reveals about our evolved human nature and vice versa.* Paper presented at the Annual Meeting of the American Psychiatric Association, New York.

Nesse, R. M., & Klaas, R. (1994). Risk perception by patients with anxiety disorders. *Journal of Nervous and Mental Diseases, 182*, 465–470.

Nestler, E. J., & Self, D. W. (2002). Neuropsychiatric aspects of ethanol and other chemical dependencies. In S. C. Yudofsky & R. E. Hales (Eds.), *Neuropsychiatry and clinical neurosciences* (pp. 899–922). Washington, DC: American Psychiatric Publishing.

Neuman, P., & Politser, P. (1992). Risk and optimality. In F. Yates (Ed.), *Risk taking behavior.* New York: Wiley.

Nielen, M. M., Veltman, D. J., de Jong, R., Mulder, G., & den Boer, J. A. (2002). Decision making performance in obsessive compulsive disorder. *Journal of Affective Disorders, 69*, 257–260.

Nisbett, R., & Wilson, R. D. (1977). Telling more than what we know: Verbal reports on mental processes. *Psychological Review, 84*, 231–259.

Niv, Y., Daw, N., & Dayan, P. (2005). How fast to work: Response, vigor, motivation and tonic dopamine. *Advances in Neural Information Processing Systems, 18*, 1019–1026.

Niv, Y., Duff, M., & Dayan, P. (2005). Dopamine, uncertainty and TD learning. *Behavioral and Brain Functions, 1*, 6.

North, N., & O'Carroll, R. (2001). Decision making in spinal cord damage: Afferent feedback and the somatic marker hypothesis. *Neuropsychologica, 39*, 521–524.

Ochsner, K., & Gross, J. (2004). Thinking makes it so: A cognitive neuroscience approach to emotion regulation. In K. Vohs & R. Baumeister (Eds.), *The handbook of self regulation* (pp. 229–255). New York: Guilford Press.

Ochsner, K., & Gross, J. (2005). The cognitive control of emotion. *Trends in Cognitive Sciences, 5,* 242–249.

O'Doherty, J., Kringelbach, M. L., Rolls, E. T., Hornak, J., & Andrews, C. (2001). Abstract reward and punishment representations in the human orbitofrontal cortex. *Nature Neuroscience, 4,* 95–102.

Odonogue, T., & Rabin, M. (1999). Doing it now or later. *American Economic Review, 89,* 103–124.

Oliver, A. J. (2003). Putting the quality into quality-adjusted life years. *Journal of Public Health Medicine, 25,* 8–12.

Padoa-Schioppa, C., & Asaad, J. (2006). *Neurons in orbitofrontal cortex encode economic value independently of context.* Paper presented at the Annual Meeting of the Society for Neuroeconomics, Park City, UT.

Park, S. B. G., Coull, J. S. T., McShane, R. H., Young, A., Sahakian, B., Robbins, T., et al. (2002). Tryptophan depletion in normal volunteers produces selective impairments in learning and memory. *Neuropharmacology, 33,* 575–588.

Parrot, W. G., & Schulkin, J. (1993). Neuropsychology and the cognitive nature of the emotions. *Cognition and Emotion, 7,* 43–59.

Paulus, M. (2005). Dysfunction of reward systems in psychopathology: Clinical and research implications. *Biological Psychiatry, 57,* 74S.

Paulus, M., Hozack, N. E., Zauscher, B. E., Frank, L., Brown, G. G., Braff, D., et al. (2002a). Behavioral and functional neuroimaging evidence for prefrontal dysfunction in methamphetamine-dependent subjects. *Neuropsychopharmacology, 26,* 53–63.

Paulus, M., Hozack, N., Zauscher, B. E., Macdowell, J., Frank, L., Brown, G., et al. (2002b). Parietal dsyfunction is associated with increased outcome-related decision-making in schizophrenia patients. *Biological Psychiatry, 51,* 995–1004.

Paulus, M., Rogalsky, C., Simmons, A., Feinstein, J., & Stein, M., et al. (2003). Increased activation in the right insula during risk taking decision making is related to harm avoidance and neuroticism. *Neuroimage, 19,* 1439–1448.

Payne, J., Bettman, J. R., & Johnson, E. (1993). *The adaptive decision maker.* Cambridge, England: Cambridge University Press.

Phelps, E. (2003). *Cognition–emotion interactions in the amygdala.* Paper presented at the Annual Meeting of the Society for Biological Psychiatry, San Francisco.

Piazza, P. (2005). *Addiction-like behaviors in the rat: Insight into the true nature of addiction.* Paper presented at the Annual Meeting of the American Psychiatric Association, Atlanta, GA.

Pirsig, R. (1991). *Lila: An inquiry into morals.* New York: Bantam Books.

Platt, M. L., & Glimcher, P. W. (1999). Neural correlates of decision variables in parietal cortex. *Nature, 400,* 233–238.

Pliskin, J. S., Shepard, D. S., & Weinstein, M. C. (1980). Utility functions for life years and health status. *Operations Research, 28,* 206–224.

Politser, P. E. (1985). Radionuclide detection of biliary atresia: An illustration of a structural method to guide test assessment. *Medical Decision Making, 5,* 437–446.

Politser, P. E. (1991a) Do decision analyses largest gains grow from the smallest trees? *Journal of Behavioral Decision Making, 4,* 121–138.

Politser, P. E. (Ed.). (1991b). Special issue on structuring decision analyses. *Journal of Behavioral Decision Making, 4,* 79–152.

Politser, P. E. (1991c). Structuring decision analyses: Statistical and psychological evaluations. *Journal of Behavioral Decision Making, 4*, 79–82.

Preuschoff, K., Bossaerts, P., & Quartz, S. (2006a). *Human insula activation in a monetary gambling task reflects uncertainty prediction errors as well as uncertainty level.* Paper presented at the Annual Meeting of the Society for Neuroeconomics, Park City, UT.

Preuschoff, K., Bossaerts, P., & Quartz, S. (2006b). Neural differentiation of expected reward and risk in human subcortical structures. *Neuron, 51*, 381–390.

Real, L. (1996). Paradox, performance and the architecture of decision making in animals. *American Zoologist, 36*, 518–529.

Redelmeier, D. A., & Kahneman, D. (1996). Patients' memories of painful medical treatments: Real-time and retrospective evaluations of two minimally invasive procedures. *Pain, 66*(1), 3–8.

Rescher, N. (1993). *A system of pragmatic idealism Vol 2: The validity of values. A normative theory of evaluative rationality.* Princeton, NJ: Princeton University Press.

Richards, J., Zhang, L., Mitchell, S., & de Wit, H. (1999). Delay or probability discounting in a model of impulsive behavior: Effect of alcohol. *Journal of the Experimental Analysis of Behavior, 71*, 121–143.

Rilling, J., Glenn, A., Jairam, M., Pagnoni, G., Goldsmith, D. R., Elfenbein, H. A., et al. (2005). Exploring individual variation in the neural correlates of social cooperation and non-cooperation. *Biological Psychiatry, 57*, 1S–212S.

Robbins, T. (2003). *Neural substrates of impulsivity and decision-making cognition in humans and animals.* Paper presented at the Annual Meeting of the Society for Biological Psychiatry, San Francisco.

Robbins, T. (2005). Controlling stress: How the brain protects itself from depression. *Nature Neuroscience, 8*, 261–262.

Robbins, T., & Everitt, B. (1992). Functions of dopamine in the dorsal and ventral striatum. *Seminars in the Neurosciences, 4*, 119–127.

Robinson, S., Smith, D., Mizumori, S., & Palmiter, R. (2005). Distinguishing whether dopamine regulates liking, wanting, and/or learning about rewards. *Behavioral Neuroscience, 119*, 5–15.

Rogan, M., Leon, K., Perez, D., & Kandel, E. R. (2005). Distinct neural signatures of safety and danger in the amygdala and striatum of the mouse. *Neuron, 46*, 309–320.

Rogers, R. D. (2003). *The neuromodulation of emotional cues in human choice.* Paper presented at the Annual Meeting of the American Psychiatric Association, San Francisco.

Rogers, R. D., Everitt, B. J., Baldacchino, A., Blackshaw, A., Swainson, R., Wynne, K., et al. (1999). Dissociable deficits in the decision-making cognition of chronic amphetamine abusers, opiate abusers, patients with focal damage to the prefrontal cortex, and tryptophan-depleted normal volunteers: Evidence for monaminergic mechanisms. *Neuropsychopharmacology, 20*, 322–339.

Rogers, R. D., Lancaster, M., Wakeley, J., & Bhagwagar, Z. (2004). Effects of beta-adrenoreceptor blockade on components of human decision making. *Psychopharmacology, 172*, 157–164.

Rogers, R. D., Tunbridge, E. M., Bhagwagar, Z., Drevets, W. C., Sahakian, B. J., & Carter, C. S. (2003). Tryptophan depletion alters the decision-making of healthy volunteers through altered processing of reward cues. *Neuropsychopharmacology, 28*, 153–162.

Romo, R., & Salinas, E. (2003). Flutter discrimination: Neural codes, perception, memory and decision making. *Nature Reviews. Neuroscience, 4*, 203–218.

Rorie, A., & Newsome, W. (2005). A general mechanism for decision making in the human brain. *Trends in Cognitive Sciences, 9,* 41–43.

Rottenstreich, Y., & Hsee, C. (2001). Money, kisses and electrical shocks: An affective psychology of risk. *Psychological Science, 12,* 185–190.

Rubinsztein, J. S., Fletcher, P. C., Rogers, R. D., Ho, L. W., Aigbirhio, F. I., Paykel, E. S., et al. (2001). Decision-making in mania: A PET study. *Brain, 124,* 2550–2563.

Rushworth, M., Walton, M., Kennerley, S., & Bannerman, D. W. (2004). Action sets and decisions in the medial prefrontal cortex. *Trends in Cognitive Neuroscience, 8,* 410–417.

Ryan, R., & Deci, E. (2001). On happiness and human potentials: A review of research on hedonic and eudaimonic well-being. *Annual Review Of Psychology, 52,* 1141–1166.

Saigh, P. A., & Bremner, J. D. (Eds.). (1999). *Posttraumatic stress disorder: A comprehensive text.* New York: Allyn & Bacon.

Sanfey, A., Hastie, R., Colvin, M., & Grafman, J. (2003). Phineas gauged: Decision-making and the human prefrontal cortex. *Neuropsychologia, 41,* 1218–1229.

Sanfey, A., Rilling, J., Aaronson, J., Nystron, L., & Cohen, J. (2003). Probing the neural basis of economic decision-making: An fMRI investigation of the ultimatum game. *Science, 300,* 1755–1758.

Satoh, T., Nakai, S., Sato, T., & Kimura, M. (2003). Correlated coding of motivation and outcome of decision by dopamine neurons. *The Journal of Neuroscience, 23,* 9913–9923.

Sayette, M., Loewenstein, G., Kirchner, T., & Travis, T. (2005). The effects of smoking on temporal cognition. *Psychology of Addictive Behaviors, 19,* 88–93.

Schkade, D., & Kahneman, D. (1998). Does living in California make people happy? A focusing illusion in judgments of life satisfaction. *Psychological Science, 9,* 340–346.

Schultz, W. (2002). Getting formal with dopamine and reward. *Neuron, 36,* 241–263.

Schultz, W., & Dickinson, A. (2000). Neural coding of prediction errors. *Annual Review Of Neuroscience, 23,* 473–500.

Searjeant, J. (2002). Actress Winona Ryder Pleads Not Guilty to Theft Fri Jun 14, Reuters news service. Retrieved May 30, 2002, from http://story.news.yahoo.com/news?tmp l=story&cid=638&ncid=762&e=2&u=/nm/20020614/en_nm/crime_ryder_dc_2

Seo, H., & Lee, D. (2006). *Neuronal signals related to gains, losses, and utilities in the medial frontal cortex of monkeys.* Paper presented at the Annual Meeting of the Society for Neuroeconomics, Park City, UT.

Shafer, G. (1976). *A mathematical theory of evidence.* Princeton: Princeton University Press.

Sharpe, L. (2004). Patterns of autonomic arousal in imaginal situations of winning and losing in problem gambling. *Journal of Gambling Studies, 20,* 95–104.

Shiv, B., Loewenstein, G., Bechara, A., Damasio, H., & Damasio, A. R. (2005). Investment behavior and the negative side of emotion. *Psychological Science, 16,* 435–439.

Shizgal, P. (1999). On the neural computation of utility. In D. Kahneman, E. Diener, & N. Schwartz (Eds.), *Well-being: The foundations of hedonic psychology* (pp. 500–524). New York: Russell Sage Foundation.

Siegel, S., Hinson, R., Krank, M., & McCully, J. (1982). Heroin overdose death: The contribution of drug associated environmental cues. *Science, 241,* 436–437.

Siegel, S., Krank, M., & Hinson, R. (1988). Anticipation of pharmacological and nonpharmacological events: Classical conditioning and addictive behavior. In S. Peele (Ed.), *Visions of addiction: Major contemporary perspectives on addiction and alcoholism* (pp. 85–88). Lexington, MA: D.C. Heath.

Slevin, M., Plant, H., Lynch, D., Drinkwater, J., & Gregory, W. (1988). Who should measure quality of life: The doctor or the patient? *British Journal of Cancer*, *57*, 109–112.

Slovic, P. (2000). What does it mean to know a cumulative risk? Adolescents' perceptions of short-term and long-term consequences of smoking. *Journal of Behavioral Decision Making*, *13*, 259–266, 273–276.

Slovic, P. (2001). *The perception of risk*. London: Earthscan.

Slovic, P., Finucane, M., Peters, E., & MacGregor, D. (2004). Risks as analysis and risks as feelings: Some thoughts about affect, reason, risk and rationality. *Risk Analysis*, *24*, 1–12.

Solomon, R. (1980). Opponent-process theory of acquired motivation: The costs of pleasure and the benefits of pain. *American Psychologist*, *35*, 691–712.

Spitzer, M. (1999). *The mind within the net*. Cambridge, MA: MIT Press.

Stone, V., Cosmides, L., Tooby, J., Kroll, N., & Knight, R. (2002). Selective impairment of reasoning about social exchange in a patient with bilateral limbic system damage. *Proceedings of the National Academy of Sciences, USA*, *99*(17), 11531–11536.

Stout, J., Rock, S., Campbell, M., Busemeyer, J., & Finn, P. (2005). Psychological processes underlying risky decisions in drug abusers. *Psychology of Addictive Behaviors*, *19*, 148–157.

Strange, B. A., Hurleman, R., & Dolan, R. J. (2003). An emotion-induced retrograde amnesia in humans is amygdala and β-adrenergic dependent. *Proceedings of the National Academy of Sciences*, *100*, 13626–13631.

Swanda, R. M., Haaland, K. Y., & Larue, A. (2000). Clinical neuropsychology and intellectual assessment of adults. In B. J. Sadock & V. A. Sadock (Eds.), *Comprehensive textbook of psychiatry* (pp. 689–701). Philadelphia, PA: Lippincott, Williams and Wilkins.

Tecott, L. (2000). Monamine neurotransmitters. In B. Sadock & V. Sadock (Eds.), *Kaplan and Sadock's comprehensive textbook of psychiatry* (pp. 49–59). Philadelphia, PA: Lippincott, Williams and Wilkins.

Thaler, R. (1980). Toward a positive theory of consumer choice. *Journal of Economic Behavior and Organization*, *1*, 39–60.

Thaler, R. (1999). Mental accounting matters. *Journal of Behavioral Decision Making*, *12*, 183–206.

Tobler, P., Fiorillo, C., & Schultz, W. (2005). Adaptive coding of reward value by dopamine neurons. *Science*, *347*, 642–645.

Tom, S., Fox, C., Trepel, C., & Poldrack, R. (2007). The neural basis of loss aversion in decision making under risk. *Science*, *315*, 515–518.

Tomb, I., Hauser, M., Dedlin, P., & Caramazza, A. (2002). Do somatic markers mediate decisions in the gambling task? *Nature Neuroscience*, *5*, 1103–1104.

Tranel, D., Bechara, A., & Denburg, N. L. (2002). Asymmetric functional roles of right and left ventromedial prefrontal cortices in social conduct, decision-making and emotional processing. *Cortex*, *38*, 589–612.

Tricomi, E., Delgado, M., & Fiez, J. (2004). Modulation of caudate activity by action contingency. *Neuron*, *41*, 281–292.

Turhan, C., Sivers, H., Thomason, M., Whitfield-Gabrielli, S., Gabrieli, J. D., Gotlib, I. H., et al. (2004). Brain activation to emotional words in depressed vs. healthy subjects. *Neuroreport*, *15*, 2585–2588.

Ursu, S., & Carter, C. (2004). Outcome representations, counterfactual comparisons and the human orbitofrontal cortex: Implications for neuroimaging studies of decision-making. *Cognitive Brain Research*, *23*, 51–60.

Usher, M., Cohen, J. D., Servan-Schreiber, D., Rajkowski, J., & Aston-Jones, G. (2000). The role of the locus coeruleus in the regulation of cognitive performance. *Science, 283*(5401), 549–559.

Usher, M., & McClelland, J. (2001). The time course of perceptual choice: The leaky, competing accumulator model. Psychological Review, *108*, 550–592.

Vaiva, G., Ducrocq, F., Jezequel, K., Averland, B., Lestavel, P., Brunet, A., & Marmar, C. (2003). Immediate treatment with propanolol decreases posttraumatic stress disorder two months after trauma. *Biological Psychology, 54*, 947–949.

Van Osch, S., Wakker, P., van den Hout, W., & Stiggelbout, A. M. (2004). Correcting biases in standard gamble and time tradeoff utilities. *Medical Decision Making, 24*, 511–517.

Volkow, N. (2004). *The role of dopamine as a mediator of saliency in the normal human brain*. Paper presented at the Annual Meeting of the American Psychiatric Association, New York.

Volkow, N., Chang, L., Wang, G. J., Fowler, J., Leonido-Yee, M., Franceschi, D., et al. (2001). Low level of brain dopamine D2 receptors in methamphetamine abusers: Association with metabolism in the orbitofrontal cortex. *American Journal of Psychiatry, 158*, 377.

Volkow, N., Wang, G., Fowler, J., Telang, F., Maynard, L., Logan, J., et al. (2004). Evidence that methylphenidate enhances the saliency of a mathematical task by increasing dopamine in the human brain. *American Journal of Psychiatry, 161*, 1173–1180.

vonWinterfeldt, D., & Edwards, W. (1986). *Decision analysis and behavioral research*. Cambridge, UK: Cambridge University Press.

Wagar, B., & Thagard, P. (2004). Spiking Phineas Gage: A neurocomputational theory of cognitive-affective integration in decision making. *Psychological Review, 111*, 67–79.

Walton, M., Rudebeck, P., Bannerman, D., & Rushworth, M. (2007). Calculating the cost of acting in frontal cortex. *Annals of the New York Academy of Sciences, 1104*, 340–356.

Weber, E. (2006). *Choice under uncertainty*. Lecture presented the Stanford Summer School on Neuroeconomics, Palo Alto, CA.

Wiedmann, G., Paulie, P., & Dengler, W. (2001). A priori expectancy bias in patients with panic disorder. *Anxiety Disorders, 15*, 401–412.

Wilson, T., Hodges, S., & LaFleur, S. (1995). Effects of introspecting about reasons: Inferring attitudes from accessible thoughts. *Journal of Personality and Social Psychology, 69*, 16–28.

Winstanley, C., Theobald, D., Dalley, J., & Robbins, T. W. (2005). Interactions between serotonin and dopamine in the control of impulsive choices in rats: Therapeutic implications for impulse control disorders. *Neuropsychopharmacology, 30*, 669–682.

Wohlford, G., Miller, B., & Gazzaniga, M. (2000). The left hemisphere's role in hypothesis formation. *The Journal of Neuroscience, 20*, RC64:1–4.

Wooley, S., & Goethe, J. (2005). *Association between SSRI side effects and adherence to modern SSRIs*. Paper presented at the Annual meeting of the American Psychiatric Association, Atlanta, GA.

Wu, G. (1999). Anxiety and decision-making with delayed resolution of uncertainty. *Theory and Decision, 46*, 159–198.

Yates, F. (1990). *Judgment and decision-making*. Englewood Cliffs, NJ: Prentice Hall.

Yu, A., & Dayan, P. (2005). Uncertainty, neuromodulation and attention. *Neuron, 46*, 681–692.

Author Index

Note: Some author names may not appear on a particular page as they are included in an et al. citation.

Subject Index

IMPUSIVITY -
MALADAPTIVE

- IMPULSE: EVOLUTIONARY
SIGNIFICANCE ?

ANTICIPATORY avoid ✓

THE in
USES(?) MODEL

MOOD

TIME DISCOUNTING
CONSEQUENCE DISCOUNT

IMPLICATIONS
FOR ADVERTISM

TEMPORAL
IMMEDIACY

SO at costly
so too is
the uses?

SENSORY

POSTTERN
(FIT
NOT FIT
PRODUCT

SOMATIC
TRIGGER
PEOPLE FIND IT
EASY TO SAY